INVENTING

LESBIAN CULTURES

IN AMERICA

INVENTING

LESBIAN CULTURES

IN AMERICA

Edited by ELLEN LEWIN

BEACON PRESS / BOSTON

Beacon Press
25 Beacon Street
Boston, Massachusetts 02108-2892

Beacon Press books
are published under the auspices of the
Unitarian Universalist Association of Congregations.

02   01   00   99   98   97   96   8   7   6   5   4   3   2   1

Text design by Iris Weinstein
Composition by Wilsted & Taylor

Library of Congress Cataloging-in-Publication Data
Inventing lesbian cultures in America / Ellen Lewin (ed.).
p.   cm.
ISBN 0-8070-7942-1 (cloth). — ISBN 0-8070-7943-X (pbk.)
1. Lesbianism—United States.   2. Lesbians—United States—Social life
and customs.   3. Lesbians—United States—Identity.   I. Lewin, Ellen.
HQ75.6.U5156   1996   96-12406
306.76'63—dc20

FOR LIZ,
WHO MAKES EVERYTHING POSSIBLE,
AND IN MEMORY OF SAM

CONTENTS

INTRODUCTION

If the women's and gay liberation movements of the 1970s can claim no other accomplishments, they can surely take some credit for the redefinition of homosexuality as something other than a psychiatric illness. Once the personal politics of the era took hold, sexual orientation could no longer be defined as an individual problem, a compulsion lacking in both meaning and intention. In particular, the idea that lesbianism might be more of a political stance than a sexual preference suggested that being a lesbian—whether that was defined in terms of behavior or identity—could somehow be chosen.[1] But once chosen, it was unclear how being a lesbian could best be demonstrated. Was having sex with other women enough, or did one's allegiances have to be revealed in some more observable way? What, anyway, did we have in mind when we referred to "sex"?[2] And if lesbian culture was learned and acted out in lesbian communities, as Kennedy and Davis have argued,[3] how did women experience it beyond the boundaries of local institutions such as bars and house parties? In other words, how did a concept of "lesbian" come to be generalized beyond immediate and personal experience?

Feminist scholarship on lesbianism in the 1970s and 1980s had

1

tended to globalize and universalize its properties, merging them with qualities associated with femaleness.[4] Adrienne Rich, in her influential 1980 article "Compulsory Heterosexuality and Lesbian Existence," claimed that we could understand lesbianism in terms of two overlapping concepts: "lesbian existence" and "lesbian continuum."[5] The former described female-female sexual behavior, while the latter referred to a range of affiliations and collaborations between women that did not necessarily have explicit sexual content. Its significance was that it enabled a view of lesbianism that transcended not only national and cultural barriers, but time and history. Similarly, Lillian Faderman's historical study of lesbianism proposed a universal definition that could be applied in a variety of historical contexts and that did not depend on evidence of sexual behavior.[6] Both of these approaches supported a politics of unity and sisterhood, and claimed that lesbians' primary loyalty ought to be to other lesbians and that the political impact of lesbianism resided in its implicit or explicit resistance to male domination.[7]

As anyone who follows developments in lesbian and feminist publishing and scholarship knows, those days of unity and sisterhood are far behind us. Recent debate and the books sparked by it dispute the ahistorical and universalized images of lesbianism that were once so widely accepted, and focus instead on sources of difference and on the meaning and experience of lesbianism in various cultural contexts.[8] Most prominent among the new publications aimed at general audiences are the almost dizzying array of books addressing feminism or lesbianism in particular ethnic communities. Beginning with the influential volume *This Bridge Called My Back*,[9] anthologies and other works concerned with cultural diversity have appeared regularly and now compete with more universalist understandings of what it means to be a lesbian or, indeed, a woman. A glance at a few of these titles offers a sense of the evolving multicultural lesbian narrative: *Home Girls: A Black Feminist Anthology; Nice Jewish Girls: A Lesbian Anthology; Chicana Lesbians: The Girls Our Mothers Warned Us About; Making Face, Making Soul—Haciendo Caras: Creative and Critical Perspectives by Women of Color; Compañeras: Latina Lesbians; Piece of my Heart: A Lesbian of Colour Anthology; Making Waves: An Anthology of Writings By and About Asian American Women; Afrekete: An Anthology of Black Lesbian Writing*.[10] Even as this manuscript is written, many more such books are making their appearance, sometimes drawing on writing by both lesbians and heterosexual women, or both lesbians and gay men, in assembling and codifying particular ethnic perspectives, or in defining the contributors along some other axis of difference—social class, age, disability or health status, specific sexual practices or role behavior, participation in a "recovery" movement, or parental status.[11]

All of these works offer varied forms of testimony by which women and lesbians offer versions of how "lesbian" and other specifics of their personhood intersect and shape each other. If anything may be said to unify them as a genre, it is their reliance on what, paraphrasing the political scientist Kathleen Jones, we might call "the authority of experience." "Feminists," Jones explains, "have insisted that authentic knowledge must be grounded in women's experiences; only descriptions rooted in these experiences can claim to provide authoritative readings of women's lives."[12] The authenticity and individuality of personal experience thus place it beyond question or analysis. Narratives—including poetry and prose, fiction and autobiography—have titles like: "Coming Out at the Sushi Bar," "A Black Girl Thing," "An Asian Lesbian's Struggle,"[13] "Jewish Lesbian Mother," "Some of Us Are Arabic,"[14] "Lesbian Grandmother,"[15] and "Trying to be Dyke and Chicana."[16] As Shane Phelan explains in *Identity Politics*, "Women of color are not to be taken simply as the voices of diversity breaking in upon the uniform consciousness of white women, but as writers who remind all of us of the tentative, constructed, but historically real and particular nature of our identities."[17]

Further complicating this landscape has been the emergence of "queer" as an identity largely at odds with existing notions of "gay" or "lesbian." Given a voice by the burgeoning field of queer studies (which in turn has largely been inspired by postcolonial studies, postmodernism, and the rise of cultural studies), it has tended to question the solidity of all received categories at the same time that it has endowed the newly constituted notion of "queer" with increasing concreteness. "Queer," as Allan Bérubé and Jeffrey Escoffier point out, "is meant to be confrontational—opposed to gay assimilationists and straight oppressors while inclusive of people who have been marginalized by anyone in power."[18] Queer identity and queer theory alike emphasize dimensions of resistance and subversion to be found in their departure from the "normal," conceptualizing themselves as a thorn in the side of both the established social order and the academy.[19] "The notion of a 'queer community,'" historian Lisa Duggan writes, ". . . is often used to construct a collectivity no longer defined solely by the gender of its members' sexual partners. This new community is unified only by a shared dissent from the dominant organization of sex and gender."[20]

All of these recent discussions owe much to the rise of the constructionist perspective in social theory, a view that has been particularly influential among some scholars of gender. Eschewing the inherent biologism of traditional, essentialized definitions of sex and gender, these theorists have usefully alerted us to the performative, strategic elements of how individuals represent themselves as men and women, or as gay and straight, or perhaps as something in between or outside of these categories. They warn us to be skeptical of assumptions of binarism in gender and to question the naturalism that attaches to ideas of sex as the simple outcome of biological forces. Along the same lines, these scholars have assailed definitions of sexual orientation that depend on genetic or other biological mechanisms for explanations, while transsexuals and transgendered persons have gained increasing prominence in the still-evolving queer pantheon.[21]

But while these approaches have all responded to what they see as excessively rigid dichotomizations of sexuality and gender, the new terminologies they have instituted have merely reconfigured homosexuality in terms of more benign, but still unproblematized, attributes we might readily recognize as "culture." Sometimes characterized as "lifestyle," a term that has unfortunate consumerist associations, at other times as "community," a term that verges toward imposing boundaries on images of social reality, the new ways of thinking about homosexuality tended to assume the existence of a distinct way of life or a sense of shared purpose. Michael Bronski, for example, spoke of "gay sensibility,"[22] while Susan Krieger wrote about "identity" in a "women's community," describing the overlapping understandings and histories shared by lesbians who live in a small midwestern city.[23]

These ideas resonate with anthropological ideas about culture, in the sense that the discipline views tribes or other population groups as inventing, perpetuating, and adapting ways of life, ideas, and expectations, as well as producing material expressions as a function or ne-

cessity of their humanness. From this angle, "acceptance" or "tolerance" of homosexuality is not very different from a kind of cultural
relativism. Just as people of other/minority nationalities and ethnici-
ties have their ways or cultures that are perfectly legitimate (even if
they are opaque to members of the majority), so have gays and lesbians
come to be seen as people who have cultures and communities that
shape their experience and values. As Richard Herrell has evocatively
described in his analysis of the evolution of the Chicago gay pride parade, gay and lesbian community activities began to take on the trappings of ethnic celebrations, with such events as gay pride day (mark-
ing the anniversary of the 1969 Stonewall Rebellion) coming to
strongly resemble ethnic festivities such as carnivals and parades.[24]

Like notions of ethnicity, gay/lesbian culture often tended to be
conceptualized as a free-floating system, operating on its own principles and having well-defined boundaries. Identifying gay/lesbian cultures depended on being able to assign individuals unambiguously to
either the homosexual or heterosexual world, and assumed that once
in that domain individuals would more or less stay put. Yet writing on
gay culture also has acknowledged the ways in which its development
has been inextricably tied to the shape of the wider culture, whether
that means availing itself of opportunities afforded at particular historical moments or responding to repression.[25]

To understand the process whereby the idea of "lesbian culture"
has been promoted, popularized, and, indeed, internalized by late-
twentieth-century Americans, we need to think both in terms of
identity politics and the processes whereby ideas about community,
nation, tradition, and history are formed and codified. Benedict Anderson has noted in *Imagined Communities* that national identity tends
to be constructed as natural or unchosen. "In this way, nation-ness is
assimilated to skin-colour, gender, parentage and birth-era—all those
things one cannot help. . . . Precisely because such ties are not chosen,
they have about them a halo of disinterestedness."[26] The presumed authenticity of nationality reveals itself in images of awakening described by people becoming conscious of their nationality for the first
time; studying one's national language (or folklore or music), for example, is recalled as a process of " 'rediscovering' something deep-
down always known."[27]

In a startlingly similar fashion, the solidification of lesbian identity has been dependent on a process of discovering both history and culture, a process that has accelerated as publishers compete to feed a market hungry for books on gender and homosexuality. Numerous works in lesbian/gay scholarship, particularly many studies produced by historians, have been consumed not only by academic specialists in the field, but also by lay readers eager to "reclaim" something they can recognize as "the lesbian and gay past." The literature now includes works on men and women, works that focus on particular historical periods or parts of the world, comparative works, and highly specialized studies. Building on their predecessors in women's history, authors of lesbian/gay history have generally used the methods and approaches of social history to portray those previously invisible and to give voice to those once silent.[28]

The process of giving voice to lesbian and gay history bears a striking resemblance to the solidification of identity that emerges from the tradition of the "coming-out" story as it appears in post-Stonewall Europe and America. While each story has unique features, Bonnie Zimmerman has noted aptly that the stories have a conventional structure, reminiscent of the bildungsroman, that points to shared notions of personal development and causality.[29] Kath Weston's penetrating analysis of a group of coming-out stories reveals their performative qualities and the ways the stories are used to illustrate lesbian/gay ideas about family and kinship.[30] The conventional shape of coming-out stories varies for men and women, with men's stories tending to be founded in childhood sexual exploits and women's more focused on relationships and the overlapping of intimacy and sexuality. Men's narratives typically illustrate ideas about homosexuality as an innate condition, while women's are often more concerned with choice and the political ramifications of being or becoming lesbian.[31] In either case, the stories adhere to conventions that have the reassuring contours of tradition, another marker of nationality and community.[32]

Both narratives that focus on the unified "nationality" of lesbians (or of gay people in general) and those that elaborate differences have been used by contemporary theorists to support the claim that gay, lesbian, or queer identity all spring from resistance and subversion of hegemonic gender politics and that corresponding forms of "identity politics" may thus be understood to have revolutionary implications.

Such views move the question of sexual orientation from a personal proclivity to the stage of political protest, making such "personal politics" the equivalent of the "everyday" forms of resistance that have attracted so much attention in various works by anthropologists, historians, political theorists, and cultural theorists.[33]

Moving from the obvious fact that homosexuality stimulates intense hostility among those we might identify as the guardians of convention, queer theorists and other proponents of "gender subversion" conclude that lesbian, gay, or queer identity alone constitutes a form of resistance to heterosexist domination and thus can be counted as a conscious (or unconscious) political move.[34] Leaving aside the question of the extent to which such views reflect at least a modicum of wishful thinking,[35] it must be clear that they also rest on a relatively undifferentiated notion of how identity is constructed and fail to consider the complications suggested by the daily proliferation of newly hyphenated forms of lesbianism (or, indeed, of nationalities in general). Just as cultural identity is perpetually being renegotiated and, in a sense, rediscovered, so its relation to dominant values may be in constant flux. Identification as a "lesbian" may have a particular meaning in one context, but may shift rapidly as the individual takes into account the other dimensions of her identity.

In all these cases, what is at stake is a definition of boundaries, and to the extent that boundaries between identities are increasingly permeable, the notion of stable identity itself must come to be questioned seriously. If the boundaries of identity are unclear and constantly shifting, and if membership in particular identity-defined groups is contested and strategic, then the naturalness of any sort of national or other culture-based aggregation must be doubted. Adoption of gay or lesbian identity must be no more definitive of the self, in a sense that can be politically manipulated, than the choice or discovery of any other identity, be it indicated by race, ethnicity, religion, politics, occupation, health status, or any other quality that can be performed or otherwise revealed.

How are these subtleties of intent and identity to be discerned? Although many of the arguments I have cited may be said to be exciting, even exhilarating, ventures into the world of political speculation, most suffer from a failure to engage with the meanings real people attach to their real-life experience, the intersection of ideology and behavior we tend to call "culture." This insufficiency has been magnified by the approach most of the few anthropological inquiries into homosexuality have taken.[36] To the extent that anthropologists have examined homosexuality at all, they have, with some notable exceptions, concentrated on describing the distribution of various sexual practices around the world, employing what Kath Weston has aptly called "ethnocartography," a kind of salvage ethnography bent on preserving the record of sexual diversity wherever and however it may appear.[37] These studies have not fully engaged with the complicated problem of defining the object of inquiry, assuming as they do that "homosexuality" is a stable category waiting to be compared cross-culturally. At the same time, however uninspiring the plodding concreteness of work in this genre, and the penchant of its practitioners for sometimes tedious enumeration, it appears that it is precisely the "empirical" element it embodies that might be of use in trying to unravel the meaning of "lesbian" in American cultures.[38]

For it is not what "lesbian" might ideally mean or how it might be constructed that should concern us, but how this element of identity is perceived and experienced by real women, and how it intersects with other sources of identity and belonging. Should "lesbian" (or "homosexual" or "queer") be conceptualized as an identity analogous to nationality or ethnicity or race? That is, does it imply membership in a group that agrees on its boundaries and organizes to pursue its interests? We have noted that displays of gay identity, such as the now-common gay pride parades, partake of symbolic strategies closely akin to those deployed by ethnic communities. But Steven Epstein has noted that the ethnic model of gay and lesbian identity easily slips toward a kind of essentialism that disguises the varied approaches to identity that appear among people all claiming to be some variant of gay or lesbian (or queer). At the same time, however, a strictly constructionist interpretation of gay identity may impede effective political mobilization and undercut efforts by gay people to generate a more positive basis for self-identification than sexual difference.[39]

What about how actual women conceptualize themselves and how that shapes the way they move through their daily lives? And what can the effort to define lesbian cultures in America tell us about the ways in which cultures are constituted by individuals who face particular threats to a cohesive identity, and about the ways in which community and other social forms are generated and recognized? This volume seeks to explore these issues by examining some of the many, varied ways that people may use a particular idea of lesbian to construct themselves, to understand how they are connected in the world, and to devise notions of community and belonging that help them make sense of their experience. While the quest for an authentically cultural understanding of "lesbian" draws directly on an anthropological perspective, the volume also benefits from the contributions of literary and historical scholars as well as from a number of efforts that demonstrate the possibilities for collaboration across disciplinary boundaries. That is, all the essays in this volume engage the question of how lesbian identities and associated cultures are formed, recognized, and go on to shape or determine courses of action, strategies, and, indeed, politics.

In asking these questions, the volume acknowledges race, class, and ethnicity as sources of cultural diversity, as in the biographical and historical essays by Elizabeth Kennedy and Rochella Thorpe, but it also takes up cultures as the creations of many types of identities and experiences. Cultures in this sense are viewed as both named and self-conscious entities, the bounded, recognized and recognizable units most students of the subject are concerned with, and as unconscious, temporary, and perhaps even fleeting phenomena.

Thus, Deborah Amory's paper on a San Francisco disco, Club Q, deals with a moment that most clearly in retrospect appears to have constituted a distinct cultural development. A particular kind of co-alescence formed among those women who met and danced and performed their identities at Club Q, and that did and did not carry over or reflect other aspects of these women's lives. Similarly, in Ellen Lewin's paper on lesbian wedding ceremonies, women who choose to celebrate their relationships in this way are seen as participating in an emergent cultural form, one that has arisen independently in a thousand places and that seems to have no organized center or agreed-upon objective, but that nonetheless displays certain symbolic consistencies. And Ellen Herman's treatment of popular psychology identifies elements of lesbian cultures that affect lesbian mothers more than others and that also overlap with cultural movements having broad significance in the wider society.

In other cases, self-awareness seems to be a more central part of cultural formation, perhaps when the need for resistance is more dramatically evident. Esther Newton's paper on the changing position of lesbians in male-dominated Cherry Grove speaks to how women define their belonging and not-belonging in a community where they are minority female but majority gay. And Alisa Klinger's account of the role of feminist presses in solidifying notions of cultural variation among lesbians takes up the formation of culture as a conscious act of political import, perhaps the hallmark of lesbian politics in the last decade. Kath Weston writes about the limits of community, about its failure, in a particular kind of instance, to provide the cultural supports that might enable an individual woman to survive economic and emotional challenges. She thus points to a mythical aspect of lesbian culture that only becomes critical when it fails to materialize.

The papers in this volume certainly do not exhaust the possibilities for cultural productivity among Americans who identify (or may be identified) as lesbian. There are no contributions dealing with recent political work done by lesbian AIDS and breast cancer activists and how involvement with these two health crises shapes notions of what it means to be lesbian.[40] A more exhaustive volume might include analyses of lesbian/gay political activists of various stripes, and their interaction with non-gays/lesbians with whom they share particular objectives, for example as they came together during the Clinton presidential campaign or in other electoral battles.[41] The growing visibility of openly gay and lesbian elected and appointed officeholders of varying political persuasions points to the development of more complicated ways to think about what lesbian/gay politics might mean in the future.

A more comprehensive approach might include papers dealing with aging,[42] with immigration, with the arts, with the various sexual practices that have been contested bitterly over the course of the "sex wars,"[43] with particular occupational groups or sports to which lesbians have had historical ties (such as some of the blue-collar trades or softball),[44] on the new visibility of transgender lesbians,[45] or with specific regions of the country that put their unique stamp on lesbian cultures. And, perhaps because other volumes have been so effective in presenting the voices of lesbians from many different ethnic groups, there is no attempt here to address ethnic and racial factors in all their breadth, or to achieve adequate representation of all voices that might be heard. At the foundation of the efforts in this volume to help to determine how lesbian cultures are generated is a recognition that the basic questions being asked have been defined by struggles already under way, and that whatever can be said here must be considered in the context of the extensive literature on which this effort is based.

In looking both at present conditions and at the recent past, the contributions take up the question of how memory or a belief in memory aid in the construction of culture, how the recollection of shared experiences in the past helps to generate the present. Lesbian cultures, if they may be said to be "genuine" (in Sapir's terms)[46]—that is, "harmonious, balanced, self-satisfactory"[47]—must do more than simply facilitate survival or enable lesbians to withstand attacks on their physical existence. They must allow for a sense of collective meaning, a sense enhanced by an integration of history into the formulation of identity. To return to Sapir's formulation, "No greater test of the genuineness of both individual and communal culture can be applied than the attitude adopted toward the past, its institutions, its treasures of art and thought."[48] As we see in many of the papers in this volume, constructions of the past are a vital aspect of how lesbians imagine the present, whether they believe the present to be continuous with or disruptive of that past. The very notion that culture might attach to the activities, alliances, and identities that make up the experience of being lesbian imbues our daily struggles with dignity and stability even as we recognize the insubstantiality of culture, its fleeting existence in our consciousness as we seek meaning for our lives.

PART ONE

•

INVENTIONS

CHAPTER 1

"But we would never talk about it": The Structures of Lesbian Discretion in South Dakota, 1928–1933

ELIZABETH LAPOVSKY KENNEDY

But we would never talk about it" is a refrain in Julia Boyer Reinstein's account of her life that expresses her frustration in trying to explain her life as a lesbian to contemporary lesbians, including her daughter. Boyer Reinstein was born in 1906, on the cusp of the last generation of New Women.[1] She is an "ordinary" bourgeois woman who lived as a lesbian school teacher in Deadwood, South Dakota, and Castile, New York, during the 1920s and 1930s; as a married woman in Buffalo, New York, from the 1940s through the 1970s; then again as a lesbian. When I first began recording Boyer Reinstein's life story, I had a simplistic understanding of what "never talking about it" meant. Influenced by gay-liberation categories, I stereotyped Boyer Reinstein and her friends as not being "out"—not having the courage to be public. But as her story unfolded, I realized that the phenomenon of being "in the closet" was much more complicated than I had assumed. During the 1920s and 1930s Boyer Reinstein was an active lesbian within a community of lesbian friends. She had few, if any, negative feelings about being a lesbian, and she was "out" to her immediate family, who was supportive of her. Yet, she did not publicly disclose being gay. She was always discreet, she never drew public attention to her relationships with women, and, when necessary, she developed convenient covers to use with those outside her immediate family. She never—or at least rarely—talked about being a lesbian, not even to her friends and family. These incongruities challenge the binary opposition of being "in" or "out" and suggest that lesbianism in the early twentieth century took various and complex forms.

This essay explores private lesbianism in Deadwood, South Dakota, during the 1920s and 1930s through the lens of Julia Boyer Reinstein's life story.[2] I am tempted to say this essay documents how Boyer Reinstein constructed her closet, because of the graphic picture such a concept presents and the ease with which it would connect my work with that of some contemporary theorists. However, I am afraid using the term "closet" to refer to the culture of the 1920s and 1930s might be anachronistic.[3] Boyer Reinstein herself uses the concept of the closet today, but she never fails to remind me that neither she nor her friends thought about life in those terms in the past. My goal is to reveal the social formations of the period, to understand in particular how class, protestantism, and the teaching profession shaped Boyer Reinstein's preference for discretion and secrecy. I hope to reveal how Boyer Reinstein managed discretion in her family and in her profession while still pursuing a rich lesbian social life, and how she and her friends were not interested in bringing lesbianism into the public but in constructing a private world in which lesbianism could flourish.

I am intrigued by these issues because of my recent research on working-class lesbians during the 1930s, 1940s, and 1950s, who had an apparent drive to end the necessity of secrecy, to reveal the closet by breaking out.[4] The contrast between Boyer Reinstein and these working-class lesbians highlights that discretion is a distinct social formation and raises provocative questions: Is discretion always oppressive? Is rupturing the closet always liberatory? But before exploring the social construction of discretion in Boyer Reinstein's life, I frame the subject by reviewing scholarship on discreet lesbians in the early twentieth century.

Until now, research on twentieth-century lesbians has focused primarily on the development of a public lesbian identity and has inadequately documented and analyzed the more private forms of woman-to-woman relationships. A variety of factors have conspired to make research on the lives of women, such as Boyer Reinstein, who were completely private about their lesbianism a low priority. First, if lesbian life by definition is not public it is difficult to identify. Successful discretion leaves few traces for study. The major sources have been autobiographies like Elsa Gidlow's *Elsa, I Come with My Songs*[5] or personal memoirs such as Boyer Reinstein's where the author/narrator consciously attempts to place the privacy of her past lesbianism in the context of today's public lesbianism. Such sources are extremely rare. Usually, personal letters, diaries, and memoirs will continue the pattern of discretion created during a lifetime of "never talking": They express deep love for women, but they leave no traces of how the authors considered themselves in relation to lesbianism. The rarity of the sources tends to present "invisibility" as an individual choice rather than as a social formation.

Second, research on lesbian and gay history was born as part of the gay and lesbian liberation movement and has adopted that movement's emphasis on being out as a path to liberation. This perspective contains an implicit negative judgment of all those who were not out, no matter the historical period, and in extreme form caricatures those who lived before Stonewall as leading secretive, furtive, and deprived lives.[6] Such an attitude does not encourage probing questions about the social formations that shaped private gay and lesbian living. Queer theory, with its emphasis on deconstruction, has challenged the identity-based politics of gay liberation and its emphasis on being out, clearing the way politically for scrutiny of earlier, less public, forms of lesbian identity.[7]

A third reason for the paucity of scholarship on lesbians who led private lives in the early twentieth century is the framework of analysis developed by feminist scholarship on the New Woman. Ironically, the rigorous, detailed research that has done so much to reveal the

forces shaping the ferment around women's lives at the turn of the
century has developed categories that camouflage some lesbians. The
groundbreaking work of Carroll Smith-Rosenberg characterizes the
older generation of the New Woman as entering the public sphere
while still locating their emotional lives in the female world of love;
the younger generation made sexuality an active part of their self-
definition and became the heterosexual "sex radical" women of Greenwich Village or "mythic mannish women," the icons of twentieth-
century lesbianism.[8] The "mannish" woman was sexually interested in
more "feminine" women. By definition, she was not private about her
lesbianism; rather her appearance drew public attention, stigmatizing
her in the eyes of the straight world, and identifying her to those
women who might be interested in connecting with her. In this framework, women who located their lives with other women but who were
not mannish or did not associate with mannish women are assumed to
be part of the tradition of the first generation of the New Woman:
women who did not identify themselves on the basis of their sexuality
but who created deep erotic, though nongenital, ties among women.
Such an analysis has the benefit of heightening the importance and
power of women's traditions, but at least from the perspective of Boyer
Reinstein's life, they underplay the profound effect the sexual revolution had on twentieth-century women. This approach is buttressed by
Esther Newton's pioneering study of "mannish women" that explains
the appropriation of masculine identity as a way for women to break
from the nineteenth-century tradition of women being asexual.[9]
Through masculinity women claimed active sexuality for themselves
and expressed interest in other women. This argument suggests there
cannot be other forms of lesbianism in the early twentieth century because it would be difficult for women to announce their sexuality.[10]

The existing historical record provides tantalizing glimpses of
various ways women were private about their erotic love for women.
Some women seem to have eschewed the label lesbian entirely, and we
have no idea about how they understood their sexualities. Other
women indicated that they considered themselves lesbians but were
completely private; for some, this was due to the fear of exposure in a
hostile environment, others, like Gidlow and Boyer Reinstein, preferred ambiguity and discretion. Leila Rupp's article "'Imagine my
surprise'" is the classic discussion of the women who gave no recogni-

tion to the word "lesbian."[11] She describes the fragmentary evidence of women who were lifelong couples and who expressed love of one another, women who developed deep crushes on charismatic leaders, and women who had affairs with each other while both or one was married, none of whom identified themselves publicly as lesbian. In some cases, anecdotal evidence suggests they were actually offended at being labeled lesbians after the rise of the lesbian feminist movement in the 1970s. Rupp points out that it is wrong to interpret these women as remnants of the nineteenth-century culture. They were, after all, living in a century when women were considered sexual and women identified themselves publicly as lesbians. She explores the irresolvable dilemma of either naming such relationships as "lesbian," despite the subjects' denial of the label, or completely disassociating these relationships from public lesbianism. In the end, Rupp calls for more careful documentation and interpretation.

Boyer Reinstein provides an interesting perspective on these relationships for which we usually have only fragmentary evidence, and the analytic dilemmas they raise. Her life story raises the possibility that the evidence we have of women who vehemently denied that they were lesbians, even though they formed lifelong couples with other women, should be interpreted as an assertion that their sexuality was not a public matter, rather than as a denial that they have a sexual interest in women. The question is not so much whether they would label themselves as lesbians in public, but whether they privately considered themselves as having sexual/romantic interests in women, and therefore as different from women who were sexually interested in men, and most importantly how they constructed discretion in order to live in a social environment that was hostile to intimate relationships between women.

In her overview of twentieth-century lesbian history, Lillian Faderman provides many examples of women who, like Boyer Reinstein, were conscious of being lesbians but were still extremely circumspect. They also emphasize the custom of never talking about being lesbians. Faderman quotes a woman describing her experience in the late 1930s at the University of Washington:

> "Although several of us were in couples, no one ever talked about their love lives. We could unload with problems about families, jobs, money, but not lesbianism. If two women broke up they wouldn't discuss it with

the group, though they might have a confidante who was also part of the group. It was our attitude that this sort of relationship was nobody's business. We all really knew about each other of course. But the idea was, 'You don't know if someone is a lesbian unless you've slept with her.' You didn't belong if you were the blabbermouth type."[12]

Faderman gives another example:

Sandra, who worked in a Portland department store during the early 1930s, tells us of having been part of a group of eight women—four couples—who went skiing every winter between 1934 and 1937. "I'm sure we were all gay," she remembers, "but we never said a word about it. Talking about it just wasn't the thing to do. Never once did I hear the L word in that group or a word like it—even though we always rented a cabin together and we all agreed that we only wanted four beds since we slept in pairs."[13]

Faderman, like most scholars up until now, interprets these women's discretion as I originally interpreted Boyer Reinstein's: They were silent because of fear of exposure and consequent oppression. And indeed Faderman might be correct in these cases. She provides evidence that at least some women who were private longed to be more public. However, Boyer Reinstein's life provides yet another possibility.

Julia Boyer Reinstein was born in Western New York; six weeks later she and her mother joined her father in Wolesley, Saskatchewan, where he worked as an electrical engineer. When she was 1½ years old, her parents divorced and her mother returned to Western New York with Julia, living first in Castile and then in Warsaw. Raised by her schoolteacher mother and by her great-aunt and -uncle, who owned a newspaper in Warsaw, Julia grew up in the bosom of a respected Daughters of the American Revolution family.[14] When Julia was a teenager, her mother married the owner of the general store in Silver Springs; Julia continued to live during the week in Warsaw but on weekends joined her mother and stepfather. Julia remembers her childhood as primarily happy, despite the inevitable discomfort caused by the stigma of her parents' divorce and her unusual height for a girl—Julia claims that by the time she was eleven she had already reached her adult height of six feet. She developed a warm and open relationship with her mother that continued throughout her mother's life.

Part of her parents' divorce agreement was that Julia and her father would have no contact until she was eighteen. He remarried and settled in Deadwood, South Dakota, and became a very successful owner of the Consolidated Power and Light Company, eventually moving in the highest circles of western society.[15] Julia's life was dramatically altered when he contacted her in 1926, when she was 20. She started spending her summers with him, and after she finished college in 1928, she went to live with him in Deadwood where she stayed until his premature death on July 1, 1933. (During that period, she continued her closeness with her mother through regular visits.)

Julia's father recognized and accepted her lesbianism at their first meeting, when he visited her at Elmira College. Here is how Julia tells the story:

> The second day he saw me, we were both of us in Elmira, and we were talking about me growing up and one of the things he asked me about was about my boyfriends. . . . And I said, "I've had my share of men friends, but they didn't mean anything to me. . . . I don't particularly care for them. If I have to have somebody for a prom or something of that sort I can always get one of the boys from Warsaw, from Cornell or Syracuse or wherever, to come down and be there for the weekend." But I wasn't interested in boys, . . . and I had never met anybody that I cared enough to even think about getting married, although some of my friends were already getting themselves pinned or engaged or what have you. And my father questioned me a little bit about why I didn't. I said, "They just never interested me, they never interested me." I didn't tell him I was a lesbian. I knew it. Oh, yes, I knew it, I had been playing with it, you see, for two years in Elmira, quite openly at college. . . . But I remember the second afternoon, we were both of us sitting in this hotel room talking, about . . . the girls he had met, and I was telling him about who this one was and who that one was, . . . and he said to me, "They're all alike, aren't they?" And I looked at him and I said, "We're all in college, you know." He said, "You know what I mean." He said, "I've known you were a homosexual . . . practically from the time I met you. You gave yourself away in your letters." See, for about six weeks, from the time my father first called me until I first met him, I wrote him a letter every day (and of course, I'd love to know what happened to those letters. . . . I imagine he destroyed them, I imagine he did. They certainly weren't in the house when he died). . . . He said, "But it's all right with me."

Julia developed an intense relationship with her father, and became the apple of his eye. She believes that in some sense he liked her being a lesbian because she could give him more attention:

> Oh yes, in fact, I think he even heaved a sigh of relief, too, in many respects, when he got me out to Deadwood, because he was very adept at turning the fellows that were interested in me away. Well, one thing is he absorbed me so that I was—My life was his life and his was mine there for those years.

She went everywhere with him, to business meetings in big cities and to the wilderness to look for new power plant sites. He was showing off his new daughter. He felt that she had the mind and the reflexes of a man, and appreciated her company. Julia did not consider herself masculine but considered his judgment a compliment.

Julia's lesbian identity continued to blossom beyond the college environment. In Deadwood, South Dakota, she created several different sites of lesbian connections. She had affairs with women when she traveled with her father, she developed flirtations with some of the local girls who were her age, and in 1931 she met another teacher, Dorothy, who became a serious love in her life. Despite these connections her lesbianism remained private, protected by the complex structures of discretion.

Julia remembers her father's business trips as very exciting. She saw new places and met many people, one of whom was Amelia Earhart. Julia's memories of the weekend she met Earhart encapsulate the privilege her father's social position brought her, and also the erotic excitement of meeting other women who might be lesbians.

> Well, my father had his own airplane, and of course, when I was out in South Dakota he was . . . acquiring, as president, and managing a string of small electric companies, because in those days the villages would have their own electric plants. And it would serve the area about it, but there was nothing in between. . . . There [were] five in the Black Hills, then there were four in Nebraska, and there was one in Missouri, and there was one in the panhandle and on down. So that he was driving or flying—first driving and then flying—after he got his own plane, a great deal of the time. Of course, that's when I was with him and doing the same thing, being with him at the same time. . . . He conceived the idea that if he had a helicopter he could get to these places without these long drives or having to fly. Because none of these little towns had airports,

you see, so he had to land in a field and get off the field. So he announced to me that this one weekend we would be spending the weekend in Rapid City because Amelia Earhart was going to bring a helicopter from Denver up to demonstrate . . . She represented a helicopter company.

So she arrived at the hotel, and she and I were assigned to one room and my father had the next room over. Of course, I was terribly excited because [this was] Amelia Earhart, [and] here I was still in college. And she landed at the airport, Rapid City, . . . where my father had his plane. And this very attractive gal got out of this helicopter in a flying suit. . . . Soft-voiced, but it had a timber to it, and there was a little bit of authority about her. She knew what she was doing, and she spoke with authority. So I was very awed, and I stood in awe all that weekend. I wish now I hadn't. . . . I had thoughts immediately when I saw her, but I put them in the back of my head. . . . Anyway, she arrived up in the afternoon, and we went to the hotel and settled down, and that night we had dinner together . . . She was talking about her flights, and of course I was listening. . . . And I didn't talk to her about it. She included me in her conversations and asked me about Elmira; [she] knew about Elmira. She was interested in the fact that it was a girls' school and that it was as old as it was. But the conversation was strictly straight. . . . They talked about motors and all that sort of thing, which I knew nothing about. . . . Well, we sat around in the bar, I remember, that night, but it was very casual. And strangely enough, even though my father introduced her to people there, and they were impressed, it didn't cause any great stir.

We got ready to go to bed, and so I took my shower, got out, she went in, and, of course she came out in pajamas, without a robe. . . . And we chatted. We both had books or things to read and so we went to bed. And she said something about sweet dreams, and I said equally, and she patted me on the shoulder, or on the—not on my head, but on my shoulder, and I lay there half the night wishing to goodness that I had nerve enough to go over and sit on the edge of her bed, but I didn't. . . .

The next morning, . . . I was an early riser so I was out of the bathroom before she got up. When she came out, she was in a bra and shorts, and the shorts were men's shorts . . . yes, they were boxer shorts. And of course, that impressed me immediately, and it gave me a chance to see what her body looked like. And I wanted to be very helpful, I remember I did straighten out her [collar]—She went into slacks and a shirt, and it was a man's shirt. And then we went down to breakfast. And somehow or another we got to talking about the young people, and I don't know, I still don't know, whether—I don't think I mentioned the fact that I was a lesbian, but I think I did probably everything that would let her know that I was. I remember she smoked, and I'd light her cigarettes and things of [that] sort. I was very attentive, but at the same time I was in awe of her, because she was Amelia Earhart.

So we went flying. And of course, it was one of those bubble . . . helicopters. It wasn't very large, and so I was in the back seat. . . . My father and [s]he were flying, and of course then I couldn't say anything, because I just had to listen and be amazed at how she handled it herself. And then [she] showed my father, and, of course, he handled it also . . . We did the hills all over, and it was the first time I had seen what became Mt. Rushmore from the air. Of course it was just a rock then, but there was talk about doing something to the rock. That was also one of my father's projects. Then . . . we landed and had lunch. And when we went walking . . . where we had lunch at a lodge in the hills, she took hold of my arm— we went arm and arm walking around the woods. . . . I had a feeling of intimacy, but I couldn't, I didn't dare go beyond it. She was still Amelia Earhart. She was personal and yet she was impersonal.

Then we had dinner again, and the three of us sat in our bedroom for the evening, and my father always had a bottle of scotch, and we were drinking some scotch. And when we got ready to go to bed [after my father left] she undressed in front of me and I did likewise, but I didn't dare make a move. I thought, if she's interested and she is a lesbian, and I know she is, she's going to have to make the first move. So I got into bed first, and she came over and sat down on the edge of the bed and talked about the weekend, that she had a pleasant weekend and my father was a great guy. . . . He and she and I had talked about his meeting me, so she knew the story of how we had been separated in my early childhood. And she leaned over and kissed me goodnight. And I wish now, I could have easily put my arms around her, but instead I just put my arm up on her shoulder and she kissed me. And it was, I think back now and I don't know, I don't know, it was more than just a casual kiss, and yet it wasn't an intimate one. But I had the feeling, I went to sleep that night feeling that, well, we knew we were each other is what we were . . . I felt that that night. But, of course, I couldn't do anything.

So when we got up the next morning, she was getting ready to fly

back to Denver. While we were at the airport she always had her arm through mine, or her arm across my shoulder, because she stood fairly tall, but not too tall—she came above my shoulder. And her flesh was just hard, muscular hard. Of course there wasn't any extra on her. When I saw her dressing, I realized she was just a wonderfully organized woman. And she kissed me goodbye when she got into the plane and took off. (My father did not buy [a helicopter] because it flew too slow for him.)

Julia's not exactly sure how, but before that weekend she had heard through her college associates that Earhart was a lesbian. "I knew when my father said we were going to [meet her] I was excited, because I thought, here is a famous lesbian woman that I can meet." Her memories seventy years later are still vibrant, evoking a concrete sense of Earhart's body and style. They also convey Julia's persistent attempts to establish common ground with Earhart, without ever talking about the topic of lesbianism directly, and her strong interest in having an affair with her, despite her shyness in the presence of such an accomplished woman. Julia loved sharing this wonderful meeting with her friends. "I was in seventh heaven. All my friends knew about it, too— that I slept in the same room with her and she kissed me goodnight." Her friends also thought she should have been more forward. A few years later when Julia told her new friend Dorothy about the weekend, Dorothy was disappointed: "Oh dear, you spoiled it. Why didn't you make a move?"

Julia never had any further contact with Amelia Earhart, and her excitement did not lead to impaired judgment about the meaning of the meeting.

My feeling . . . was . . . that . . . it was primarily a business weekend for her. She had flown up to sell a helicopter, and it was up to her to sell it if she could, and I just happened to be . . . there. [Laughter.] No, I never thought of it [as becoming more serious]. And I don't think my father thought of arranging it as that, he just was taking me to meet Amelia Earhart, he knew I would be interested and he was interested.

For Julia this was just one of many adventures as she came into her womanhood as a lesbian, as a college student, as the daughter of a father who was a prominent citizen and business owner, and as the daughter of a mother who was strongly independent yet part of an established small-town protestant family. Julia is very clear on how stimulating that period was for her, so that weekend was one among many, rather than one that had a particular lasting effect on her life.[16]

> There were too many other things going on; it was just one of those events. I think back now and realize that I piled and put into those years with my father what lots of people would have put maybe a lifetime into. . . . And it was exciting, and I could talk about it to other people and brag about it. . . . But I didn't think of it as being terribly important. It was just one of those things that was happening to me.

Julia's father never thwarted her lesbian desire; in fact he encouraged it, as long as it remained hidden—like his extramarital affairs. Julia remembers her affairs with other women as an integral part of accompanying her father on his business trips:

> Those years were hectic years, but they were wonderful years. I've often thought about them since then. My father would take me, for instance, to Denver, and he would be with people from the big electric companies, and then we would go out to dinner and go to the nightclub afterwards. And invariably, . . . I knew, one of the women in that ten or fifteen that were at the nightclub with us was the woman he was going to sleep with that night. I would find out which one it was. . . . Invariably, there was a lesbian among them. . . . I would team up with her. . . . I don't know [how he arranged that.] And I never questioned it, I just accepted it. This gal would separate herself from all of the men and women. Some of them were wives and some of them weren't, you know. Some of them were secretaries, some of them were executives from some other place. . . . And then once I met her, of course, why the next time, why you just teamed up again, that's all.

On hearing those stories, at first I assumed that Julia and her friend for the evening would just spend time together without specific sexual intentions. But Julia corrected me and said most often they did have a sexual encounter in the hotel where she and her father were, each in their separate rooms. "See, I was young and it was exciting to me, and they were always older people, older women. They might be in their late twenties or their early thirties or even their forties. Some of them were charming, and some of them became very good friends of mine after my father died and I came back east."[17]

Lillian Faderman documents that in New York City during the 1920s women were beginning to define themselves as sexual beings and were willing to explore sexual relationships with other women.[18]

The many rendezvous Julia had during trips indicate this was happening in cosmopolitan centers throughout the U.S., including the west. Usually Julia saw the women of these affairs only when she was away from Deadwood with her father, and primarily in the evening. But she did spend full days with some of them. When Julia was in Denver, Bonnie, a married woman who raised terriers, might join her for a day of shopping and for the evening. Julia would even accompany Bonnie to her house to care for the dogs, if Bonnie hadn't made any other arrangements; but Julia never met Bonnie's husband.

As Julia matured she became less dependent on her father to arrange her contacts. She could attend a meeting and identify someone she was interested in immediately, as she did with Columbia:

> Oh dear, there was Columbia, who was a secretary to one of the presidents of the electric company for the city of Minneapolis. And she was my age. She was out at a big conference that was held in Rapid City, [a] very big conference, and there were several of the secretaries, because they were supposed to work . . . in the administration part of the conference business area. But I stole Columbia from that area; we barged all over the Black Hills together for five days. Then she came back one summer, she and I took off, went down to one of the local spas in the lower Black Hills and spent a week down there. . . . When I came back east, we carried on a correspondence, and she finally migrated out to the West Coast and I lost track of her. So I never knew what happened to her, but she never married, to my knowledge.

Julia also had continuing contact with a woman who had nursed her back to health when she became sick on one of her father's business trips. "She lived in McCook, Nebraska. And she came up and visited me for about two weeks one summer. She was very much a lady. You would never have known it to look at her that she was a lesbian. Never known it—until she went to bed." Julia also accompanied this nurse on a trip to visit her family in Minnesota. Neither Julia nor any of these partners was ever interested in making their relationships more serious. In fact, she does not call them relationships or affairs, but "escapades," indicating their frivolity. These women had other commitments to family or business. Julia was not in love with them, and to the best of her knowledge none of them wanted something more serious from her. Julia reminisces: "Columbia and I just knew we liked each other, and it was fun being together and that was it." Julia did not consider most of these women lesbians, despite their sexual predilections, nor did they consider themselves as such.

During the period Julia was accompanying her father and meeting women interested in making love with women, she also developed a social life in Deadwood. Julia describes Deadwood as an unusual town. Despite its size and isolation, it was very lively, up-to-date, and open-minded.

> Deadwood was just different. . . . Once a month there was a dinner dance in the hotel—everybody who was anybody went to the dinner dance, and the reservations were limited because the center of the big dining room was cleared so that you could dance in it. . . . The Shriners always had a big ball, and when we had a ball, I want you to know, there was a grand march. You see, it was done properly. The theater was in sections, like the big theaters that were built . . . it would probably hold six hundred to seven hundred people. But it had its grand circles and its boxes, and strangely enough, it had good theater, [which] would come up from Denver . . . for five nights and then go back down to Denver. There was a lot of social life, and it was cultured, and the library was an excellent library. But our lives were—All I can say is we were just loose-knit . . . , "[doing] pretty much what you wanted to do."

The dress code in Deadwood was quite lax, and allowed space for women who did not want to dress in a typical feminine manner. "See, the thing is, we could dress casually there in slacks, in riding trousers, riding things, so that they didn't think anything about that." But for such public events as dances and theater, women were expected to be fashionably dressed as ladies who could mix in the best society. Julia loved dressing up and was quite good at it. She understands that some of the resentment that her stepmother had towards her was the way she came from nowhere into Deadwood as a very fashionable woman.

> Here I was, coming from the east, with a mother who had dressed me exotically from the time I was a child, and I knew how to dress and be strikingly dressed, differently dressed, and had dressmakers who could . . . make me clothes that fitted me. And my mother, . . . if she saw a pattern she liked and some cloth, she would just like as not turn it over to a dressmaker, who was a wonderful, wonderful dressmaker, who could make me a dress, ship it to me and it would fit me perfectly. Some clothes were always six months to a year ahead of South Dakota, which made me unusual. And I don't blame her [my stepmother] for resenting me. And my

father took me, very obviously was showing me off, and I was a brat enough to like it, too.

In this context Julia made friends with several local girls of her age and class. They took advantage of Deadwood's social life, attending the theater and dances. They also went on outings together, sometimes to accompany Julia's father on a short trip, and played bridge with the family. She was particularly fond of Dorothea, who was not a lesbian although she had an extended affair with Julia. Julia would have liked to have made it more serious, but Dorothea was not interested. She thought it would be too difficult to lead a life outside of marriage.

Originally, Julia's father wanted her to remain a woman of leisure who accompanied him on his trips, learning about and helping with his business. Once the depression hit, his perspective was particularly sensible, since there were few jobs available for a young female college graduate. Although Julia was enjoying her life of leisure, she was not completely comfortable in it. When one of her circle of friends who was teaching in a mining camp became sick, Julia applied and was hired to replace her. "I liked it, I liked it. And I thought it was exciting to be living in this little mining camp." Julia was reappointed the second year, after which her father pressured her to leave and return to a life of leisure. She decided to use this time to study in Chicago. Her father, wanting her close by, used his influence to find her a teaching position in Deadwood. She was offered one at the last minute, and she took it.

Julia's mother had insisted that she prepare herself at Elmira College to be a teacher. She remembers her mother saying:

"I'm going to ask one thing of you—I want you to take enough education courses so that you will qualify for a teacher's license." And evidently, I had looked skeptically at her, because she ended up by saying, "Remember, Julia, that if I hadn't had my teacher's license I never would have been able to have taken care of you and grandma. . . . I had my license and I could teach, and I want you to be able to teach."

In this environment Julia took for granted that she would be competent and independent—and in fact, all the women on her mother's side of the family were. Not only was her mother a teacher, but her great aunt, who had helped to raise her, had been a teacher in Nebraska before her marriage, and was a suffragist and a member of the Woman's Christian Temperance Union. In time her father, too, came to accept her teaching, and even encouraged her to pursue her master's degree during the summers.

It was while teaching in Deadwood that Julia met Dorothy. This was a turning point in her life, and it was her first serious love. Until this time Julia considered herself isolated from other lesbians. She did not consider her "escapades" as having provided a lesbian friendship or relationship. "And frankly, other than my own personal feeling, and until Dorothy came into my life, I had very little to do with any lesbian people after I left college. See, I was isolated." Thus, in looking back Julia clearly distinguishes between sexual encounters with women and more stable lesbian relationships in a context of continuous contact with lesbians, even if the word was never spoken.

Julia still vividly recalls how she met Dorothy:

Six or seven [teachers lived in the big hotel in town] . . . They always went over to the hotel for lunch at noon, and those teachers always came over from the hotel and came in the . . . side door of the school so they had to go past my first grade. I was always assigned to be in the doorway with the first graders as they came in. And there were three or four teachers who came in, and I spotted this one, and I was immediately attracted. She taught Latin and French. It was Dorothy—her blue eyes and her hair. She had dark—her hair was curly, and no matter what she did with it, no matter what she did with it, it curled. No matter how she had it cut or whether it was wet or dry it curled. And she had the most beautiful blue eyes. She was tall, rather slender, and she dressed very nicely—she had wonderful taste. And there was just something about her along with the others, they all came in, in a group, she just was there and that was it. So during that year when I was teaching first grade . . . I got so I didn't go home for lunch, I would go over to the hotel with the girls and the teachers there and have lunch with them, so that I got to know Dorothy. And Dorothy was, she was quiet and she had a wonderful wit, and it was sharp. We liked the same kind of poetry, and the teachers, because there were these seven or eight of them up there, they hung together, they did things together.

Julia and Dorothy began their life together in 1930. Her relationship with Dorothy did not dramatically change Julia's relationship with her father. She continued to travel with him, though to a more limited extent, since her teaching job didn't allow her time off during the week. And she no longer had affairs with women on these trips. Now she and her father aided and abetted each other's sexual interests in other ways. She was a cover for her father, just as he was for her. Dorothy's roommate, Helen, became quite smitten with Julia's father, who began an affair with her. Normally he didn't have affairs with women in Deadwood, so he had to be careful.

> What happened was, Helen fell for my father. So for all that winter and spring it was a foursome. Dorothy, Helen, and I would start out in Dorothy's car, my father would start out in his car, we would meet some place or another, and I don't know when my father got home and Dorothy and I didn't care. So it was a nice foursome, it worked out very nicely. And you'll see some pictures of Helen and Dorothy and me and we all were having fun. . . . That's the reason why she's in the pictures, because we were together, the three of us were traveling together a great deal of the time.[19]

Julia was unquestionably protective of her father. She says, "Dorothy and I kind of kept [Helen] under, kept her locked down." Julia's father helped her materially as well. For instance, Dorothy was in a deteriorating relationship with a teacher in Rapid City when she met Julia. A stumbling block to ending the relationship was the fact that the two had bought a car together. Dorothy used the car regularly but did not have the money to buy her partner out. Unknown to Julia and Dorothy, Julia's father went to see Dorothy's partner and paid off the car. He wanted his daughter to be happy.

There were no other lesbians among the teachers in town, but there were three other "odd" couples, which is the term Julia thinks she and her acquaintances would have used back then. She and Dorothy became friends with one such couple who were closest to them in age and class. One of the women was the daughter of a doctor in town. And after college, "she brought [home] this obvious—so obvious that it was too obvious, almost—dyke, and they settled in," Julia recalls. "Then I know there were eyebrows raised." But there were no sanctions. Rather, the doctor bought his daughter a building for a beauty parlor, and in time she and her partner set up a sauna, with a ladies' afternoon once a week. Julia remembers the importance of the sauna to their lives as lesbians:

> Well, they decided that they would start a sauna of their own, so they established a sauna in connection with their hair salon, and it was quite

popular with the ladies, because they didn't have to go up to where the big sauna was, which was obviously for men, built for men and masculine. And they [the couple] lived in the apartment, in one of the two apartments upstairs over it, and they rented out the next apartment. Well, when Dorothy, the first year that I went to teach in Deadwood and I met Dorothy, and fell in love with her and she with me, I was having the girls do my hair. And Dorothy said, well she always had somebody in Rapid City do her hair, [but] she would try them, and so we both of us used to go to the sauna together. And of course that led us immediately to the fact that the other two were lesbians, so there were the four of us. We would very often go late in the afternoon for our sauna and then the four of us would have dinner together. Now we talked about everything but being homosexuals . . . Never talked about it. Maybe occasionally, Heidi [who] was the older of the two of them, Heidi would say, well, I left something good down in Denver . . . , something like that, but it was never, we never talked about it. And this is what I keep saying to so many, many people, in that period of time it just wasn't talked about. We knew it existed, we accepted it or didn't accept it, but it was there.

Julia and Dorothy's close group of friends included Helen, and a substitute teacher and her self-employed husband. Julia recalls that this was a forward-looking straight couple who shocked the town of Deadwood when the man had a vasectomy, because he and his wife had two children and didn't want more. Together these friends were adventurous and fun-loving. One of Julia's favorite stories is about the evening they decided to alter a sign by the road leading out of Deadwood. The sign said "Prepare to meet thy God." They climbed the rocks and changed it to "Prepare to make thy goddess."

Julia was very happy during this period of her life:

The second year I taught in Deadwood was kind of a wonderful year, because we [Dorothy and I] were together; my father aided and abetted me. Of course I was aiding and abetting him. And we [Dorothy and I] were both of us talking about . . . starting our master's, and we decided we'd go to Wisconsin instead of Chicago. Helen decided she'd go to Wisconsin and start her master's degree, the three of us would go. That was the year that . . . the couple that had the hair dressing [salon] opened the sauna, and Dorothy and Helen were going to take an apartment, which would have made it much nicer for the three of us. And I knew that it was a bad year for my father, because he began to do some heavy drinking. He was

traveling an awful lot, to New York and Chicago and St. Louis, so I knew
there was a lot of stress, as far as the depression, the stock crash happened. But I was in such . . . euphoria is right. Lots of things just went
over my head—you know, this was it.

Julia's father died suddenly as the result of an infected tooth, right
before she was to leave for Wisconsin for summer school. Two weeks
later she left Deadwood permanently.

Julia's life in Deadwood goes against much of the received wisdom
about women in this period: her sexual energy; her ability to live an
active and full lesbian life while not being public; her Protestant up-
bringing, which supported as well as repressed her lesbianism; and her
positive relationship with her parents. Since this is only one woman's
life, we could view it as exceptional and disregard its implications for
women's and lesbian and gay history. But her life was not isolated—it
involved friendships and relationships with many other lesbians at all
stages of her life. Julia has wonderful photographs documenting her
friendships, loves, and escapades, and her daughter, Julia Reinstein,
has met many of the people in these stories. Julia's life, therefore, can
be taken as a starting point for reevaluating or rethinking lesbianism
in the 1920s and 1930s.

From the perspective of the late twentieth century it is extraordinary that such extensive lesbian activity could remain a private part of
an individual's life and not become public. Julia's memories of life in
Deadwood suggest that this was possible not only because of her own
careful discretion, but also because the complicity of heterosexuals
sustained the blurred line between ignorance and knowledge about
matters of sexuality. Together these created the interstices where lesbian life could flourish. Julia herself has often wondered how she and
her friends managed to live the life they did. Fifteen years ago she and
an old friend talked about it:

> The only conclusion we could come to was the families had money. They
> had social prestige, and we were not too obvious. I think that was it. They
> may have talked about us behind our backs, and probably did—in fact I
> know they did, because mother got upset a couple times when somebody
> made a crack about "Julia not marrying Bob Sterns in Castile," who was
> five years younger than I and gay. He taught with me in Castile, and I
> guess we covered for each other. He went around with me and everybody
> thought we should get married. And a couple people said something to

mother about it and made mother angry. But under normal circumstances that was all it was [talk]. We never felt discriminated against.

Julia's discretion, her not being "obvious," was governed by two rules—first, to publicly behave as a respectful heterosexual daughter, to the extent that was possible without marrying, and second, to never talk about lesbianism. While they constructed female-centered lives, Julia and her friends followed most of the social rules of heterosexual society. They socialized with their parents. They played bridge with family members and went to the theater and to the many dances. At these dances she and Dorothy could dance together, because there were usually more women than men and women often danced to-gether. But they also danced with others, including some men. This did not trouble Julia, who loved to dance and loved to dress in the man-ner of a "proper lady." Good behavior was expected of women of her class, particularly of teachers. She was used to these gender expecta-tions and did not find them terribly confining. For a woman like Julia, being a lesbian was just one aspect of her life, albeit an important one. Coming out publicly, being more obvious, would have been more of a burden than a freedom. In most ways her discretion did not limit her life or make it unpleasant. By accepting these rules, Julia received all the benefits and privileges of her class. Furthermore, they allowed her to live without stigma.

Proper behavior for a daughter of this class was unquestionably a key ingredient for acceptance. The partner of the doctor's daughter did not follow these rules by the way she looked or behaved, and Julia remembers "there were some eyebrows raised." In time, the town ex-cluded her from its social circles.

But the one who came up from Denver, she didn't like to play cards and she didn't like social work, she was an outdoors person anyway. . . . She'd just take off and hide. . . . And we just accepted it. When there was a party, she just wasn't invited—that was all, we knew she wasn't going to come. She wouldn't come, so we never invited her.

Julia is uncertain what happened to this couple, but she knows they did not remain in Deadwood in the bosom of the doctor's family. A few years after Julia left, the couple followed a religious cult to New York City.[20]

What does it mean that Julia and her friends never talked about lesbianism? They felt that the only appropriate setting for the discussion of love between women was in the context of an intimate relationship between lovers. Lesbian couples who were friends rarely talked about lesbianism together. They never talked, for instance, about the four "odd" couples in the town. Julia explains, "Now at that point, even after I got out of college . . . we didn't talk about lesbianism. We just didn't talk about it, and I don't know why. . . . It's very curious." And lesbianism was certainly not talked about with heterosexual people. Although Julia's father and mother knew about her lesbianism and were comfortable with it, giving her freedom and support, they rarely talked about it. Julia thinks that in her entire stay in Deadwood lesbianism was not mentioned in public. She could only recall one vague reference: once, her group of friends that included the forward-looking straight couple had planned to take some peyote (plans that never came to fruition), and the man wondered about the effect of peyote on "you girls." Nothing more was said, but Julia assumed that he was referring not to their gender but to their lesbian relationships.

Julia and her friends' avoidance of the subject, and even the term "lesbian," in conversation seems to be a general strategy of all private lesbians. It seems reasonable that lesbians should avoid public discussion of the topic, due to social norms about the privacy of sexuality and the stigma attached to being lesbian. But why would lesbians avoid discussion among friends? Faderman suggests that the prohibition showed whether you could be trusted to keep quiet in the public realm ("You didn't belong if you were the blabbermouth type"). But it seems that the prohibition is even deeper than that. By using the word "lesbian" they would hasten the naming of themselves as a distinct kind of person and the inevitability of her emergence in the public world. The consequences of this naming would be dramatic—it would mean losing extensive social privileges, perhaps the most important of which was acceptance by family and society.

Discretion was not simply an organizing principle in Julia's behavior, but also in her family's. Thus, in Deadwood, her father attempted to accept and protect her, and other townspeople willingly ignored or avoided the obvious signs that she was not a typical heterosexual daughter. Her family respected her privacy and supported her pursuit of the life she wanted. This protection is key for keeping lesbianism in the private realm. In effect, they created a buffer zone between Julia and the judgments of the outside world. In addition, the privacy was

maintained by other heterosexuals' ignorance, or if they were knowledgeable, their complicity in supporting her parents' position. Julia
tries to capture this complicated environment between those who
"know" and those who don't.

> Yeah, then there was another couple that I didn't know too well. One of
> them was obviously [lesbian]. She and her father and her uncle worked a
> very little . . . gold mine. And then they had a housekeeper, and I heard
> some of the women saying disparagingly, "Oh well, she probably goes to
> bed with Andy's father," like that. But the girl and the housekeeper were
> lovers. . . . I knew it, but the rest of the town—see, again, the town was
> so square that they didn't. There was a definite difference between the
> men who were in the mining game, or that kind, and the women who
> were there because their husbands were there.

Julia assumes that many of the wives in the town were more igno-
rant than the men. She thinks her stepmother did not suspect her
lesbianism, because she was a strict catholic who had a very limited
knowledge about the world or about sexuality or even her own body.
At the same time we can assume that there were also people in Deadwood who, like Julia's father and the many women she had slept with
in larger cities, were knowledgeable about the existence of lesbianism
because the topic was discussed in medical journals, newspapers, theater, and literature of the times. Such people seemed to accept it, like
Julia's father and the father of the woman who owned the beauty parlor, treating it like marital indiscretion. They assumed that sexual life
was private and one could do what one wanted as long as one had the
power to protect oneself. Those who did not accept sexual relations
among women chose to ignore Julia's behavior because they did not
intend to challenge the morality and respectability of the daughter of
one of the wealthiest men in town. The family's reputation meant that
others would not be too critical, and also that the family would stand
behind their own, as long as nothing was too obvious. People might
have talked, or "raised their eyebrows," but nothing much came of it.

Since Deadwood was a relatively new and booming western town,
it is possible that it offered more interstices for lesbian life than more
traditionally conservative small towns in western New York. But that
doesn't seem to be the case. With few additions and variations the
same social formations of discretion seem to be at work for lesbians

and heterosexuals when Julia returned to western New York after her father died. Julia was discreet and behaved as a proper lady, she and her friends did not talk about lesbianism, and her mother and stepfather protected her, welcoming her partner Dorothy into her house. That system was effective even while Julia was teaching in Castile, New York, a most conservative town (the only town in Wyoming County that forbade the sale of liquor). During this period a new ingredient was added to the construction of discretion: the use of a gay man as a cover. When Julia and Bob, a gay teacher in the same school, became good friends, members of the town assumed they were engaged. Interestingly, this ruse was invented mostly by heterosexuals, either out of their ignorance or their desire to facilitate complicity, rather than by Julia and Dorothy themselves.

Boyer Reinstein's construction of and comfort with discretion was certainly not unique. She had a set of friends who more or less managed their lives in the same way. But there is evidence that similar patterns of discretion existed in the lives of other lesbians in the early twentieth century. Elsa Gidlow, who also recognized her lesbianism at a young age, lives a multifaceted, sexually active life in which her lesbianism is important but quite private. Born in 1899 in England, she forged a lesbian life in Canada as an adolescent and later in the United States (New York and California). Her childhood in a large working-class family was marked by poverty, and as a woman supporting herself in the early twentieth century without an education, she spent many years in poverty. Her goals and accomplishments in the literary world, however, brought her in contact with a middle-class circle of friends with similar interests. Gidlow was always clear about her interests in women but was not public about it. She also had ties with some gay men who fostered her artistic work and offered her support at key times in her life. She never had a community of lesbian friends; she avoided the bars and did not cultivate a "masculine" identity. It was not that she ever denied who she was, she simply did not announce it or discuss it. Her friends respected each other's privacy. In contrasting her early life with the culture of gay liberation, she writes:

I am not saying it was better then, although in some ways it was more comfortable. Perhaps it was the San Francisco circles we moved in, but

it did seem that in those days civilized persons respected one another's privacies. Some may call this elitist. I can only say if live-and-let-live good manners are elitist, let's learn from elitism.

I think it was more comfortable then because we did not have to be ever-conscious of being in somebody's sexual spotlight. However, speaking for myself and other women I knew intimately, we were *not* repressed and we were not ashamed of our erotic needs. There are too many erroneous assumptions today concerning women of earlier decades. What was important to me and my intimates then, as it continues to be, was not orgasm, but shared loyalties. I and my lesbian friends took it for granted that our primary loyalty and support was to women.[21]

At the core of her characterization of her life is the idea of respect for privacy that was shared by lesbians and heterosexuals in her circle of friends. They simply did not discuss the details of each other's private lives. In addition, Gidlow is questioning the value of identification by sexuality alone, and the stigma that results from being known only as a sexual being. This explanation of how lesbians and heterosexuals constructed discretion is quite parallel to Boyer Reinstein's. The major difference is that Gidlow did not come from a wealthy family and she never developed a close circle of lesbian friends. It was not her family who protected her, but rather the artistic circles that she moved in, reinforcing the common assumption that artists have been traditionally hospitable to homosexuals.[22] This suggests that the structures of discretion are varied and dependent on specific social contexts.

Boyer Reinstein's memories and reflections indicate that the sites of lesbian desire were multiple in the first half of the twentieth century; that they included the rural areas of New York and South Dakota; that they were intertwined with traditional Presbyterian families, even families who were Daughters of the American Revolution; that they were compatible with the profession of school teaching. In most cases private lesbians consciously considered themselves sexual beings and built meaningful relationships that included sexuality, but this was only one aspect of their lives. Their lesbianism was hidden at that time, and therefore to history, by complex structures of discretion that played with the fundamental division between public and private in modern American life and allowed them to escape being characterized primarily on the basis of their sexuality. This evidence suggests that in the 1920s to 1930s the social dichotomies of heterosexuality and homosexuality were not yet hegemonic. Concomitantly, the closet was not fully institutionalized. For many segments of the upper class all sexuality was a personal matter; public hints were gracefully ignored. Lesbian liaisons were not much different from heterosexual infidelities. In some contexts the traditions of discretion were very freeing, allowing lesbians to lead lives fully incorporated into the dominant society while still developing woman-centered spaces. But, unlike the protection offered extramarital affairs, such arrangements were fragile, easily disrupted by forces outside an individual's control. In certain situations discretion can become quite restrictive and limiting.

Julia Boyer Reinstein's life dramatically shows these limits. After almost thirty years as an active lesbian, a confluence of circumstances left her isolated with the traditions of discretion offering her no way out. She started a new teaching job in Buffalo in the 1940s, away from her friends and family, and her girlfriend left her for someone else. It was not easy for her to find other female companionship unless she was willing to become more public, which she was not. In time the pressure from a widower became overwhelming, and she married. Without the interstices created by the protection of family and the good behavior of friends, the "closet" slammed shut, requiring women to embrace the stigma of lesbianism, to live completely hidden lives governed by fear of exposure, or to leave lesbian life completely. In some respects the increasing public presence of lesbians as the century progressed made it less and less likely for a fluid relationship between public and private, knowledge and ignorance, and in and out of the closet to persist.

This rigidity is a concrete manifestation of what is meant by the dichotomy between heterosexual and homosexual becoming hegemonic. Boyer Reinstein's life in South Dakota (like that of Gidlow) is rich with sexual possibility and connections among women, yet it is suffused with discretion. As such it helps us, the descendants of gay liberation and identity politics, to see beyond a dichotomized sexuality, and it allows us to imagine what it might mean to live without the stigma of sexual difference.

CHAPTER 2

"A house where queers go": African-American Lesbian Nightlife in Detroit, 1940–1975

ROCHELLA THORPE

During our interview about lesbian life in the 1940s and 1950s in Detroit, Ruth Ellis[1] discussed where and how lesbians socialized back then. Ruth, an African-American lesbian "in the life" in Detroit since the 1930s, recalled that lesbians gathered "in somebody's home, yeah. 'Cause they didn't have anything like the beer parlors or anything . . . that gays could go to. . . . They didn't have any."[2] But Detroit was home to several lesbian bars during this period, and virtually all the white lesbians interviewed for this study were aware of them. This essay addresses the reasons why Ruth, whose home was a lesbian and gay social center for many years, did not know, and did not need to know, that bars for lesbians existed in Detroit before the 1960s. In doing so, it attempts to address larger questions about the way historians of lesbians have defined public and private space, and the impact these definitions have had on the history that has emerged.

Most historical writing about lesbian social life has focused on the importance of bar culture in shaping lesbian communities, especially for working-class lesbians. In fact, historians of lesbian life have posited bar culture as the first, indeed the only, site of a burgeoning lesbian subculture in the 1950s. Cut off from any knowledge of their predecessors, lesbians struggled to hold onto the ties they had made in wartime, making the best of what little the conservative cold-war era had to offer them. For instance, Lillian Faderman has written that for lesbians during this period, "There was little to inherit from the past in terms of safe turf, though safe turf was crucial to lesbians as a despised minority."[3] Janet Kahn and Patricia Gozemba describe lesbian bars in the 1950s as "the only public, although often hidden, space in which people acknowledged their gayness."[4] And Elizabeth Kennedy and Madeline Davis call 1950s gay and lesbian bars "the public manifestations of gay life at the time."[5] These arguments, however, are based on sources that deal overwhelmingly with white lesbians.

This essay looks beyond bars for lesbian social activity, and in doing so suggests that one reason historians of lesbians have not been successful locating lesbians of color might be that they have assumed bars have been the center (both theoretical and actual) of lesbian communities.[6] Broadening the lens to include other kinds of socializing reveals the importance of race in shaping the social activities in which lesbians chose to engage. By looking back to the vibrant social life of the Harlem Renaissance, this essay demonstrates the importance of race- and class-based cultural traditions in the choices made by Detroit lesbians.[7]

In addition, this essay begins to problematize the definition of "public" culture as it is referred to by historians of lesbians. The public nature of lesbian social life was compromised by the fact that lesbians needed to hide their sexual orientation from an often harsh heterosexual world. Lesbian bars, which were legally registered as public establishments where liquor was sold, just like heterosexual establishments, were public mainly in the legal sense. The social characteristics that made most bars public—advertising, open discussion of evenings

spent there, open admission—were not necessarily desirable for a lesbian bar. Lesbians who frequented bars did their best to protect each
other and to create a culture that would buffer them from the public
aspects of life in the bars. But when race is added to the equation, the
definitions change once again. What does "public" mean for people
who have been denied access to public space due to economic and political oppression? Is a lesbian space less public if it is racially segre-
gated? And finally, how did African-American lesbians adapt their social institutions to effectively resist racial prejudice from white lesbians
and homophobic reactions from their black communities? This paper
shows the ways that African-American lesbians created semi-public
spaces that met their social needs and circumvented the problems created by a racist, homophobic society.

Although social life is an area of social history that is often difficult
to document, historians have assembled vivid descriptions of African-
American social life throughout the twentieth century. This has been
possible especially for the 1920s, when the jazz culture of Harlem and
the black cultural renaissance moved many participants, both black
and white, to record their experiences at the clubs and parties that
were popular at the time. Most famous are the flashy dance halls in
which white travelers could go "slumming" for the evening, eating
traditional black southern food and hearing both famous and lesser-
known jazz musicians. But these clubs, despite their Harlem locations,
were often owned by European Americans and catered to white cus-
tomers. Researchers have also documented another form of African-
American social life, grounded in the needs and limitations of African-
American people: the rent party.

According to one historian, rent parties were an alternative to the
"classier Harlem night spots," and were frequented by people who
could not afford or would not have fit in with the more public night
life there.[8] Printed advertisements served as invitations and were distributed in black-owned businesses, bars, and on the street. Party-
goers enjoyed food, music, and alcohol (especially important during
Prohibition) for a fraction of the admission charge at high-priced
clubs. Rent parties benefitted their hosts as well, since they helped off-
set the high rent of Harlem apartments or other expenses.[9] For someone looking to make money with little overhead cost, rent parties provided the means. And because these gatherings were less selective of

their guests than clubs were, hosts could be relatively assured of a profit.[10]

Rent parties were often a place where sexuality was expressed more freely than in clubs or dance halls, which were easier targets for vice squad surveillance. Historian Eric Garber describes the importance of these "private" parties to the lesbian and gay subculture in Harlem. Garber points out, "Private parties were the best place for Harlem lesbians and gay men to socialize, providing safety and privacy."[11] Garber claims that in the "relatively tolerant" climate of African-American jazz culture, "black lesbians and gay men were able to build a thriving community within existing African-American institutions and traditions."[12] Buffet flats, which combined wild parties with rooms for rent in private apartments, "offered a variety of sexual pleasures cafeteria-style."[13] These pleasures were not confined to Harlem, however; Garber gives one example of a buffet flat in Detroit during the 1920s that Bessie Smith and her niece, Ruby, visited. Ruby Smith recalled,

> They had a faggot there that was so great that people used to come there just to watch him make love to another man. He was that great. He'd give a tongue bath and everything. By the time he got to the front of that guy he was shaking like a leaf. People used to pay good just to go in there and see him do his act. . . . That same house had a woman that used to . . . take a cigarette, light it, and puff it with her pussy. A real educated pussy.[14]

In such a sexually permissive milieu, lesbianism was just one of many experiences to be had.

The strength of this cultural tradition is evidenced by the fact that in the mid-twentieth century, most Detroit African-American lesbians' social lives continued to revolve around parties in private homes.[15] Unlike their historical precedents, however, these parties were exclusively gay and lesbian. Certain homes became frequent gathering places, where people would congregate on a regular basis to eat, drink, dance, and talk. Hosts would sometimes charge admission, sometimes not.

Unlike their Harlem rent-party predecessors, lesbian party hosts in the 1950s and earlier often avoided printed invitations, probably because is was difficult to control who might eventually see them. Party locations were usually relayed by word of mouth, and lesbians

relied on their networks to find these centers of social activity. Ruth
Ellis, who went on to host legendary parties at her own home, remembers meeting women when she arrived in Detroit from Springfield, Illinois, in the 1930s:

> [W]e got acquainted with a couple of girls, one of 'em worked in a restau-
> rant and we used to go there to eat, and come in contact with 'em. Then
> they knew other girls, and they'd introduce me to these other girls. And
> you just kept meeting different people in that line. . . . We went to visit
> the girls' houses, had parties, and then we'd meet other girls, maybe we'd
> go to somebody else's house.[16]

Margaret Lorick recalls that in the 1940s "[W]e would more or
less find places . . . where groups of gay people could be together. . . .
And most of our partying was done in our homes, my house or at E.'s,
or we knew some gay men and we would have parties at their house
down in Flint and then they branched us off to Detroit and that's
where we met Ruth."[17] For African-American lesbians, making a first
contact with someone involved in the gay social scene could be crucial.
Unlike white lesbians, who could hear about a bar and show up without knowing anyone else there, black women had to form connections
with other lesbians in order to know where to socialize. Once that ini-
tial connection was made, however, their choices of where to socialize
could increase dramatically.

Some hosts gained widespread reputations. Ruth Ellis and her
partner, Babe, became well known to African-American women in the
life in Detroit. Women came from all parts of Detroit, other cities in
Michigan, and as far away as Cleveland and Dayton, Ohio, to attend
their parties.[18] Ruth recalls that "[A]fter we had lived around different
places, we finally found this home and we bought it. Then all the gay
people would come to our house. That was known as 'a house where
queers go.'"[19] When Margaret Lorick heard about the parties—two
gay men told her "[t]here's a place in Detroit where we know a lady
where you can go and have parties at her house"—she was excited at
the prospect of a place where there were "all gay people." Soon she was
driving down from Flint every weekend to attend parties at Ruth's.
For Margaret and Alice Miller, Ruth's was a place to relax, have fun,
and eat good food. Ruth would play music in the basement, serve
drinks, and "cook up these great big pots of food—like sometimes she
had string beans in one, carrots in another, and some kinda meat or

hot dogs or something like that," or she would cook spaghetti enough for everyone.[20]

One of the most important activities at Ruth's parties was dancing. Dancing, as important to courtship for lesbians as it was for heterosexuals, was something that African-American lesbians could hope to do only in private or at lesbian and gay parties. Women could attend heterosexual clubs and sit and listen to music, but if they wanted to dance, especially slow dancing, they had to dance with men. In fact, Margaret said women were expected to dance only with men who asked them. "If you don't dance with them it's something wrong with you. . . . it is that way with black men, you know. If a woman comes to a bar and she's with three women sitting together, they don't get up and dance, . . . then what's wrong with you, you know, 'cause you there to drink and have a good time." Pressure to conform to heterosexual expectations in these clubs was so great that refusing to dance with men sometimes led to violence. One night when Margaret was out with her friend E. and E.'s sister, Margaret repeatedly refused to dance with a certain man. The situation escalated:

> This man, he got real smart and E.'s sister say, "She said she didn't wanna dance now get on with yourself." [The man] said, "Don't she like men?" [S]he said, "Maybe if she does, so what, she don't like you!" It went on and on and on. . . . One night she got in a fight with him and then I think we took it up, . . . and they threw us out the bar.

Dancing was such a contested area of public life for lesbians that it became an important part of socializing once lesbians were in a safe environment. Margaret and Alice remember at Ruth's, "Dancing, that was the biggest part of it. We would be dancing all night long." Slow dances were the most popular, since not everybody knew how to jitterbug. Black women swayed together to the music of Nat King Cole, Jimmy Longford, Sarah Vaughn, Dinah Washington, Ella Fitzgerald, and Della Reese, among others.

Ruth and Babe's home also was a place where women could meet friends and lovers. For Margaret, one of the best things about going to Ruth's was the open and friendly atmosphere. "I always know that we was always welcome when we went there and they was all looking forward to us coming," she said. Margaret recalls that her social networks expanded quickly, and that she met lesbians and gay men "from all walks of life—all backgrounds and all kinds of people. . . . I even met a lawyer, and I met some gay men that were in real sophisticated jobs and things." Ruth reminisced that the people who attended her parties were "mostly people we knew. Then we'd keep meeting different people, and that would add to the crowd."

Ruth's guests had diverse occupations. Margaret would eventually earn a master's degree, but at the time she was meeting teachers and lawyers at Ruth's house, she was working in a factory. Ruth worked in a printshop, and later ran her own printshop out of her house. Babe was a cook, and Alice had a series of factory jobs. But when asked what kind of people came to her parties, Ruth replied, "They were pretty nice people. Mmm-hmm, pretty nice people." Her description of her guests in terms of their personalities rather than their occupations conveys the spirit of the gatherings. In the lesbian and gay culture that flourished at these parties, there was a kind of social status that had to do more with values and self-respect than economic class. Because an invitation to Ruth's came through contact with someone who was already a part of the crowd, her guests had been in a sense screened for their compatibility. As a result, black lesbians trusted the people who went there. At Ruth's parties people introduced themselves with their first and last names and talked freely about their occupations. Margaret said "They weren't afraid about using their own names. . . . I guess they felt like this was just like a clique and everybody would keep all this information there. I don't think it ever got out to their jobs or anything." Although telling a new acquaintance their full name and where they worked left African-American lesbians vulnerable to a vindictive call to their employers or to gossip, at Ruth's people were willing to take that risk because they all understood the importance of confidentiality.

African-American lesbians used their wartime and postwar prosperity to the advantage of their communities. Although their wages remained low, compared with those of white and black males and white females, World War II marked the first time jobs other than domestic or institutional service were open to African-American women. In Detroit, as in other major cities, it took vocal political agitation by black organizations before African-American women were offered factory positions, and even then opportunities remained very limited.[21] But economic conditions in Detroit, as well as strong black organizations and lending institutions, meant African Americans were more likely to own their own homes, or have decent housing than was the case in most other cities.[22] Margaret remembers that "most all the people that I met, they all had houses—and they had nice houses." And although black women workers were "demobilized and redomesticated" after the war, overall, African-American women made economic gains that would continue to grow through the 1970s.[23]

Gay men were always welcome at Ruth's parties. African-American lesbians felt a common bond with "sissies," as black gay men were called, derogatorily, by heterosexuals. When Ruth and Babe first came to Detroit in 1937, they often went to parties with both "girls and . . . gay boys." Margaret said, "[When] we went to parties, there were always some men there." Alice said she enjoyed the gay culture that men would bring to the parties: "They take over. Doin' a floor show for you!"

Ruth and Babe's home was a two-family flat, and they rented out the bottom floor to gay men. On weekends, they would sometimes "open up the whole house, with gays." Ruth particularly remembered her fiftieth birthday party, in 1949: "I had a big party and a big yard, and it was in July and it was hot, and they were all over the house, outside and inside."

Gay men may have been crucial in expanding the social circles in which black lesbians traveled. Gay men first introduced Margaret to Ruth's parties, and they often brought other men to the parties.

Although most African-American lesbians socialized in private homes in the 1940s and 1950s, some spent time in predominantly white lesbian bars. Nearly all the white women I interviewed who frequented these bars said there were only a few women of color, mainly African Americans, in these bars. Judy Utley remembers that "there was one [black] woman that used to come to Fred's. I think she was a phys ed teacher or something. But she's the only one I can ever remember that was there. Black and white didn't mix back then, and they don't mix that much now."[24] Brandy McGuire at first remembered that, "[I]n Detroit you just automatically get to know blacks—I can't recall that many Hispanics or anything. It was either just black or white. But back then [it] wasn't such a big issue about your race. And everybody got along." But when questioned further, Brandy said "there weren't that many blacks, come to think of it, [it] was mostly white," and that the African-American women in the Palais were

mainly women that played ball on teams with white women.[25] Some
of the black lesbians who went to "white" bars might have been with
white friends, or were having a drink with other softball team members, but weren't regular patrons.

Why did only a few African-American lesbians choose to socialize
in lesbian bars in the 1940s and 1950s? Certainly the appeal of house
parties for those women lucky enough to know about them was a compelling reason. But prevailing racism in Detroit was a powerful de-
terrent.

Documenting racism can be a difficult task for historians, and, for
several reasons, this study is no exception. Only one white lesbian expressed overt racism in an interview. When asked how much contact
she had with women of different races, Mable Stewart Merritt explained, "[T]his is going to sound like exactly what it is: being a bigot.
I could not sleep with a black woman any more than I could sleep with
a cat and have sex. I just could not wake up in the morning and see that
lying next to me." Merritt attributed these feelings to the way she had
been raised. Although she said these attitudes have changed, and that
young white lesbians today are more open to interracial socializing,
she described herself as "from the old school. . . . I prefer staying with
my own color."[26] Although Merritt, an exceptionally forthright
woman, was the only white lesbian in this study to make such a statement, it seems highly likely she was not alone in her beliefs.[27]

Many lesbians of color interviewed for this study described incidents of overt racism that made them feel unwelcome in predominantly white bars. For instance, Anita described the practice of bouncers demanding several forms of identification from black women at the
door.[28] Ronnie pointed out that in white bars African-American lesbians had to stay "basically in the background. . . . [White women in the
bars were] very prejudiced, and they let you know that they are prejudiced." She said although an African-American woman might go to a
white bar, she would not find many other black lesbians there. "If you
go in the bar you might find one or two, three or four blacks in there
or hang out with that crowd, but other than that, you don't find 'em
going." According to Ronnie, white women "claim that a lot of [blacks
in one place] are trouble, and they don't wanna be bothered with that
type of atmosphere." In keeping with this belief, white bouncers were
reluctant to admit black women who would not easily fade into the

background. Ronnie describes an incident in which a male bouncer at a white lesbian bar denied her admission because of both her feminine appearance and her color. Ronnie was out with a white friend, who dropped her at the door of the bar while she parked the car. The bouncer told Ronnie there was a private party going on and shut the door in her face. When she returned moments later with her white lesbian friend, the bouncer explained that Ronnie "didn't look like she was gay. We thought she was heterosexual." Although feminine white women had a place in white lesbian bar culture as femmes, Ronnie's race somehow negated the possibility that she could be a femme lesbian. As Ronnie put it, "Well, they figured, it's this black woman, she's dressed up and what's she doing here?" Incidents like these kept many African-American lesbians from patronizing white lesbian bars, especially when house parties provided an appealing alternative.[29]

But not only overt racism deterred black women from spending time in white lesbian bars. Subtler racist attitudes might have made black lesbians feel unwelcome or invisible. For example, with few exceptions, white women in this study believed that as lesbians they were less racist than heterosexuals. Linda Emery claimed that "when you're gay, it changes your perspective on how you view people. Your whole life may be hard because of your sexuality, so it's very hard to discriminate against someone else for their color, for their livelihood, or whatever, because you know that you're going through it, too."[30] Some white women suggested racism was not a problem in the bars. For example, Brandy Maguire believed that although her family was racist, she and her friends were far less so. She said, "I never really thought about [racism among lesbians] till you brought it up—never made a big deal out of it. . . . Because we were such a close-knit circle . . . everything was acceptable because you didn't have much choice." Many white lesbians assumed that the experience of living as lesbians in straight society created a common ground with lesbians of color that was more powerful than their differences.[32]

This kind of attitude, in which similarities are believed to outweigh differences, is considered by many white people to be a nonracist way of thinking. Many scholars and activists of color have described their frustration at this position, which legal theorist Patricia Williams describes as "this absurd type of twisted thinking, racism in drag, [which] is propounded not just as a theory of 'equality' but as a standard of 'neutrality.'" According to Williams, this claim of neutrality limits the ways people of color can express themselves, since to define oneself as black contradicts the logic in which the "neutral" white person is not racist. In fact, neutrality does not render everyone race-free, but instead constructs everyone as white. She writes, "Blacks who refuse the protective shell of white goodness and insist that they are black are inconsistent with the paradigm of goodness, and therefore they are bad."[33] Neutrality, then, increases the likelihood of silence about race and racism, and allows white people to believe that racial oppression is nonexistent.

Cultural critic bell hooks prefers the term "white supremacy" for this insidious form of racism. Hooks believes that white supremacy (or neutrality, in Williams' description) is "the ideology that most determines how white people in [the postsegregation United States] perceive and relate to black people and other people of color." Hooks, like Williams, fears this ideology "masks how all-pervasive white supremacy is in this society both as ideology and as behavior." She warns,

When liberal whites fail to understand how they can and/or do embody white-supremacist values and beliefs even though they may not embrace racism as prejudice or domination (especially domination that involves coercive control), they cannot recognize the ways their actions support and affirm the very structure of racist domination and oppression that they profess to wish to see eradicated.[34]

In both Williams' and hooks' formulations, so-called neutrality is as powerful a form of racism as more overt expressions of racial prejudice.

Certainly, it is not the intent of this study to accuse particular Detroit women of racism. But it seems important to note that the lack of awareness about racial problems in white lesbian bars in Detroit existed precisely because race was never adequately dealt with as an issue in these bars. African-American lesbians who had been discriminated against might have felt it would be inappropriate to discuss these experiences with white women, or that they would not be believed, since white lesbians thought of their bars as a haven.[35] Indeed, bar culture was both dear to the white lesbians who participated in it and under fire from heterosexual society. Nonetheless, to declare the bars a safe place for all would be to ignore the very real experiences of African-American lesbians. As cultural historian Bernice Johnson Reagon has pointed out, dealing with differences among people is never comfortable or safe.[36] And Patricia Williams explains eloquently that "the hard work of a nonracist sensibility is boundary crossing, from safe circle into wilderness. . . . It is the willingness to spoil a good party and break an encompassing circle, to travel from the safe to the unsafe."[37] Unfortunately, in securing their own safety in the bars, white lesbians left little space for African-American women.[38]

This point is demonstrated most clearly by a close look at the few black lesbians who did feel at least a conditional acceptance in white lesbian bars. Karla said she "never had a bad experience" in white bars, and recalls that "they seemed to get along fine, you know, blacks and whites. . . . It wasn't too much prejudice among the gays anyway—not too much." Compared with West Virginia, where she lived for a while, Karla said she found the racial situation in Detroit more comfortable. She thought it was possible, however, that this was because she only became romantically involved with other African-American women. "When I was in Detroit, I never hardly go with any white girls. I can't think of one that I did, it was always when I was outta town."[39] Possibly, African-American lesbians who seemed to pose a threat to racially separate dating practices triggered white lesbians' racist fears.

Sandy's experience seems to support this analysis. Of all the lesbians of color I interviewed, Sandy—a biracial woman whose mother was white and whose father was African American—had the best experiences in white bars. Paradoxically, Sandy attributes her acceptance by white lesbians to her identification with black culture. Sandy said she passed as black in white bars because "the only time I had trouble was when they found out who my mother was. They never knew I had any white blood in me." (This, however, is also testimony to the power of selective cognition among white lesbians, as Sandy's skin is so fair that her current lover, an African-American woman, claimed "she's mixed, but she looks white—if you see her you gonna think she's white.") Sandy's choice to define herself as black worked to her advantage because, she said, "I've always liked black women."[40] Because she kept her racial background a secret and only became involved with African-American women, Sandy did not violate what may have been a taboo in white lesbian culture—black lesbians using white bars as a place to pick up white lesbians. As a biracial woman who witnessed daily the discrimination her parents faced for their interracial relationship, Sandy was perhaps especially sensitive to such taboos. And taboos they were, rooted deep in the same racist and sexist stereotypes whites used to justify lynchings in the first half of the twentieth century.[41] The myth that African-American men stalk and rape white women underpins much of contemporary racism, and lynching can be seen historically as an expression of white masculinity. As historian Jacquelyn Dowd Hall has argued so persuasively, the rhetoric that white men lynched black men in order to protect white women was the battlefield of one of the most difficult struggles of antilynching movements.[42] For white butches, who wanted to appear as capable as any man of protecting their women, African-American studs in white bars may have seemed a considerable threat.[43] As studs, Karla and Sandy had to prove their intentions were nonsexual and emphasize their common oppression as gay women, rather than their racial differences.

Sandy might also have felt comfortable socializing at a white lesbian bar as a result of her first contact with gay culture, at the Palais, where her father—a bisexual black man who had been involved in the gay life for years—took her soon after she divorced her husband. She remembers the experience vividly: "He introduced me around. And I got to lookin' around and I said 'Oh, my god' when I seen all these women. He said, 'I told you you were gay.'" Sandy learned about gay life from her father and from white lesbians at the Palais, and she became a regular there. The "smallest stud in the bar," Sandy recalled that she became the "mascot" there. "I had protection everywhere I went." On one occasion, at least, Sandy needed it—an ex-lover sent a group of studs to the Palais to rough her up because she had broken off their relationship. But the Palais women came through for Sandy: "[T]he next thing I know, I'm be picked up off the floor, put behind the bar and told to stay there, and all the [Palais] studs surrounded these ones who came in the door—they had shotguns, baseball bats, 45s, 38s and 32s and 25s." The Palais women "ended up clearin' that bar out, they took it outside, and honey, you seen studs scatterin' everywhere, the ones that come to get me was runnin' like that Satan was after their behinds." The lesbians at the Palais protected their own, and clearly they felt Sandy was one of them. She remembers the Palais as "a close-knit family type" bar. Apparently, for some African-American lesbians who avoided sexual relationships with white women and emphasized the bonds all lesbians shared, socializing in white lesbian bars could have its rewards.

By the late 1960s, some African-American lesbians had begun to socialize at bars frequented mostly by black gay men, at bars patronized by men and women, and at new bars for black lesbians. Karla's first experience with black lesbian culture was in the primarily black gay men's bars. George's Inca Room was one of her favorite gay male bars in the early seventies. Like many African-American lesbians, Karla felt accepted by gay men and appreciated their culture. She spent most of her early socializing with men because "it was more of them that were together and closer than it was women. You might see two women to every ten gay men. It was more gay men then that was out in the open, and you know, I knew a lot of 'em." Toni fondly remembers her earliest experiences with gay culture in the 1960s when she was under the legal drinking age and would sneak into the Royal Bar, which featured drag shows. "It was the female impersonators in there, and I mean, you couldn't tell if they were women or men, because they were so good. A female impersonator named Sonia used to sing, I mean sing beautifully." Toni also remembers evenings at Studio 51 and Todd's, where the clientele was predominantly male.[44] Ronnie spent many evenings at Bingo's, a large, upscale black men's bar with drag shows on weekend nights. Drag shows may have been the aspect of gay men's culture that made bars possible, because straight couples would go for the novelty of seeing female impersonators, thereby supporting the gay bars where men, and some women, would meet. And by the late 1960s, many black lesbians socialized at Foster's, a mixed bar on Linwood Avenue in which singer Althea Barnes often performed. Sandy described the scene at Foster's:

> It was a together place. We could get out there and dance. We could communicate with each other 'cause it was a small bar. Everybody was everybody's friend, there was no, "Oh, that's my woman" and "I'm gonna hit on your woman," it was nothin' like that, it was a friendship, communicating bar, where everybody knew everybody and we were all close.

Although many lesbians of color enjoyed the supportive community and good times they had in the company of gay men, others felt some discomfort with gay male culture, which they saw as different from their own. Anita said, "I figure, it's not against men, but their lifestyle is very much different from most women. And I think that women do themselves an injustice and a disservice associating themselves politically and socially. I think that we are much different."

Anita said the qualities she valued in friends were not shared by the men she knew: "I don't find men as being fair; I find that their ability to be fair is limited by their ego. And I just can't placate and cater to a man's ego." For some lesbians, what they perceived as promiscuity among gay men created a barrier to close friendships with them. Ronnie had long-term friendships with gay men, and said, "We got along just fine—as long as they respected me, I respected them, that was all that matters." But then she said she found out "they were male prostitutes, a lot of 'em," which was a turning point in how she perceived her friendships with them, and began to treat them only as friendly acquaintances: "I see [gay men friends] and say hi and bye, and we might sit down once in a while and have a couple a drinks, somethin' like that while we were out, but that's about it." Ronnie also sensed tension between drag queens and femmes in mixed bars. "Drag queens and lesbians just don't rate because whereas he's tryin' to be a woman, you're already a woman [and] he gets jealous." African-American gay men were fine to socialize with some of the time, but sometimes black lesbians preferred to spend time in their own bars.

By the 1970s this had become a possibility. Karla recalls, "[C]omin' to the seventies, you had women openin' bars, women managing 'em." The new black lesbian bars existed on a shoestring—closing and opening frequently, changing locations every few years—in contrast to white bars like the Palais, which catered to lesbians continually from 1949 to 1975. These bars were not owned by black women, but were rented from white bar owners whose clientele had participated in the white flight to the suburbs in the 1950s.[45] Yet despite the tenuousness of their existence, these bars represented a new era in a thriving black lesbian culture in Detroit. The time was ripe for black lesbian bars—Detroit's black population was overwhelmingly young, housing was increasingly scarce,[46] and many African Americans had money to spend; unemployment for black workers in Detroit dropped sharply between 1961 and 1965 when auto plants hired more African Americans as whites moved to the suburbs. By 1965, the median family income for blacks in Detroit was nearly twice the national average.[47]

The Barbary Coast and Club Exclusive were the popular night spots for African-American lesbians in the 1970s and catered primarily to them. Club Exclusive offered drinks and dancing in a small, unassuming space. Ronnie tended bar at Club Exclusive, which she remembers was owned by a married heterosexual man who rented to a lesbian. According to Ronnie, it wasn't nearly as nice as clubs like Bingo's, partly because the owner had no incentive to make improvements. "It could've been better if the owner woulda kinda pitched in and fixed it up, but all he saw was dollar signs." Because there were so few public spaces for black lesbians, the owner knew they would frequent his club as it was. Club Exclusive had an especially difficult time staying open, not because of lack of business, but due to outside forces. The club's first site was closed by authorities because the building failed to meet inspection code standards, and the club was met at its second location with a petition from (mostly black) neighbors saying they did not want a gay club in their neighborhood. It was understandable, therefore, that the woman who managed the bar would want to avoid pressuring the owner to make improvements.

At the Barbary Coast, on Thursday nights the crowd was men and women, but on Friday and Saturday nights the clientele was predominantly female—Sandy remembered that on Saturday nights it was the most popular hangout in Detroit for black lesbians. She said that was "where I met a whole lot of women, a whole lotta women. I mean, it was jumpin' every weekend." Women paid a cover charge at the door and could dance all night. Sandy remembers that, unlike the Palais, "The Barbary Coast was not really a liquor drinking bar. It was a party bar where you could go to meet somebody." The atmosphere in these new gay bars was significantly different than their predecessors, the white lesbian "family-type" bars that opened in the days before disco music attracted hordes of young people to the dance floors.[48]

Although these new bars were predominantly the domain of African-American lesbians, a few white women also socialized there. The presence of white women in black lesbians' social spaces was a change from earlier days. Gatherings at Ruth's house were exclusively black, except for the occasional guest of an African-American gay man.[49] Ruth recalled, "[T]here's several white men that has come to the house, but I never knew of any women. Cause you know the men go out and they'll pick up anybody, anything." Ruth said that before the early 1980s, she never knew any white lesbians. Alice and Margaret said they, too, had just gotten to know white lesbians in the previous few years. Unlike black women who went to white lesbian bars a couple of decades earlier, these white lesbians had their own bars but instead chose to socialize with black women. Also, unlike African-American lesbians, whose presence in the Palais was tolerated because they made no sexual advances toward white women, these white women were in black lesbian bars for the purpose of dating African-American women. White lesbians who socialized with African-American lesbians did so because they were looking for sexual or romantic relationships with black lesbians. Some of these white women became well-known for their exclusive attraction to black women.[50]

This new public night life for African-American lesbians embodied other changes, both negative and positive. The growth of bar culture meant that lesbians could find places to socialize through word of mouth, as well as gossip and rumors among heterosexuals, rather than depending on a personal introduction to a party host. And because the clientele was more anonymous, women visiting a bar for the first time could observe lesbians and gay men from a bit of a distance while deciding if the life was for them. Anita first encountered lesbians when her neighbor, a bisexual woman, took her to the Casbah, a once predominantly white bar located in a neighborhood that was shifting from white to black. The clientele of the Casbah reflected the neighborhood around it, and when Anita first visited the bar, she said, "It was different people from different walks of life, different backgrounds; it was one of those party bars, and people were very open and very friendly." Anita had confided in her neighbor that she had been to several doctors about her problem with frigidity, and the neighbor thought she knew the cause of Anita's problem, even if the doctors and Anita did not. The neighbor told her, "I don't think you're frigid. I think you need to go somewhere with me. If you don't want to stay, we won't stay." Anita thought they were going to "a group session with frigid women, a support group." She described their eventual destination:

> So she took me one night to this place and it was a bar. And I'll tell you how dense I was. I was sitting there and drinking my little drink and noticed that all of the women were coming in, and I thought, well maybe later the men will come in. . . . And then I noticed there were no men coming in, and it dawned on me; and she said, "Do you know where you are?" and I said, "Yes, I do." And she said, "Do you want to go home?" and I

said, "No, I don't." At that point it wasn't interest in another woman as sexual; it was just a different experience.

For Anita, being able to observe gay people in the informal atmosphere of the Casbah allowed her to control her introduction to the lesbian world, and to learn about lesbians while maintaining what was for her a safe heterosexual identity. She recalls "I started talking with different women, and I found myself being turned off by real aggressive women." When she felt threatened by a woman, she would tell her she was straight, hoping to cool their ardor. Instead, she said, "it seemed to create a challenge" to the kind of women she wanted to discourage. She remembered, "That's how eventually I met an older woman, and I determined when I wanted to be brought out." The knowledge she gained at the Casbah about lesbian culture gave her the confidence she needed to make sure her first sexual experience with a woman was a good one. Karla also learned about lesbian life through the bars; she said even though she had already had sexual relationships with several girls, "bout the time I got 18, 19, I started goin' to bars. So that's how I kinda learnt, is through goin' to bars." In the sixties and seventies, bars helped lesbians of color learn about what it meant to be gay in Detroit.

Bar culture had its drawbacks, however. Lesbians who socialized in bars opened themselves up to the possibility of violence, police raids, or the chance that they would be seen by someone indiscreet or malicious. Ronnie blamed the risk of antigay violence as "one reason why a lot of us didn't frequent too many gay bars." As she recalled, black men would "be sittin' outside the gay bars and they would harass you goin' in the bar, harass you comin' out the bar, and some [lesbians] have been robbed." Women had to be careful going to and from the bars, because any public display of affection between women could provoke homophobic violence. According to Ronnie, violence was most likely "if they caught them . . . two girls holdin' hands or hugging or kissing," when they "probably got a little tipsy." "They beat up a couple like that. They were holdin' hands walkin' down the street and some guys jumped on 'em and broke they bones in they bodies." Some African-American lesbians avoided such risks by avoiding the bars. Ronnie said, "[Y]ou don't have to even be bothered with that scene, period, if you didn't even go around it, so why make yourself familiar with it?"

Bars did not foster the trust among their clientele that house parties had. Middle-class lesbians in particular became reluctant to socialize in bars in favor of private parties. Since bars were open to the public, heterosexuals wandered in unknowingly or came purposefully, and
lesbians had little faith in their discretion. Margaret Lorick said she
was wary about going [to bars] "because in Flint I didn't want anybody
to know, 'cause . . . even though you have a gay bar a lotta straight
people comin' there, they see you." Margaret knew the social and professional price she would pay if the wrong people found out she was a
lesbian. "[Y]ou probably woulda been ostracized by straight people
that . . . you had friends with . . . they woulda just cut you off." As a
teacher, she feared it "would get out to the parents or something. . . .
And they couldn't fire me or anything from my job, but they [would]
make it difficult for me on my job." Ronnie remembered that in the
1970s, middle-class African-American lesbians "hung out with people
who . . . had the same type of profession, they didn't wanna hang out
with somebody who was . . . all ADC [Aid to Dependent Children] or
. . . somebody who was moochin' offa other people, you know. And
they basically hang out with they own kind, like any other culture . . .
like a heterosexual couple, you know, if you were middle class, you
middle class. It's just life, I guess."

Characteristics of bar life seem to have magnified growing class
differences among African-American lesbians. Many African-American lesbians, especially studs, began to use nicknames in the bars to
protect their real identities. These nicknames were usually masculine
and suggested a tough and daring character, like Deville or Fleet-
wood.[51] These nicknames reinforced stud-femme roles, but they were
also a response to the increased risk of exposure in a lesbian bar. Ronnie said lesbians also used these nicknames because many of them "had
jobs, you know, work in the plants and things, post office and things
like that and I'm quite sure for their social security number they used
they regular name, they didn't use the little nickname that they carried
in the street." This response to the very real threat of homophobia
could make bar life alienating in some ways. Ronnie lamented that a
lesbian "might end up dead and you probably wouldn't know they real
name until they died."

The bars gained a reputation for being rough places that middle-
class black lesbians were unlikely to frequent. Indeed, many African-

American lesbians described incidents in bar culture involving violence or illegal activities. Toni said violence in bars was one reason she
avoided them. "I would go to the bar, . . . but, see, . . . they were just
different than me. [T]hey believe in fightin' and cuttin', you know.
Livin' real hard."[52] Sometimes violence would erupt between two
women over jealousy and competition for a woman's attention, or because a relationship had gone awry.

Police raids of African-American lesbian bars in Detroit were extremely rare, due to a notoriously corrupt police force eager to accept
payoffs from bar owners.[53] Bars, then, became places where other
"vices" flourished. Joan Nestle has written about what she calls "an
historical sisterhood" between lesbians and prostitutes. According to
Nestle, prostitutes and lesbians share an outlaw status as women and
repression by the state and social movements aimed at controlling
vice, and both have been subject to control by the psychiatric profession. In addition, lesbians and prostitutes have historically shared
"red-light districts" in cities, as well as survival strategies that evolved
into cultural norms.[54] In discussing lesbian nightlife in Detroit, most
of the African-American women interviewed for this study commented on the sex trade in the bars, which offered a variety of sexual
pleasures for those who sought them, but remained discreet enough
that those who wanted to could remain only vaguely aware of them.
Some lesbians worked as dancers, pimps, or prostitutes in the predominantly male sex industry in Detroit, collapsing the gap (however
small) between the two worlds.

Despite the thriving gay and lesbian bars available to African-
American lesbians, house parties still remained favorite social activities, although their character had changed somewhat. In the early
1970s many parties took place in houses in the Palmer Park area of
Woodward Avenue. Palmer Park gained a citywide reputation for gay
activity, both from its centrality as a gay male cruising spot and for the
large numbers of gay men and lesbians who lived in the area. In the
seventies, house parties took place near Palmer Park and in other parts
of the city. Karla remembered that several house parties would be going on at one time: "It might be three over here on the West End and
maybe three or four on the East Side. [T]hey'd be in different locations and it'd be different groups of people that do it." These parties
were often larger and more anonymous than they had been twenty

years before at Ruth Ellis's house. Called "blind pigs" or "after-hours parties," these events had more of the public qualities of Harlem rent parties than did the gatherings at Ruth and Babe's house. Karla described a blind pig as a party where "they sell liquor after hours, you know, after the bars close. [I]t opens about 2 [A.M.] . . . you go there and still drink and everything." Renee McCoy recalled, "[t]hey'd basically be rent parties because they'd charge you to come in and you'd go to these house parties afterwards and pay to come in and buy food there." Ronnie said, "You tore up the people's house by the time they left havin' so much fun!" After hours parties offered dancing, drinking, eating, and talking as their main activities.[55] Because these parties began after the bars closed, African-American lesbians and gay men could participate in both the public bar scene and the house party tradition.

Ronnie recalled that people who were hosting after-hours parties used their knowledge of popular lesbian and gay bars to advertise their events with flyers and via word of mouth. The lesbian, gay, and mixed bars provided safe places for hosts to advertise their parties just to other lesbians and gay men, as well as tapping into a population hungry for social events. Renee McCoy recalled that "[a]t the bars they would pass out little cards" advertising the locations of after-hours parties. Once the word was out, party hosts had only to provide drinks, food, and a place to party in order to turn a profit. Ronnie said she charged between one and three dollars at the door, depending "on how I felt and . . . how much crowd could I draw in."

House parties in the late 1960s and the first half of the 1970s not only carried on this traditional form of African-American social life, but also were a practical alternative for people who wanted to make money by hosting social events but were unable to open a bar. This was difficult due to lack of capital, the difficulty and expense of obtaining a liquor license, the dangers in assuming a public role in the black community as the owner of a lesbian bar, and the strength of the house party tradition. Ronnie summed up the reasons for widespread practice of hosting house parties: "What it really is about [is] black people not havin' very much." She pointed to the difficulties faced by lesbian and gay African Americans who aspired to owning their own bars. According to Ronnie, "It's hard for them to get a . . . liquor license. Either they done got a felony on 'em or something is wrong where they can't get a liquor license, . . . or . . . they don't have enough money to buy a building." Blind pigs gave people with knowledge about lesbians and gay men the opportunity to make some money while fulfilling a need for late-night social spaces.

For some black lesbians and gay men, holding after-hours parties was a serious business venture in which their knowledge of the needs of men and women in the life could be parlayed into a tidy profit. Karla remembered that people who had met each other at a gay bar "might get together and open a house just strictly for that." Ronnie, who held parties in her apartment, said

> [I]t was a pretty nice profit. Because it was not really a lot of places for us to go so we had to have something to do. And then if you wanted to be bothered with the crowd . . . you made a nice profit out of . . . it. It helped me along because I had kids and I needed extra money, you know, and this was another way for me to deal within the gay community. . . . I didn't have to be bothered with heterosexual people . . . except for the ones who like to always party with us. I sold drinks and food . . . even though it was illegal, I did it.

The history of African-American lesbian social life is one of both change and continuity. For African-American lesbians, bars represented not a long-needed site of lesbian unity, but rather an adaptation to the changing character of the larger African-American community. Far from being a people without a usable history, African-American lesbians drew on African-American history and tradition as a basis for developing their social spaces. Bars emerged not from a void of activity, but as a change from earlier, no less thriving, forms of social life. Furthermore, as economic factors permitted, bars evolved from house parties to include shared gay and lesbian spaces, to bars where the clientele was mostly black lesbians. And house parties continued to be an important tradition, even as lesbians adapted their older form to fit the new bar-dominated social scene. By focusing on forms of social life outside public bars, this study reveals a history of vibrant creativity and adaptability. For historians of sexuality, exploring this history can sharpen our questions, challenge even our most basic assumptions, and move us toward a better understanding of the dynamics of our communities.

CHAPTER 3

Writing Civil Rights:
The Political Aspirations of
Lesbian Activist-Writers

ALISA KLINGER

But for me, a Black Lesbian Feminist Poet, the politics is not just close at hand, it is the printer's ink on the paper.

JEWELLE GOMEZ

One thing about books is that they can get places that bodies can't.

CHERRÍE MORAGA

At a time when it is no longer easy to read all the volumes by or about lesbians dispatched by the independent, commercial, and academic presses, it is undeniable that discursive production has become a fundamental feature of North American lesbian culture. What is less readily apparent is the pivotal role multiethnic and multiracial lesbian writers and book-trade workers have played in the politicization of lesbians from diverse geographical, cultural, institutional, and sociopolitical locations. The distinctly political cast of multiracial and multiethnic lesbian personal and fictional narratives and the revolutionary investment of lesbians in textual production and distribution over the past twenty-five years, have made writing and reading vital tools for constructing a loosely defined but internationally recognizable North American lesbian community.[1]

By constituting themselves as a diverse community of activists, contemporary multicultural lesbian writers and publishers differ dramatically from the modernist lesbian literati of the 1920s and 1930s, whom Shari Benstock names the "women of the Left Bank," and from the lesbian pulp paperback writers of the 1950s and 1960s, who were, with such important exceptions as Ann Bannon and Valerie Taylor, frequently men writing soft-core pornography for a male readership.[2] Now that electronic technology is indelibly changing our relationship to print, I will risk appearing nostalgic in order to map the vast collective accomplishment of an extensive network of Canadian and American lesbian writers, editors, publishers, printers, distributors, and booksellers operating outside of established literary channels. Using literature as a locus for organization and collaboration, these women assembled lesbians not only at bookstores, public readings, and book clubs, but also at the Women in Print, International Feminist Book-fair, OUT Write conferences, and the Impact Benefits and Lambda Literary Awards ceremonies. Together lesbian cultural workers deployed the print page itself in the struggle for lesbian liberation and cross-cultural understanding, creating in the process an enduring array of innovative textual practices and publishing arrangements.

In choosing to focus on the late 1960s, 1970s, and 1980s as a discrete, bountiful, and highly politicized period in lesbian book history, I am not suggesting that there has been an appreciable decline since then but rather a greater commercial investment in the overall quantity of lesbian writing, publishing, and bookselling.[3] Clearly, such widely acclaimed lesbian writers as Dorothy Allison, Cherríe Moraga and Gloria Anzaldúa, Minnie Bruce Pratt, and Sarah Schulman—recipients, respectively, of a National Book Award nomination, the Before Columbus Foundation American Book Award, a Lamont Poetry Selection prize, and the Words Project for AIDS Award—suggest the extraordinary promise for the continued expansion of the lesbian literary canon. Lesbian printed materials not only line the shelves of 135 feminist bookshops in the United States and Canada, but also are increasingly profitable for commercial bookdealers and filmmakers attuned to their crossover audience potential. However, the death of Audre Lorde (in November, 1992), prolific author and cofounder of Kitchen Table: Women of Color Press, poignantly demarcates the passage of a substantial chapter in the history of lesbian print culture. My account of the traffic in lesbian books focuses on the politically pragmatic narratives and cross-cultural literary exchanges that, like Audre Lorde's life as a "Black Lesbian Feminist Warrior Poet Mother," imbued lesbian literature with its power to effect progressive social and political change.[4]

Before the fledgling New Queer Cinema began enlarging the tiny cast of unabashed celluloid lesbians and before the mainstream media discovered potentially lucrative aspects of lesbian and gay culture, print was the cherished currency of lesbian cultural exchange. Recognizing that "lesbian writing plays a tremendous survival role and culture communication role for the lesbian reader," Joan Nestle, a cofounder of the Lesbian Herstory Archives (who housed the renowned collection in her New York apartment for more than seventeen years before it was moved to its own brownstone in the Park Slope district of Brooklyn), contends that lesbian literature is "one of the pillars of our political movement, and of our eventual survival as a community."[5] The centrality of print media to the expansion of queer culture, Michael Bronski claims, resides in "its relatively cheap technology and the possibility of private consumption."[6] The example set by *Vice Versa*, the first magazine for lesbians, or "gay gals," as they called themselves, indicates that the opportunity for self-publishing and for private circulation were also as much factors in the postwar era debut of Lisa Ben's *Vice Versa* magazine in June 1947 and the ensuing lesbian fascination with printed matter. At a time when obscenity laws meant that lesbian and gay male materials could not be sent to a printer or to newsstands, Lisa Ben (an anagram she used for a pen name when she began writing for *The Ladder* in the 1950s), began composing, editing, and typing *Vice Versa* at her office typewriter. The foremother of the women-in-print movement of the second wave, Lisa Ben anticipated the seditious practice of "liberating" supplies from one's place of employment that subsequent generations of "paper lesbians" used to advance the cause.[7] Lisa Ben explains how while working as a secretary in Hollywood she was able to single-handedly produce multiple issues of the free magazine:

> I put in five copies at a time with carbon paper, and typed it through twice and ended up with ten copies of *Vice Versa*. That's all I could manage. There were no duplicating machines in those days, and, of course, I couldn't go to a printer. . . . Then I would say to the girls as I passed the magazine out, "When you get through with this, don't throw it away, pass it on to another gay gal.[8]

During the prefeminist era the Daughters of Bilitis (DOB) publication, *The Ladder*—the first national lesbian periodical in print from 1956 to 1972—also validated lesbian readers who by "cruising the libraries" hoped to discover some reflection of themselves. As Lee Lynch's description of the complex, highly mediated process of self-recognition suggests, print was one of the few reliable avenues out of the closet for a generation of lesbians:

> [I]dentifying variant books was as subtle, frustrating, and exciting a process as spotting lesbians on the street. Success depended on a vigilant

desperation. I *had* to find reflections of myself to be assured that I was a
valuable human being and not alone in the world. . . . Then, in a magazine
shop in Greenwich Village, I found *The Ladder.* This small, rough periodical was not full of unhappy endings. I sensed that its very existence pro-
claimed a kind of healthy survival I hadn't imagined possible. . . . [It] allowed entry into a legitimate universe.[9]

The Ladder was particularly crucial for many lesbians' sense of cultural
identification and expression during the postwar era, because the per-
secution tactics of Joseph McCarthy's House Committee on Un-
American Activities, which identified homosexuals and communists as
subversives, had driven lesbianism well underground. In 1970, Rita
Laporte, the national president of DOB, and Barbara Grier, the editor
of *The Ladder* from 1968 to 1972, revamped *The Ladder*, disassociating
it from the DOB organization and turning it into a much more politicized magazine, attentive to the emergence of women's liberation and
political lesbianism.

With the rise of the women's liberation movement, an unprecedented number of newspapers, journals, and newsletters that were devoted, or at least attentive, to lesbian concerns were launched. Bought
or borrowed, such ambitious periodicals as *Amazon Quarterly, Chrysa-
lis, Feminary, Conditions, Lavender Woman, Feminist Bookstore News,
Lesbian/Lesbienne, Sinister Wisdom, Azalea, Connexions, Heresies, Open
Door: Rural Lesbian Newsletter, Calyx, Fireweed, La Vie En Rose, Aché,
Hot Wire, Dyke, Rites,* and *Common Lives, Lesbian Lives* found their way
into rural and urban lesbians' hands. The periodicals proved to be a
nurturing milieu for author development, providing established and
upcoming lesbian writers with a peer cohort comprising editors, re-
viewers, and readers. The classified sections of lesbian newspapers,
journals, and newsletters, moreover, routinely ran the calls for submis-
sions that generated the material for prospective lesbian anthologies
and single-author works. While lesbian literary history during the
late sixties and early seventies was being made and recorded primarily
on the freshly drafted pages of lesbian journals, magazines, and news-
sheets, by the mid-seventies and -eighties debates about lesbian diversity, community organizing, and political activism were generating an
increasing number of book-length works and lesbian-feminist publishing collectives.[10]

Despite the repressive cultural, political, and economic climate of the Reagan-Bush and Mulroney era, countless lesbians infiltrated the prohibitive marketplace of publishing and bookselling in a unified effort to develop an autonomous lesbian-feminist publishing network that went hand-in-hand with lesbian writer-activists' relentless analysis of the interstices of subjectivity, agency, and power. The feminist appropriation of A. J. Liebling's slogan, "Freedom of the press belongs to those who own the press," became the rallying call for an entire women-in-print movement, galvanizing women to learn how to edit manuscripts, run printing presses, paste up copy, bind books, and operate bookstores.[11] The rapid proliferation of alternative publishing houses—including Naiad, Persephone, Diana, The Women's Press Collective, Aunt Lute, Spinsters Ink, Sister Vision: Black Women and Women of Colour Press, Daughters Inc., Firebrand Books, Kitchen Table: Women of Color Press, Cleis, New Victoria Press, Seal, and Press Gang Publishers—provided lesbians with unparalleled opportunities and forums for their self-expression.

Operating, at least in theory if not always in practice, as egalitarian, nonhierarchical, nonprofit, and ideologically correct enterprises—juggling socialist and feminist principles with the laws of capitalism—lesbian-feminist presses and publishers actively repudiated the elitist, discriminatory, and censorious practices of the mainstream (male-controlled) commercial presses. Although the women-in-print movement was by no means impervious to some of the flaws of the commercial presses and retail outlets (often working without contracts and selling subsidiary rights without authorial consent), its historic undertaking enabled "literature"—discourse itself—to perform simultaneously the work of cultural awareness, political cohesion, and social activism. In her introduction to the new edition of *Lover*, Bertha Harris contextualizes lesbian-feminist literary production in the early 1970s:

> The presses eked out a hand-to-mouth existence. The costs of the publications often barely covered the production expenses. Nobody got paid; skills, including fundraising, were learned on the job. Decisions were usually made collectively. Hardship was the rule, burnout was the norm; but the staying power was in some cases enormous, and it was almost exclusively fueled by the adamantine convictions which had got the presses

going in the first place: that well-wrought words on a page could, by speaking the unspeakable, create and organize radical political activism.[12]

No women's institutions—cultural, community, or commercial—more dramatically exemplify the viability and endurance of lesbian politics and culture over the past twenty-five years than the lesbian-feminist publishers, presses, and booksellers.

Because of the profound impact lesbian books and feminist bookshops have on our individual socialization and collective visibility, they are an unmistakable feature of lesbian fictional and autobiographical landscapes. In *Exile in the Promised Land: A Memoir*, Marcia Freedman recalls that her partner, Ayala, wanting to bring lesbianism literally out of the closet, had jokingly suggested that they call their makeshift bookshop in Haifa "The Closet" and decorate the windows with books suspended from hangers.[13] Despite the significant geographic vicissitudes of global lesbian culture, when Veronica, the lesbian hero of Terri de la Peña's novel *Margins*, wants to come out to Siena, she decides to take her to the Sisterhood Bookstore in southern California:

> **Her eyes shone as she pointed out well-remembered titles—novels by Katherine V. Forrest, Jane Rule and Ann Allen Shockley; poetry by Judy Grahn, Audre Lorde and Adrienne Rich; non-fiction by Gloria Anzaldúa and Cherríe Moraga. . . . "Whenever I feel discouraged, alienated, I stand here and look at all these books, remember these writers—and my spirits rise."**[14]

The revolutionary investment of North American lesbian writers in the actual means of textual production enabled them to self-consciously represent themselves and their readers as literary and political subjects for the first time. Concomitantly, paper lesbians' concerted entry into print enabled them to inculcate themselves and their readers into the political culture of the nascent sexual liberation movement. Although, as Jane Tompkins argues, "in modernist thinking literature is by definition a form of discourse that has no designs on the world . . . not attempt[ing] to change things, but merely to represent them," contemporary lesbian writers endeavored expressly to create utilitarian or "usable" art—writing that would be assessed in terms of its functionality rather than its "artistic" or entertainment value.[15]

Gloria Anzaldúa proclaims in the "Creativity in a Coping Strategy" portion of her introduction to *Making Face, Making Soul*:

**[W]hen tongue and hand work together, they unite art and politics. . . .
For many of us the acts of writing, painting, performing and filming are
acts of deliberate and desperate determination to subvert the status quo.
Creative acts are forms of political activism . . . and are not merely aesthetic exercises. We build culture as we inscribe in these various forms.**[16]

For many lesbians, including Chrystos, a Native American political activist and activist-writer whose disclaimer is inscribed in the deliberately disjunctive cadence of her contribution to *Making Face, Making Soul/Haciendo Caras* "art" and "literature" are luxuries associated dubiously with the institutional structures of Western culture:

**I've always written from some compulsion, the necessity to make some
damn sense somewhere   a tool of survival   never been art
to me.**[17]

By positioning themselves as activists, multiethnic and multiracial lesbian writers endeavored to negotiate the gulf between art and politics as they socialized lesbians into movement work. They were thus both attempting to recuperate the value accorded literature in their cultural traditions and insisting on a conception of writing and a philosophy of publishing that endorsed literature's relevance and usefulness to particular communities of readers. Their published texts, injected unapologetically with personal and autobiographical content, constitute a historical document of lesbian life, literature, and liberation in the late twentieth century.

The use of print by multicultural lesbian activists to establish strategic political identities and affinities and to articulate passionately their aspirations for civil rights and elemental social change has been the crux of lesbian liberation politics. The "social situatedness" of lesbian activists who emerged as a writing community in the late seventies and eighties—their experiences of erasure by and invisibility in a variety of liberation movement groups—indicates why their interest in writing was as much motivated by their exclusion from movement politics as their estrangement from the dominant literary tradition. In her characterization of the contributors to *This Bridge Called My Back: Writings by Radical Women of Color*, Norma Alarcón argues that

[a]s a speaking subject of an emergent discursive formation, the writer
in *Bridge* was aware of the displacement of her subjectivity across a multiplicity of discourses: feminist/lesbian, nationalist, racial, and socioeconomic. The peculiarity of her displacement implied a multiplicity of positions from which she was driven to grasp or understand herself and her
relations with the real, in the Althusserian sense of the word.[18]

The contributors to *Bridge* and to other such oppositional texts recognized "the considerable difference between them and Anglo-American women, as well as between Anglo-European men and men of
their culture" ("The Theoretical Subject[s]," 28). The disenfran-
chisement many lesbians experienced from the civil rights movement,
the women's movement, and the gay liberation movement can be
understood as a pernicious by-product of the conflict of interest
created when liberation groups promote communitarianism while
fighting for the individual's right to autonomy. The construction of an
affirmative identity, and a recognizable political interest group based
on that identity, necessarily requires a community of supporters. Yet
the commitment to inclusion, strength in numbers, and solidarity frequently renders liberation groups unable to recognize and effectively
represent significant differences, particularly those relating to sexuality, race, ethnicity, and class, among individual members. The political rallying by liberation groups for acceptance of their "difference"
and for recognition of their equal entitlement to the rights and privileges of citizenship has frequently been at the expense of those with
multiple, interlocking subjectivity claims. Lesbians, a subconstituent
group of the civil rights, women's, and gay liberation movements, invariably found aspects of their identities affirmed at the expense of
others.

While lesbians were experiencing simultaneously strong affinities
with a range of gender, sexual, racial, ethnic, and cultural identity
groups, liberation groups that privileged a particular kind of "oth-
erness" over others were consistently ignoring or invalidating the
manifold identities of their multiethnic and multiracial lesbian members. In other words, by treating them only as a constituency to be re-
cruited, liberation groups, as a consequence of their practical and
philosophical essentialism, were performing what Judith Butler calls
a distinctly "colonizing gesture": "colonizing under the sign of the
same those differences that might otherwise call that totalizing con-

cept into question."[19] Galvanized by their displacement within feminist and gay male organizations in particular, and by their collective desire for political recognition, multicultural lesbians from a wide range of social locations staged "paper uprisings" that unequivocally made discourse the terrain for provocation.

   Their creation of discursive communities, then, was instrumental to their efforts to constitute themselves as a recognizable political "subculture." Jean-François Lyotard argues in *The Postmodern Condition* that during the twentieth century there has been a perceptible disappearance of the grand metanarratives professing universal truths and a critical mass of micronarratives whose very presence contests paradigmatic notions of universality. Unlike the transhistorical and transnational scope of the metanarratives, micronarratives present "narrative knowledge"—knowledge that historically has been esteemed "unauthorized"—specific to the shared historical and social conditions of particular constituencies.[20] Moreover, micronarratives are "locally determined" (xxiv), offering "immediate legitimation" (23) and social empowerment to those traditionally disenfranchised from social and political organs of power. Although Lyotard registers some degree of nostalgia for the totalizing narratives of universal truth, his model of modern literary formations characterizes well the politicized textual culture created by contemporary multicultural lesbian writers.

Contemporary lesbian writers of activist micronarratives, unlike authors of conventional political fiction, neither present the field of politics as the sole site of institutional power relations nor focus to any great extent on the public exploits or covert actions commensurate with prohibitive government, military, and penal systems.[21] Rather, personal experiences of being excluded from or effaced by the prevailing culture invariably situate the political in lesbian activist fiction. Political action, consequently, emanates typically from community-based networks staffed by the radically disempowered.

   The real-life political concerns of lesbian activist writers themselves inform the very structures, themes, characters, and images that permeate their fictional landscapes. Foregrounding the negligible distance that separates experiences from literary rendition in many lesbian political tomes, Melanie Kaye/Kantrowitz, for example, is compelled to write an epilogue to "All Weekend No One Mentions Israel." Her apologetic disclaimer attempts to clarify the distinction between her fictional account of a family barbecue and a series of family events she actually attended. The ambiguity about what comprises fiction and nonfiction is perhaps best underscored by the quotation, "[E]vent and invention are equidistant from story and require the same arts," which she includes at the closing of *My Jewish Face and Other Stories.*[22]

Admittedly, the concern about or deference to family members that engenders Kaye/Kantrowitz's epilogue and underlies her foray into the world of fiction is an inherent feature of multicultural lesbian writing. In her "*Introducción*" to *Loving in the War Years*, Cherríe Moraga deftly articulates the issues of self-disclosure and familial reprisal that characteristically circumscribe multiethnic lesbian autobiographical, testimonial, and fictional narratives:

> **Can you go home? Do your parents know? Have they read your work? These are the questions I am most often asked by Chicanos, especially students. It's as if they are hungry to know if it's possible to have both— your own life and the life of the familia. . . . It is difficult for me to separate in my mind whether it is my writing or my lesbianism which has made me an outsider to my family. . . . So often in the work on this book I felt I could not write because I have a movement on my shoulder, a lover on my shoulder, a family over my shoulder. On some level you have to be willing to lose it all to write—to risk telling the truth that no one may want to hear, even you.**[23]

The visceral sense of risk and foreboding created by the transparently personal dimension of politically engaged lesbian fiction is also amplified by the immediacy of the first-person-singular narrative voice and the matter-of-fact tone. Lesbian tales of political enlightenment are typically narrated from the perspective of a street-smart protagonist, yet paradoxically she does not speak simply for herself but also (horizontally rather than hierarchically) for her community. The narrator's first-hand experience of civic exclusion, social injustice, and racial prejudice—in a narrative trajectory reminiscent of lesbian coming out novels that conform to the bildungsroman and picaresque pattern—takes her on a journey from mainstream society to the world of grassroots organizing, community politics, or underground resistance. Her story is not simply a tale of personal empowerment, however, but a representative expression of a communal social problem and a testament to the efficacy of activist work. Molly, the forthright protagonist of Sarah Schulman's *People in Trouble* and a literary descendant of Molly Bolt of *Rubyfruit Jungle* (1973), for instance, negotiates how to be politically effective while living at "the beginning of the end of the world."[24] The tension between action and aesthetics is sustained through her involvement both with Justice, the novel's guerrilla activist organization (modeled closely on ACT UP), and with her married lover Kate, an installation artist who clings to the outmoded idea that "challenging form is more revolutionary than any political organization ever can be" (217). Schulman, herself a participant in ACT UP since 1987 and the cofounder of the Lesbian Avengers in 1992, juxtaposes AIDS activism with "political" art not only to explore the ethics of street justice, but also to entertain what in the apocalyptic world of the novel constitutes empathic, or even simply appropriate, human conduct.

Revealing at the start that "[i]t was the exact blend of rage and fun that got [her] hooked on politics in the first place," the lesbian activist who narrates "My Jewish Face" is well-versed in oppositional tactics.[25] Like Molly of *People In Trouble*, she lends the title story of Kaye/Kantrowitz's first collection of short stories the measure of practical political erudition characteristic of multiethnic and multiracial lesbian protest narratives. By chronicling the growing political aspirations and achievements of the various characters, however, the story is a particularly rich example of how an activist sensibility imbues fiction with liberatory possibility. Kaye/Kantrowitz, herself a long-time peace activist, a former editor and publisher of *Sinister Wisdom*, a prolific poet and essayist, and the present executive director of Jews for Racial and Economic Justice, based in New York City, grooms her characters and readers alike for activist work in the contentious field of identity politics.[26] On one level, the story operates as an exercise in role-playing in which the characters, a small band of Jewish women attending an annual Midwestern feminist conference, act out how to stage a protest. On another level, the story is clearly an emotionally charged dramatization of role reversal precipitated by one actor's disruptive identity disclosure and her corresponding descent from the theater stage to the audience pit.

The story revolves, initially, around two conference attendees' ac-

count of a deleterious political theater performance they had attended
the previous evening. "Scraping the bottom of the bad taste barrel"
(144), the theater company had made a joke about the Holocaust and
some comparisons between Jews and animals. While the conference
women's sense of outrage escalates upon hearing the review of the performance, the lesbian activist—the narrator who recounts the story as
a participant of the affronted group, rather than as an isolated or distinctive subject—contemplates how to translate their collective anger
into aggregate action:

> I recognized that energy. It was people wanting to fight back but uncer-
> tain what to do. I know when people want to fight but do nothing, every-
> one's sense of possibility shrinks up a little. That restless energy is my
> idea of sheer temptation, whereas blocking that energy—out of fear, la-
> ziness or just plain lack of imagination—is my idea of sin. "What do you
> want to do?" I asked. The word *do* hung in the air, an odd moment of
> quiet. (147)

Although the women do not know it until later, one of the company
actors, Rae, has been a conscious Jew and an out lesbian for two years.
Playing the part of the Statue of Liberty in one of the skits, she is
nonetheless the very symbol of American freedom. She is also the only
company actor who is offended by and critical of the play's anti-
Semitism. "My Jewish Face" relates how the conference attendees, as
well as Rae, respond to the anti-Semitic political theater performance.

The would-be activists clustered around a cafeteria table are
somewhat ambivalent about whether they are even entitled to "act up."
Nonetheless, they consider the repertoire of serviceable activist strategies, including starting a discussion after the performance, inter-
rupting the show to give out leaflets, picketing the event, and performing their own guerrilla theatrics at the entrance to the playhouse.
In the grips of a Hamletesque state of indecision, they finally muster
the courage to go to the performance, not committing themselves to
a specific plan of action. The lesbian activist who had earlier prompted
the women to take action explains, "[w]e sat in the audience waiting
to be or not to be offended enough to do something" (149). The characters on stage make offensive remarks, giving the women their cue to
respond. From their seats, they bombard the performers with questions. As Clara exclaims boldly from the audience pit, "[T]he whole

point of political theater is that people shouldn't be passive. . . . Why do you expect us to sit quiet and listen?" (150)

Inspired perhaps by the conference women's protests, or by her own growing refusal to condone the political theater troupe's anti-Semitism, Rae saves her dramatic disobedience for the finale:

> [T]he cast gathered on stage at the front of the cafe to sing, each actor in turn, a verse about her or his character from the last skit. Each verse ended with the line, *See how you like my face,* sung three times. . . . It was [Rae's] turn. . . . She sang her verse like everyone else, concluding with *See how you like my face, see how you like my face*—she tossed her head, the words came through clenched teeth—*See how you like my Jewish-looking face.* (150–151)

After departing from the script to come out as a Jew, Rae leaves the stage and joins the women in the audience sitting in judgment of the cast. Rae as well as the conference women refuse the precarious protection passing occasionally affords white-skinned Jews when they publicly identify themselves as Jews.[27] By investing the women's declaration of their Judaism with the same fears of self-disclosure and anxieties of coming out experienced by many lesbians and gay men, Kaye/Kantrowitz not only draws a striking comparison between the dynamics of homophobia and of anti-Semitism, but also enacts the cumulative effects of intersecting axes of oppression.

The truly performative disruption of identity politics as usual liberates political theater, democratically restoring power to the audience. In so doing, the women's insurrection in effect transforms a fiction about political theater gone bad into a how-to guide for latent and aspiring political activists alike. Narrative uprisings, or protest narratives, such as "My Jewish Face" demystify activism and identity oppression by expanding and enriching the reader's political literacy. Readers are given practical advice about how to articulate their inner sense of devaluation, how to join with others to stage publicly their shared causes for protest, and how to combat discrimination within progressive groups themselves. By infusing fiction with such a distinct political imperative, multiracial and multiethnic lesbian activists were able to make their micronarratives a medium for readers to learn strategies for redressing the social injustices and racial inequities in their daily lives. Lesbian narratives of political enlightenment thus work locally to bring about civil justice. Quite literally, they inspire readers to take action while training them how to be activists.

The inextricable connection between discursive production and anti-racist political mobilization for innumerable multiethnic and multiracial lesbians also inspired a steady stream of influential collaborative writing projects, including *Home Girls: A Black Feminist Anthology, This Bridge Called My Back: Writings By Radical Women of Color, Nice Jewish Girls: A Lesbian Anthology, Yours In Struggle: Three Feminist Perspectives on Anti-Semitism and Racism*, and *Piece of My Heart: A Lesbian of Colour Anthology*.[28] The deliberately accessible lesbian-edited anthologies, perhaps more so than individual works by a single author, appreciably bridge the gap between isolation and solidarity, between literature and social consciousness. While socially relevant lesbian fiction depicts the strategic deployment of identity for personal and political restitution, the works they are included in, as well as multicultural lesbian anthologies and collections as a whole, scrutinize the concept of "identity" by consistently addressing the specificities of and interconnections among a wide range of oppressions. Unlike the preoccupation with "speaking the body," characteristic of much women's experimental fiction (such as fiction theory and *écriture féminine*), the emphasis placed on diaspora experiences of exile, migration, displacement, and self-determination by multiracial and multiethnic lesbian anthology contributors, suggests why their politicization of writing owes more to historical and materialist analyses of power than to psychoanalytical discourse.[29] The multilingualism of many contributors, moreover, produces a recurrent thematic preoccupation with enforced second language acquisition, rather than solely with phallocentrism (the dimensions of representation—the symbolic) per se. Characteristically mingling Black English, Spanish, Hebrew, or Yiddish with English, multiracial and multiethnic lesbian-feminist anthologies attempt to reclaim and recreate a cultural tongue, while resisting the imperious language of colonization and the dominant language of patriarchy. Although the contributors to the innovative lesbian-feminist anthologies share some of the linguistic inventiveness associated with experimental women's writing, their pieces manifest a distinctly pragmatic concern for the recovery of cultural history and literacy.

Authenticating by accumulation, the anthologies are a repository of the contemporary lesbian movement's collective self-representation, historical memory, and political resistance. Contributors to multicultural lesbian anthologies—invariably a combination of previously unpublished and more experienced writers who nonetheless share a similar sense of estrangement from the literary establishment yet some degree of personal agency—render print a viable medium for the production of self-knowledges *for* themselves and their readers. By reiterating, expanding, and refining their cocontributors' claims and by making explicit overtures of invitation to the reader, the plural subjects of multiethnic and multiracial anthologies renounce the Western hegemonic tradition of the autonomous (elitist) author in favor of an editor-contributor collaborative model of authorship and a people's activist conception of the writer. The sense of complicity they thereby create within and among the anthologies and between "author" and reader produces a consciousness and an ideology that is collectivist but not monolithic, narrowing the margin between public and private discourse.[30] Whereas lesbian coming-out stories, the mainstay of the American lesbian literary canon, are characteristically preoccupied with the idiosyncratic psychosexual development of an individual woman, the hybrid testimonial quality of and the cumulative effect created by the anthology pieces posits a plural self, and encourages a constitutively public mode of expression to denounce the political status quo. In other words, the experientially determined focus of any given piece in the multicultural lesbian-feminist anthologies, in combination with the variety of related accounts by other contributors who are similarly wrestling with complex questions of identity and entitlement, transforms the individualist story into a collectivist social text and communal resource. This oppositional strategy, based on a shared capacity for and approach to resistance and emblematic of multiethnic and multiracial lesbian-feminist print culture, has enabled contemporary multicultural lesbians to communicate a polymorphous concept of community, inviting to readers at varying levels of critical consciousness, self-acceptance, and political commitment.[31] The landmark lesbian-specific and lesbian-feminist anthologies, with their multi-genre mixture of short stories, diary entries, polemical essays, poems, testimonials, interviews, and oral histories "grounded in and informed by the material politics of everyday life" (Mohanty 11), are thus the very site in which the common context of struggle has been rooted for contemporary lesbians from diverse racial, ethnic, religious, linguistic, regional, and class positions.

The fervent analyses of oppression and celebrations of difference that bounded into print during the eighties reveal an unprecedented degree of dialogue, collaboration, and affirmation among lesbians who shared neither similar backgrounds nor a unified political vision that matches the writerly collectivity and readerly communitarianism created by lesbian texts themselves. Evidence of the appreciable contributions, including editing drafts, offering encouragement, printing texts, and checking galleys, multiracial and multiethnic lesbian writers were willing to make to one another's work can be found readily in the ancillary materials that accompanied lesbian discursive projects into print. Barbara Smith, for example, acknowledges a diverse group of Latina, Jewish, and African-American lesbians who assisted voluntarily in the preparation of *Home Girls: A Black Feminist Anthology* for publication. In "A Note to Our Readers," prefacing their essays in *Yours In Struggle*, Elly Bulkin, Barbara Smith, and Minnie Bruce Pratt jointly articulate the conditions that made it possible for them to enter "a growing dialogue among women" (7), while offering a discursive model of cross-cultural political coalition:[32]

> **Yours in Struggle** grew out of the three of us having known each other for several years. We are all lesbians who have worked together politically and respect each other's work. This book happened because we were able to talk to each other in the first place, despite our very different identities and backgrounds—white Christian-raised Southerner, Afro-American, Ashkenazi Jew. Each of us speaks only for herself, and we do not necessarily agree with each other. Yet we believe our cooperation on this book indicates concrete possibilities for coalition work. (7)

The acknowledgments and dedications that preface lesbian textual productions offer similarly inspiring, yet pragmatic, examples of the crucial role multicultural lesbian writers have had in the creation of an increasingly diverse and widespread activist movement and literary community. Echoing numerous appreciative lesbian readers and writers, Makeda Silvera, an Afro-Caribbean woman living in Canada and editor of the first collection of Canadian and American writing by lesbians of color, acknowledges the formidable influence that lesbian-feminist writing, in print for scarcely a decade, had on her own development as an activist-writer and as publisher (*Piece of My Heart: A Lesbian of Colour Anthology*):

> I want to acknowledge with all my heart, women who came out in print and in their lives before this anthology. Women who paved the way, who helped build respective lesbian communities to make us strong and to serve as examples. It was through such women, the editors and contributors to *This Bridge Called My Back, Writings by Radical Women of Colour* (1981) and *All the Women are White, All the Blacks are Men, But Some of Us Are Brave* (1982) that my own voice began to emerge (xix).

The far-reaching impact of multicultural lesbian discursive productions was not only felt across national borders, but, as Joseph Beam indicates, also in the gay male community. By mid-1983, Beam claims he had called a "personal moratorium on the writing by white gay men, and read, exclusively, work by lesbians and Black women."[33] In his revealing introduction to *In the Life: A Black Gay Anthology*, he explains:

> I was fed by Audre Lorde's *Zami*, Barbara Smith's *Home Girls*, Cherríe Moraga's *Loving in the War Years*, Barbara Deming's *We Cannot Live Without Our Lives*, June Jordan's *Civil Wars*, and Michelle Cliff's *Claiming an Identity I Was Taught to Despise*. Their courage told me that I, too, could be courageous. I, too, could not only live with what I feel, but could draw succor from it, nurture it, and make it visible". (13)

Admittedly, extratextual details are not the traditional purview of textual analysis or literary theory. Lesbian readers grounded in community issues, however, invariably situate lesbian cultural texts in the broader sphere of an author's (anthologist's) political engagements and community commitments, thereby blurring distinctions between inter- and extratextual materials. For queer theory—the study of a nondominant discursive culture—ancillary materials are thus richly suggestive, offering insight into the personal dimension and process of literary production. Further, the mainstream media's persistent marginalization of lesbians and almost total disregard for the integrity of their cultural practices encourages lesbian readers to support a lesbian press that reports on lesbian writers' biographies, activist credentials, and public appearances. Even details that may seem speculative and ancillary are important to multiethnic and multiracial lesbians in their continuous efforts to find affirmative representations of their identities and to construct an empowering lesbian cultural history.

Although I do not want to romanticize or minimize the palpable struggles that underpin even the most localized acts of cross-race and cross-class communication and alliance, the progressive practices of multiethnic and multiracial lesbian writers, editors, publishers, and booksellers represent an impressive collective accomplishment. Taken together, the broad range of lesbian discursive engagements, including the countless public readings, lecture series, book fairs, symposia, and writing workshops held in bookstores, coffeehouses, community centers, living rooms, synagogue and church meeting rooms, educational institutions, and conference sites not only disseminate the theoretical tools for understanding the indivisibility of interconnected identities. They also document the deeply felt commitments that fuel the struggle for progressive political change and deliver the inspiring blend of resistance and optimism necessary for an abiding vision of lesbian cultural survival.

At this cultural moment, when (white) lesbians are *Newsweek*, *New York*, and *Vanity Fair* cover girls, the recurrent literary enactments of activist politics in and the directives for political mobilization proffered by oppositional lesbian discursive enterprises may seem naive if not outmoded. Nonetheless, by creating an elaborate apparatus of literary production and what Barbara Smith terms the very "resources for struggle"[34] since the late sixties, multiethnic and multiracial lesbian writers were not only instrumental in theorizing the complex relationships among different axes of identity oppression, but also permanently demystified literary composition, textual production, and political activism for a class of people whose words and actions have historically been censured or silenced.

PART TWO

·

CONVENTIONS

CHAPTER 4

All in the Family:
Lesbian Motherhood Meets Popular
Psychology in a Dysfunctional Era

ELLEN HERMAN

One of the classics of early lesbian feminism, Dolores Klaich's *Woman + Woman*, managed to include, in almost 300 pages, only a single sentence on the "special problems" of lesbian mothers. Its index lists one reference to domestic arrangements; it reads "family, overthrowing of."

That was in the early 1970s. Less than twenty years later, motherhood[1] is the subject of a mushrooming literature produced by and for lesbians: Workbooks cover everything from obtaining sperm to managing stress; children's stories explain that *Heather Has Two Mommies*; videos profile the individuals who populate the radical edge of contemporary kinship. Within lesbian communities, motherhood is the engine behind new organizations that have spread from the West Coast eastward, and the cause of frequent, earnest conversations about whether, when, and how to have and raise children.

Of course, millions of lesbians have always been and continue to become mothers by all the same purposeful and accidental methods common to other women. Widely accepted estimates have been that at least 10 percent of all women are lesbians and 20–30 percent of all lesbians have children. That adds up to somewhere between 2.5 million and 4 million lesbian mothers in the United States today, without even counting the lovers and friends who share in the work of parenting.

Today there are indications that the sheer number of lesbian mothers may be increasing even as the very definition of lesbian motherhood—and its relationship to lesbian identity in general—is being thoroughly revised. For the first time, lesbians in large numbers are deliberately "choosing children" after coming out, a phenomenon that is causing a demographic blip known as the "lesbian baby boom." Few lesbians, it seems, are interested any longer in overthrowing the family, at least not the intergenerational one they imagine creating themselves through biological reproduction, co-parenting, adoption, or foster parenting.

Why has this happened and what does it mean about the evolution of lesbian identity, culture, and community? When and why did the central question about lesbian motherhood move from whether we will be "allowed" to retain custody of our children (assumed to be the products of heterosexual, frequently marital, relationships) to whether we will be able to create stronger and better families than the ones in which we grew up ourselves? Does the baby boom of the past decade indicate the success of gay liberation in increasing lesbian self-esteem and inaugurating an era of sexual and reproductive freedom? Or does it indicate lesbian surrender to the rules and regulations of femininity, maternity being first among them?

There are, of course, no simple answers to any of these questions. Any analysis of the shape of lesbian motherhood today must take into account a series of complex and interrelated demographic, political, and technological changes over the past several decades.[2] After a cursory glance in the direction of each of these, I will explore one particular cultural influence that is pervasive among lesbians and in contemporary American culture at large: the psychotherapeutic sensibility, and especially the popular psychological literature, about dysfunctional family systems and "adult children."

The orientation of popular psychology toward emotional acceptance, and its appreciation of the importance of growth through interpersonal relationships and life cycle stages—including parenting—help to explain (along with the absence of satisfying alternatives) the exceptionally eager reception given to this literature by lesbians. As members of a group struggling to come to terms with an emotional and sexual identity that is still severely stigmatized in American society, many lesbians have found that an apt metaphor for their frequently negative experiences of family life is "recovery." Like the effort to gain control over the ravages of alcoholism or drug addiction, moving away from parental rejection and toward self-love and supportive community is considered an empowering journey that promises mental health. While they instill hope that lesbians can overcome the psychic wounds of homophobia, the simplistic nostrums of popular psychology dangerously distort the reality of contemporary family life and offer few suggestions that can help lesbians imagine or realize new visions of what that social institution might be like.

What are the ideas of this popular psychological literature on family and family systems? How have they influenced lesbians, be they mothers, potential mothers, or non-mothers? What are the areas of tension between popular psychology and the lesbian/feminist critique of the family to which many of these same women have been exposed? These two literatures, which are reviewed in the following pages, have both been important in shaping lesbians' ideas about family even though these literatures diverge rather dramatically in their judgments of what constitutes family in the first place, what the sources of family problems are, what links families to the wider society, and whether conventional familial ideals should be embraced or rejected.

BEHIND THE LESBIAN BABY BOOM

By 1990, the first generation of post-Stonewall lesbians was up against a ticking biological clock. Having come out in an era of feminism and gay liberation, many of these women had spent their entire adult lives involved in organized efforts to counter sexism and homophobia. As the 1980s ushered this generation into its middle years, it was perhaps inevitable that the idea of lesbian self-determination would come to include the right to social or biological motherhood.

The demographic profile of family life has changed dramatically over the past several decades, and not only for lesbians. The flood of women into the labor market, skyrocketing divorce rates, and trends toward delayed marriage and lower rates of childbirth transformed the traditional nuclear family ideal of male breadwinner (earning a "family wage") and female homemaker (caring for household and children) into a statistical minority as early as 1965. By 1980, 70 percent of all Americans lived in households that looked nothing like the Ozzie-and-Harriet prototype, and real questions existed about the prevalence of that prototype in earlier historical periods.[3] But if patterns of household composition have become more varied than ever—with families comprised only of women and children becoming especially numerous, visible, and poor—the desire to experience parenthood has hardly evaporated. Rates of childlessness among women have hardly budged since the post-World War II baby boom. Motherhood has changed, but it has not gone out of style.

The Reagan/Bush years were characterized by vigorous attacks on women's hard-won reproductive rights—especially the right to an abortion—and feverish efforts to polish the tarnished image of the heterosexual nuclear family, bolster the supposedly natural authority of the male breadwinner role, and glorify stay-at-home motherhood. The election of Bill Clinton in 1992, and his appointment of Ruth Bader Ginsburg to the Supreme Court, eased anxieties that *Roe v. Wade* might be overturned in the near future, and a political climate friendlier to many public policies that feminists advocate, from family leave to more severe penalties for sexual harassment, existed for a short period.

But the changing of the guard in the White House has not been enough to dismantle anti-gay policies, some of which have grown up over decades, let alone end the exclusion of homosexuals that is at the core of many social institutions, none more than marriage and the traditional family. The Clinton administration's early effort to lift the ban on military service by gay men and lesbians, to mention only one well-known example, generated a groundswell of resistance and ended in a dismal "compromise" that maintains the closet as the only option for gay military personnel who wish to keep their jobs.

Many key battles over reproductive and civil rights, in any case, have moved away from the orbit of federal policymakers and into the heart of state and local electoral politics, where the strength of organized gay communities is patchy at best. Clinton's election may have served notice to the Christian Right that the political tide was turning on the abortion question, but it also stiffened its resolve to resist the creed of secular humanism where it seemed both most terrifying and vulnerable, in the area of gay rights, where no federal guarantees yet exist. According to David Caton, chair of the American Family Political Committee in Florida, "You will find more people willing to fight the homosexual agenda than oppose abortion."[4] Consequently, momentum has been growing in grassroots campaigns to repeal civil rights statutes, and to prohibit the passage of any "special rights" for gays. Inspired by the recent success of such a statewide amendment in Colorado (as well as municipal initiatives that rolled back gay rights in Cincinnati, OH; Lewiston, ME; and Portsmouth, NH), voters in a number of states organized ballot initiatives and the Republican sweep in the fall 1994 congressional elections demonstrated, among other things, the strength of such anti-gay political mobilization.

In addition to political developments, advances in reproductive technology have promoted pro-natalist views of women as special (and therefore deserving of differential treatment) because they are more devoted to human connection and healing, and closer to "nature" and to "life," than men. *In vitro* fertilization and embryo transfer, widely heralded by the media as brave new "choices" for which women should be grateful, served mainly to underline the conventional equation of womanhood and biological motherhood, as did controversial surrogacy cases, such as that of Mary Beth Whitehead and Baby M in 1987. The vast sums spent on and the deep reserves of feeling generated by "discovery" of infertility as a medical condition in recent years have pressured women to consider anything standing between themselves and pregnancy as an intolerable obstacle to be overcome at all costs. In such a climate, it is the desire *not* to become a mother that is best kept quiet.

These demographic, political, and technological shifts touched the lives of lesbians because they touched the lives of all women. Some developments during the 1980s, however, were disproportionately felt by lesbians. The experience of working with gay men as AIDS activists, for example, tended to banish the mood of self-protective timidity and galvanize a new militancy, embodied in such organizations as ACT-UP, Queer Nation, and the Lesbian Avengers, and in slogans like "Silence=Death" and "Lesbians Are Luscious." By exposing the depth of homophobia in America, AIDS made many lesbians and gay men more determined than ever to make gay love visible, and far less willing to compromise it behind the smokescreen of privacy.

As a consequence, there has been a wave of enthusiasm among gay activists for domestic partnership legislation, challenges to marriage statutes, and other efforts to formally legitimize the domestic arrangements of lesbians and gay men by expanding the legal definitions of "family." Many of these local campaigns have gone down to defeat, in part because right-wing groups have effectively labeled the "gay agenda" as a conspiracy to confer "special" privileges on an undeserving homosexual minority.

SAMENESS / DIFFERENCE

Lesbian mothers have been subject to all the pressures that heterosexual women and mothers have confronted during the past twenty years. Heterosexism, on the other hand, causes unique problems for lesbians who are mothers or who are considering motherhood. Rather than struggling against the assumption that reproductive biology constitutes their destiny, lesbians have had to fight the straightforward rejection of their potential for motherhood, more often than not based on homophobic stereotypes of lesbian life as tragic, loveless, and necessarily childless. What lesbians and heterosexual woman shared, according to the dominant cultural view, was their categorical and obligatory relationship to motherhood: Straight women must reproduce; lesbians must not.

Lesbians who were mothers in marriages before they came out faced the prospect of ugly custody battles upon divorce or as soon as their sexual preference was discovered. Until the late 1970s, organizations like San Francisco's Lesbian Mothers Union and Seattle's Lesbian Mothers' National Defense Fund (the latter is still in existence) offered legal assistance and support. Today the National Center for Lesbian Rights (in San Francisco) and the Lambda Legal Defense Fund (in New York) are the outstanding national resources on legal issues related to lesbian and gay parenting.[5]

Traditionally in custody battles, sexual preference was implicated as a central issue (and sometimes the *only* issue) in determining the fitness of lesbian mothers. Judges consistently expressed concern about the detrimental impact of homosexuality on children, either because of the fear that lesbian mothers would turn their children gay, because the stigma would be too much for children to bear, or because lesbian sexuality and maternal love were perceived as incompatible. One Ohio judge put it bluntly: "Orgasm means more to them than children or anything else."[6]

Many judges today remain preoccupied with these concerns, if a recent high-profile Virginia case is any indication. In September 1993, Sharon Bottoms, a lesbian mother, lost custody of her two-year-old son to her own mother, who argued that Sharon's sexual orientation was immoral and that her relationship with another woman would confuse and damage the boy. Bottoms and her partner pursued an appeal, which eventually failed. They have pessimistically warned other lesbian parents to stay far away from Virginia.

Offsetting such setbacks have been some encouraging breakthroughs in the formal recognition of lesbian familial ties. Only three days after Sharon Bottoms was declared an unfit mother because of her lesbianism, the Massachusetts Supreme Court permitted a lesbian couple, Susan Love and Helen Cooksey, to jointly adopt Love's biological daughter because they together created "a warm and stable environment which is supportive of [the child's] growth and over-all well being."[7] The court's decision made the Love/Cooksey family (and that of another lesbian couple whose case was heard at the same time) the first to legally include two parents of the same gender. (There are a number of other states in which such same-sex second-parent adoptions have been granted in recent years; California is the most notable.) The result is that courts in Massachusetts are now required to hear adoption petitions from unmarried couples—heterosexual as well as gay—though adoptions are still granted on a case-by-case basis.

The sharp contrast between the Bottoms and the Love/Cooksey cases demonstrates the power individual states wield in determining whose sexual and emotional arrangements can or cannot constitute a family in the eyes of the law.[8] Forays onto this legal frontier are critically important. But for the moment at least, their impact is more symbolic than real since the vast majority of lesbian mothers must live and struggle with the practical fallout of legal nonrecognition. Few employers or health insurance companies extend family benefits to "significant others," let alone their dependent children, so members of lesbian families either pay for additional policies or go without. Unofficial parents—partners or friends of biological and adoptive mothers—have no legal standing in the event of death or separation. Their histories of loving support evaporate before a law that considers blood and/or marriage the only valid ties. As "biological strangers," these lesbian mothers are denied even the dignity of being named a parent at all.[9]

THE STRANGE CAREER OF PSYCHOLOGICAL EXPERTISE

Because both old- and new-fashioned lesbian mothers continue to face obstacles thrown up by the sturdy doctrine of homosexual psychopathology, advocates and enemies of lesbian motherhood have all been eager to occupy the high ground of psychological knowledge. The testimony of psychological experts pervades not only the court records of lesbian custody cases and popular television talk shows, but debate among lesbians as well.

In the past twenty years, the professional consensus that homosexuality is a sickness has given way to a more pluralistic and less judgmental understanding of psychological development, sexual maturity, and mental health in general.[10] This change resulted more from political pressure than professional enlightenment. Gay activists and their allies forced the removal of homosexuality from the Diagnostic and Statistical Manual of Psychiatric Disorders (DSM-II), psychiatry's diagnostic bible, in 1973, where it had been listed as one form of pathology or another for decades. Likewise, feminist caucuses formed within most professional psychological organizations to protest scientific sexism and reorient clinical and research practices in egalitarian directions.

In the realm of theory, feminists tackled the sexist biases of conventional psychological and psychiatric perspectives and produced developmental models that tried to explain the production and reproduction of gender and sexual identities as social, rather than natural, phenomena. Clinicians, too, pioneered a variety of therapeutic alternatives—frequently called "feminist therapy" or "lesbian and gay counseling"—designed to simultaneously heal the individual pain caused by oppressive gender and sexual prescriptions and to offer a larger social critique.

By the 1980s, a certain amount of progress was evident. It was possible (at least for urban, well-educated, middle-class lesbians) to find supportive therapists (many of them lesbians themselves), to read sympathetic books about love and courtship, and to carve out spaces in their lives where they need not fear being labeled deviant or dangerous on a daily basis. Much of the skepticism about psychological expertise that accompanied the earlier equation between homosexuality and mental illness had faded.

The language of developmental theory, professional psychotherapy, and self-help—all promoted with a vengeance in the 1980s through the medium of popular psychology—have had strikingly wide appeal among lesbians. Lesbian communities have been willing and eager to invest the capital, the entrepreneurial spirit, and the education necessary to build and maintain a sensitive psychotherapeutic industry and an environment thoroughly supportive of psychological self-consciousness. Impressionistic evidence can be found in the pages of ads for therapeutic services, which typically outnumber all others in lesbian and feminist publications. More empirical data emerged in the first major national survey of lesbian health, which was conducted in the mid-1980s and documented that utilization of professional mental health services was "surprisingly high" among lesbians: about seventy-five percent of those surveyed. Its authors were careful to note, however, that lesbians' embrace of psychotherapy should be interpreted as a sign of strength, not pathology.[11]

Twelve-step programs and other support and recovery groups for addicts and codependents have also proliferated. Books by Harriet Lerner (*The Dance of Anger: The Dance of Intimacy*) and Anne Wilson

Schaef (*Co-Dependence: Misunderstood, Mistreated; When Society Becomes an Addict*) have hit the top of the charts in feminist bookstores
across the country, many of which now devote entire sections to recovery literature and paraphernalia, as do numerous general bookstores
as well. There is even a feminist newsletter called "Women's Recovery Network."

Issues like domestic violence, insistently pushed into the world of
politics by feminist activists in the late 1960s and early 1970s, have
made a marked transition from problems of power and domination to
problems of pain and healing. Recent books by feminists about sexual
abuse, for example, have adopted some of the substance of contemporary popular psychology as well as its stylistic fondness for checklists,
exercises, catchy acronyms, inspiring but simplistic affirmations, pre-
dictable emotional chronologies, and other trappings of how-to
genres. (Ellen Bass' and Laura Davis' *The Courage to Heal* comes to
mind.)

Noticeably absent are explicit references to feminism's core ax-
iom: that the contemporary family is a patriarchal arrangement in
which women and children are vulnerable to sexual abuses because of
their subordination to adult men within and outside of the household.
Today, the suggestion that codependency explains the persistence of
sexual or other abuse, that a compulsive search for self-esteem leads
women and their children to keep family secrets and betray their own
true self-interests, appears at least as persuasive—perhaps more so.

HOW FAMILY SYSTEMS DO
(AND DON'T) WORK

The literature on "dysfunctional" families, whose popularity coin-
cided with the lesbian baby boom of the 1980s, insists that something
is very wrong with the family. But where feminists tended to see male
domination and mandatory heterosexuality as problems, the new family experts see a maze of dysfunctional rules and a deep well of childhood pain that stubbornly follows people into adulthood. A society of
suffering "adult children" then fuels the tragic cycle by reproducing a
new generation of compulsively addicted or codependent children.[12]

Where feminists called for the elimination of male supremacy and compulsory heterosexuality, popular psychology urges recovery.

Earlier, feminist analysts revealed the family as a patriarchal institution that produces and reproduces relations of domination and subordination based on gender, a process that benefits men and victimizes women and children. Lesbians added obligatory heterosexuality to the critique, promoting a vision of voluntary sexuality and domesticity in order to loosen the allegedly "natural" bonds tying womanhood to heterosexuality and maternity. The goal is to make love, not biology or legal status, the essential ingredient in a family and to acknowledge a wider range of legitimate sexual and reproductive choices about whether or not to mother, with whom to mother, and so forth.

The feminist critique of the family as it emerged in the 1970s is in a state of flux. The inhospitable political atmosphere of the 1980s, the pointed criticisms of white feminists' racial biases by women of color, and the practical lessons that millions of women have learned while trying to blend paid work and family have all raised fundamental questions. Is the family actually the monster many feminists initially thought it to be?

This state of confusion helps explain why feminists and lesbians may be looking to popular psychology for answers. While feminist theorists are trying to make up their minds about whether or not to continue the attack on the family, the literature of popular psychology acknowledges that families exist and that real people and their real pain cannot wait on the answers to such questions, no matter how theoretically important they may be. It assumes that emotional experience and personal life are utterly significant, and that they cannot and should not be ignored or dismissed as peripheral matters. In this sense, popular psychology speaks a direct and eloquent truth.

Popular psychology may differ from feminism in accepting the family *as it is*, but it shares with the feminist critique a central belief: that familial relationships are largely social, and that they produce certain types of personalities and certain kinds of relationships. When people suffer and when relationships are abusive, the family process expresses a "poisonous pedagogy," according to John Bradshaw, one of the gurus of the new literature, who borrowed this phrase from psychoanalyst Alice Miller. The family "is like a multicar pileup on the

freeway, causing damage generation after generation after generation," writes Susan Forward, author of *Toxic Parents*.[13] Feminists and
psychology's popularizers share a desire to explain the reproduction of
particular emotional arrangements, but while the former direct their
attention to child-rearing, domestic violence, and economic dependence, the latter employ a gender-neutral vocabulary of (damaged and
healthy) self-esteem.

Another view shared by feminists and today's psychologists alike
is that people learn to accept just about whatever happens to them in
familial contexts as normal. "Naming" out loud the secrets of wife
beating, child abuse, or emotional anguish—whether in psychotherapy, self-help organizations, or consciousness-raising groups—is a
critical first step. Theorists contend that people must escape the emotional trap of their families of origin by seeking nonjudgmental validation before they will be able to reclaim and heal themselves (in the
case of family systems) or create a movement for social change (in the
case of feminism).

The most consistent overall themes in the new literature are as follows. The most urgent human needs are to feel good about oneself, to
experience one's emotions directly, and to grow. Parents cause children's emotional pain and manufacture their distorted identities. Personal anguish is deep and entirely legitimate. Each person is precious
and important. There is a way out of misery if one can only reach deep
down inside and discover the courage to move toward self-definition
and happiness. The ultimate goal is a conflict-free life in which love is
never painful and abuse cannot exist. Many of these notions are borrowed directly from the conceptual arsenal of humanistic psychology,
a theoretical and clinical perspective pioneered by such figures as Carl
Rogers and Abraham Maslow in the decades after World War II. Not
coincidentally, these beliefs about human psychology assume the existence of an affluent society in which basic material needs for food,
clothing, and shelter are routinely met.

The family, according to popular psychology, is best understood
as a system of rules and regulations that govern the development of
children's identity and shape what they learn about how to relate to
others. When the family rule system is out of whack, it becomes the
source of self-hatred, causing most of the bad things that happen to
good people throughout their lives. According to Bradshaw, "Family

systems fail, *not because of bad people*, but because of bad information loops, bad feedback in the form of bad rules of behavior. The same is true of society."[14] Nonetheless, the family retains a magical potential for being the source of happiness—if the faulty information loops and feedback can be reoriented toward producing people who love themselves. In short, once the family system and the individuals and relationships it produces are identified as dysfunctional, change is possible.

According to a very broad definition that includes everything from alcoholism and physical violence to anxiety and sadness, most, or even all, families today are dysfunctional. Pain is the relevant indicator. If it hurts, the experts advise—if you fear criticism, seek approval, feel dependent, guilty, or over-responsible—then your family system wasn't working and you are an "adult child."[15] Estimates of "adult children" range from a modest 90 to 95 percent of the entire population to an ambitious claim that the number of addictive and co-dependent people in the United States exceeds the total U.S. population![16]

At times the popular psychological literature sounds nominally feminist. Although lesbian and gay households are rarely ever mentioned, neither is a nuclear family configuration always stipulated as a mandatory prerequisite for good family functioning. Traditional attitudes about the propriety of women's and children's subordination to adult male authority are frequently described as dysfunctional in the extreme. People's need for unqualified acceptance of every aspect of their identity is a constant refrain. John Bradshaw, in his popular PBS series on the family, reassures, "It's ok to be gay or lesbian." Absolutely everyone, it seems, is precious and loveable.

At other times, the literature sounds antifeminist and homophobic. Bradshaw contradicts his own tolerant slogans by endorsing an ideal family comprised of mom, dad, and kids. In his view, the marital relationship dominates the family system, and the family system needs a marital relationship in order to be stable. If the marriage is good, then the kids have a chance to turn out all right because their role models are constructive. If the marriage is not good (or, one may presume, if it does not exist), dysfunction will flourish, children will be forced into compensatory positions in the family system, and their fragile sense of selfhood will be damaged.

Bradshaw's emphasis on the central role of the married, heterosex-

ual parents is typical of an important assumption found throughout
the popular literature: parents are pernicious because they are the all-
powerful architects of their children's suffering. Parental abandonment—a tragedy that takes forms from severe sexual abuse to mild
emotional neglect—is directly responsible for the destructive developmental course that is the fate of children in dysfunctional families.
In *Becoming Your Own Parent*, Dennis Wholey advises,

> **Because your child's low self-worth is being learned from you, he or she
> will not be able to live a happy life or raise a happy family. Your child will
> not know how to have fun, enjoy friendships, or even take care of his or
> her own basic needs. . . . You may have the right to wreck your own life,
> but do you really have the right to wreck the lives of others?**[17]

Because he believes that children internalize their parents at their very
worst, Bradshaw goes so far as to propose that anyone under thirty be
prohibited from having a child and anyone over thirty be required to
submit to a battery of mental tests and a program of rigorous in-
struction.[18]

If parents are entirely responsible for their children's identities,
children are entirely blameless, even as "adult children." Children are
perfectly whole and innocent at the start, and their dependence makes
them vulnerable to the "shaming" and "soul murder" that flourish in
dysfunctional systems, forcing children to develop false selves—the
precursors of addictive and codependent adult personalities—in order
to survive. The self-destructive requirements of growing up under a
toxic parental regime are frequently compared in the literature to enduring life in a Nazi concentration camp, a parallel that sheds some
light on the use of the term "survivor" as a generic label for "adult
children" and also illustrates the treacherous, but characteristic, anal-
ogies made by the expert popularizers.

In adulthood, people remain enmeshed in the dysfunctional roles
and behaviors that were foisted upon them by parents who made psychic self-denial a ticket to surviving childhood. Although they are held
blameless for the many wrongs visited upon them in youth, adults are
held responsible for taking charge of their own lives and the lives of
their children. It is in this transition that insight into the social nature
of the family blurs into old-fashioned American individualism and
self-help. In the process of excavating the perfect child within, the theory goes, adults recover their capacity to define themselves indepen-

dent not only of family, but of every other significant identity too: work, race, ethnicity, nationality, religion, etc. Recovery and personal accountability, consequently, go together. "If you are going to recover, ultimately you have to recognize your own culpability. Even though you were unconscious and blind, the potential for choice was always there for you. Ignorance of the choice is no excuse."[19] Success, in the end, is measured in emotional elbow grease. You are either strong enough to change, or you fail to take responsibility and are doomed to repeating the harmful patterns of the past.

Just as the family system is seen as both the problem and the solution, awesome parental power has a utopian future in creating happy people to match its distinguished track record in ruining children's lives.

> **You have within you the power to change your children's destiny. When you free yourself from the legacy of guilt, self-hatred, and anger, you also free your children. When you interrupt family patterns and break the cycle, you give a priceless gift to your children, and to their children, and to the children who will follow. You are molding the future.**[20]

Becoming your own good parent as an adult is considered to be an essential element in the detoxification process; it is also practice for being a good parent in the future. The path to personal recovery and the path to a functioning family system are therefore identical.

Feminists pay much more attention to who is actually raising the children than do family system theorists, but often, the verdict is the same: Reorganize the inner workings of domestic life and parental behavior—whether by drafting fathers into child care or mandating recovery—and social change is sure to follow. In the 1970s Dorothy Dinnerstein and Nancy Chodorow were among those who built on the classic psychoanalytic identification of unconscious conflicts in early childhood as the source of adult gender identity. Focusing on the consequences of exclusively female mothering, both theorists stressed the impact of norms and values internalized in childhood on adult personality, which raised hopes that change would result from cultural redesign. But they also largely ignored influences on children that were external to the family and drew sharper lines between masculine and feminine identities than exist in reality.[21]

Although the family experts counsel that new relationship rules (presumably something that cannot be learned except through social interaction) are key to establishing functional family systems, recovery—the process of self-knowledge that cuts through layers of false identity to uncover the perfect child—is described as a journey to the psychic interior. Tenacity, courage, and the will to grow are all located within, perhaps because they are safe there from the contaminating streams of family dysfunction. The resources needed for recovery are available to any person willing to explore the psychic landscape through introspection, self-help groups, professional psychotherapy, or a combination of all three methods.

The real challenge, according to much of popular psychology, lies with individual psyches, and their combination into family systems. Society is nothing more or less than one huge dysfunctional personality. "The system is like the individual, and the individual is like the system," Anne Wilson Schaef points out.[22] Sometimes though, the literature gives the distinct impression that families float freely as self-sufficient entities, sealed off entirely from the influences of other social institutions, "creating their own realities," as the saying goes.

When the family is not sealed off entirely from the rest of society, it is often considered to be the blueprint for whatever exists outside of it. For example, both Anne Wilson Schaef and John Bradshaw suggest that domestic patterns of emotional control, dishonest communication, depression, and crisis are all clearly reflected in undemocratic, confused, and ineffective government policy. If family dysfunction causes everything from slums to war, then progressive change, or even radical change, must begin, quite literally, at home. "If we love this society in which we live, we must be willing to confront the reality that it has a disease. Like an alcoholic, it is not bad and trying to get good. It is sick and trying to get well."[23] Recovery and revolution, in other words, are just two different words for the same thing.

PSYCHOLOGICAL TRUTH AND POLITICAL CONSEQUENCES

Why have these ideas been so influential within lesbian communities?

There is one obvious reason why lesbians have welcomed many of the ideas of family-systems popularizers. They confirm what gay people already know and have been saying for years: Parents can cause pain and families can be breeding grounds for self-hatred. Most lesbians (and gay men) grew up in ordinary families where heterosexuality was obligatory and its naturalness treated as self-evident. Stigmatization, isolation, or abandonment were the rewards for any children brave or foolish enough to be honest about their homosexual feelings.

Beyond this simple truth, have lesbians been convinced that *all* painful conflicts about sexual identity can be laid at the feet of their parents, and that *all* progress toward self-acceptance is due to the quality of one's personal psychological effort? Perhaps. Others, though, who have experienced the power of feminism or the gay and lesbian movement to transform lesbians' sense of self and collective identity have doubts about the validity of either total parental control or built-in psychic fortitude. Suggesting that how good (or bad) one feels about oneself is a product of one's social context and not one's innate psychic constitution—and this is exactly what I am suggesting—does not diminish belief in individual worth or potential one bit, nor does it negate the importance of parents and family in shaping identity. It simply moves the action from an internal frontier to an external one, and translates a matter of uncontrollable chance—what kind of parents you happen to have—into a question of controllable social goals: What kinds of families do we want to have and what can be done to create them?

At a time when more lesbians are contemplating more reproductive and family choices more openly than ever before, there is a clear link between easing the continuing memories of childhood and adolescent anguish and instilling confidence about the future. By addressing lingering anxieties about our families of origin directly and personally, the popular literature on the family has been read by lesbians as a promise that they can and will be good parents after all, if they only work hard enough.

The literature also offers many lesbians something else that is critically important: assurance that motherhood will not add up to an inexorable, conservative retreat from antisexist, antihomophobic convictions. Recent lesbian literature on choosing children is filled with detailed how-to information—how to get pregnant or navigate the adoption process, how to tell one's parents, how to deal with school

officials—but is remarkably thin on question related to whether lesbians will or can alter the ideological meanings of motherhood and family, questions that have been of deep concern to lesbians who consider
themselves feminists. Although they do not speak to lesbians per se,
popular psychologists do champion the creative, change-inducing potential of child-rearing and the positive social contribution of parents—functional ones, that is. They stay away from the complicated
questions that plague feminists and make wholehearted optimism difficult to sustain.

Lesbian mothers—like all parents—want their reproductive decisions to be respected and their child-rearing labor to be seen as valuable. But many lesbians also want to make their personal decisions politically significant, evidence of progress toward the goals of feminism
and gay liberation. If lesbians are now able to choose children, isn't
that a sign of an emergent pluralism in family and child-rearing
forms? Aren't we proving that an ethic of respect for people's emotional, sexual, and reproductive choices is alive and well? Won't our
children be the standard-bearers for a genuinely human culture, devoid of sexist and homophobic irrationalities? One mother put it this
way:

> We certainly are raising these children in a different way than a straight,
> heterosexual, middle-class way that children are usually brought up, and
> I think they are very, very healthy, well-adjusted, basically happy kids.
> And I think the gratification is seeing this, and seeing how beautifully
> they're growing up. . . . the antithesis of what it was like when I was
> growing up.[24]

The name of a series of support groups in New York, Lesbians Rein-
venting Motherhood, suggests that lesbians are concocting something
brand new. If lesbian motherhood can work such wonders, don't lesbians deserve political points as well as personal support when they decide to care for children?

The optimistic notion of an intrinsically progressive lesbian
motherhood may have gathered a lot of steam in the past few years, but
it is not new. Long before the current wave of choosing to have children, lesbians saw their actual or potential parenthood as an engine of
feminist social change. Lesbian mothers, it was hoped, would bring an
end to the suffocating culture of "momism," the authoritarianism of

parents, the rigidities of sexist and heterosexist socialization patterns, even (in the most overheated ruminations) the fundamental social relations of capitalism. Jill Johnston, for example, had this to say in 1972 about the advantages of "amazon mothers."

> The end of motherhood (and of course fatherhood) means the end to parent chauvinism and child oppression, an end to private property and authoritative representation. Women already are standing up and saying that being a mother in a ticky-tacky box looking after her possessions is an abnormal unhealthy situation. . . . *Possibly the only "liberated" communal families at this time are the lesbian mother households*—the total child care center. A cooperative community of little adults and big children merging identities and responsibilities and exchanging skills and information in an atmosphere of consciousness and mutual respect.[25]

Yet many young lesbians at the time consciously carved out adult identities in opposition to everything female, including motherhood, because they considered conventional feminine selfhood a prison. In the 1970s, lesbians and feminists placed a sharp emphasis on demonstrating women's *non*procreative and *non*traditional talents. Evening up the score in nondomestic, public life was considered as vital to the valuation of traditionally feminine work (like mothering) as insisting on the presence of men's labor and emotion in the family, and it had the added appeal of seeming more attainable. Similarly, within the gay movement of twenty years ago, some lesbians renounced the heterosexual obligations of conventional femininity by publicizing lesbian desire and celebrating nonmonogamous sexuality. Such boldness was based on an understanding of lesbian identity as oppositional. Many women rejected a strategy of pointing out how "normal" lesbians could be—by being or becoming mothers, for example, or by settling into long-term unions that resembled heterosexual marriages.

Lesbian mothers and mothers-to-be who seek unconditional approval for their choices have been less likely to get it from feminist writers who address the political implications of lesbian motherhood than from popular psychologists who bless the inherent virtues of good parenting. Feminists have, however, also been far less likely to blame parents and dysfunctional families for everything bad that ever happens to children, or to adults. They are more sensitive to the ties connecting families to other social institutions than are popular psychologists, who tend to draw clear, and artificial, boundaries around the domestic unit.

Feminists have pointed out that "choosing children" can be as profoundly shaped by the realities of racial and class oppression as it is by sexual preference. Many lesbian mothers had, and continue to have, children who are not "chosen," either because they are the result of heterosexual relationships or because they are unplanned and, sometimes, unwanted. Much resentment has been expressed by lesbian mothers who compare their own experiences of invisibility and lack of support within the lesbian community (especially if they had children in the 1970s or if they were or are the mothers of sons) to the flood of resources—from sperm banks to play groups—being generated by the middle-class "lavender moms" of today. They rightfully point out that endless deliberations among lesbians about whether or not to include men in child rearing ignore the fact that many millions of children have already grown up without the benefit of daddy's presence, and that the absence of men's wages has probably done more damage than the shortage of paternal hugs.

Some analysts have observed that the lesbian baby boom may prove the durability of feminine conformity even as it stretches the outer edges of reproductive freedom.[26] Being a pregnant lesbian, or the partner of one, does not guarantee that one will choose to come out and raise the consciousness of the local obstetrician or school board. Nor, of course, does it preclude it. But the real burdens and responsibilities of motherhood (not to mention the overwhelmingly ordinary assumption that motherhood implies heterosexuality) may indeed make lesbian mothers look and feel more like "normal" women and less like "deviant" ones, and generate reasons not to make an issue of our sexuality.

Do some lesbians see in motherhood a way to mend the ruptures with friends and family caused by insistence that their sexual relationships be acknowledged openly and with dignity? Perhaps clear restraints on lesbians' sexual freedom will even accompany motherhood, giving women the oldest excuse in the book—protecting the children—to compromise their own public demands for change?[27] Other lesbians will tally the costs of "normality" for their own happiness as well as that of their children, and consider them far too high.

This much is certain: Coming out as lesbian mothers is as conscious an act as coming out as lesbian lovers, and just as difficult.[28]

Motherhood comes no more freely to women in contemporary American society than heterosexuality does; both are mandatory. Because the post-Stonewall generation's sexual and reproductive choices have of necessity been deliberate, achieved through conscious will and desire rather than by custom or accident, lesbians today tend to be more sensitive to the politics of domesticity than are their heterosexual peers. This deliberateness is a good thing, and heterosexuals would be wise to emulate it. Lesbians who make strenuous efforts to attain the status of "mother" are living proof that parenting is a social achievement that involves real talent and ongoing social support, not an inevitable by-product of nature. None of this, however, makes lesbian motherhood inherently revolutionary, or even feminist. It no more guarantees that lesbian-raised children will be the vanguard of future social change than it condemns children growing up with a heterosexual parent or parents to a Barbie-and-Ken destiny.

Lesbian mothers deserve far more support and acknowledgment for their love and labor than they now receive; all parents do. So do lesbians and heterosexual women who decide *not* to have or care for children. In many ways, being a non-mother remains the supreme mark of female deviance, always requiring painstaking explanation where maternal impulses seem entirely self-evident.

Invoking "the personal is political" is not in itself an adequate rationale for lesbian motherhood. But lesbians who choose children today, hoping to alter family relationships for the better, can remind us that rearranging how children are loved and cared for is as subject to conscious choice and collective action as whether women workers will be paid the same wages as men or whether gay people will be pressured to live their lives in shame and secrecy.

In recent years popular psychology has been one factor giving lesbians (and others) the confidence to blaze new paths toward chosen families, in part by simply recognizing the obvious: Becoming a parent is an emotionally significant decision that deserves social recognition and assistance. But lesbians' new-found domestic enthusiasm will, I think, turn into hollow disappointment if they uncritically adopt many of popular psychology's simplistic themes—that the family is the source of all human pain and that the key to being a good mother or a happy human being is sheer willpower.

On the other hand, lesbians who have not forgotten or abandoned the feminist insight that the family is socially embedded may be able to extract a more useful lesson from the recent wave of popular psychology: that emotional life is itself worthy of serious attention because human experience links psychology to politics and happiness to justice. A healing approach to bruised identity is no more a substitute for a lesbian and feminist movement than political commitment can ever be a substitute for intimacy or selfhood.

Desire for children may indeed reveal our inner selves as never before, but a truly free lesbian motherhood—which neither mandates martyrdom for those who choose it nor degrades the human worth of those who do not—will not emerge from the luck of the psychic draw. It will be possible only when we reject the separation of inner and outer change as false and embrace a journey to wholeness, marked equally by personal growth and political transformation.

"Why in the world would you want to do that?": Claiming Community in Lesbian Commitment Ceremonies

ELLEN LEWIN

Although 1994 will long be remembered by many as the year in which the Republicans took control of the House and Senate and the baseball season was halted by a strike, I will remember it as the year the television series *Northern Exposure* devoted an episode to the wedding of two gay male characters. *The New Yorker* that year featured a cover illustration titled "June Grooms" of two men in formal attire standing behind a traditional wedding cake topped with two male figurines, and *Chicks in White Satin*, a documentary film about a lesbian wedding, was nominated for an Academy Award. In 1994 HarperCollins brought out a mass market paperback, *The Essential*

Guide to Lesbian and Gay Weddings, that shepherds prospective brides and grooms through the intricacies of selecting wedding invitations, rings, vows, and caterers, and what to say when your mother asks, "Why in the world would you want to do that?"

These representations in the popular media suggest that while gay and lesbian weddings may still be controversial, they have recently become visible to what seems to be an unprecedented extent. While challenges to laws that permit only mixed-gender couples to marry have been mounted in a number of jurisdictions, and may soon succeed in Hawaii, fears of lesbians and gay men rushing to the altar have sparked attempts to enact legislation forbidding same-sex unions in at least two states (South Dakota and Utah). But at the same time, growing numbers of private and public employers are implementing domestic partner benefits and courts increasingly are ruling that lesbian and gay couples should have some legal entitlements normally reserved for traditional families or husbands and wives.

While these shifts are dramatic, they have a limited impact on the legal situation of gay/lesbian couples. They still cannot qualify for benefits on the same basis as heterosexuals, they must make arrangements on a contractual basis about property, health and illness, and inheritance that are automatically accorded heterosexual couples, they cannot submit joint tax returns or apply for immigration status on the basis of marriage to an American citizen. They are less likely than heterosexual couples to have their unions be the occasions for family celebrations, to have the costs of putting on their weddings subsidized by their families, to receive wedding gifts on a scale comparable to their heterosexual siblings, or even to have members of their families of origin attend their ceremonies. But increasing numbers of such couples are choosing to solemnize their relationships in some sort of public context—through commitment rituals, holy unions, domestic partner ceremonies, or just plain weddings—creating a grassroots movement that threatens to overwhelm gay-rights activists and political strategists.

Same-sex marriage, then, has emerged as the focus of considerable debate within gay and lesbian communities. In simple—and perhaps overly dichotomized—terms, the debate is as follows: Proponents of gay/lesbian marriage claim that gaining the right to marry should be a civil rights goal as long as marital status offers significant benefits available on no other basis. Some go on to assert that demanding the right for same-sex couples to marry constitutes a type of gender resistance, in that it subverts and destabilizes conventional gender understandings and that it expands the impact of "coming out." Opponents point to a historical relationship between marriage and patriarchy, arguing that the desire to "marry" is merely accommodation in that it represents nothing more than a crass attempt to conform to heterosexist standards that devalues the unique virtues of gay culture and community.[1] One of the few popular books to examine lesbian and gay marriage, in fact, uses this debate as its focus; the volume, devoted to the personal narratives of gay/lesbian couples who have or who have not had ceremonies, was inspired, the editor tells us, by her own "conflicting feelings about marriage," by her discomfort with the idea that gay people might choose to conform to mainstream values.[2]

This debate rests, of course, on the related issue of whether or not there is any such thing as "gay culture," distinct from the other cultural contexts in which gay and lesbian people find themselves, and whether such "culture" is "genuine or spurious," to draw on Gilbert Herdt's reprise of Edward Sapir.[3] Partly because of the need to confront the stigma and dispel the invisibility that has long been attached to homosexuality, the wave of research and writing stimulated by the gay/lesbian rights movement and by feminist scholarship has largely concerned itself with documenting and interpreting the unique cultural forms that emerge in gay/lesbian communities.[4]

While this work has greatly enhanced our ability to appreciate the vitality of gay/lesbian cultural production, it has also tended to obscure the extent to which lesbians and gay men actively partake in the wider cultural arena, crossing the boundaries of the gay/lesbian community to interact with other people (relatives, friends, co-workers, or neighbors) as well as to participate in a range of activities we might consider "culture." In other words, gay/lesbian lives are rarely played out in rigidly bounded communities. Instead, the rhythm of activity that marks individual stories reveals their movement between gay and straight worlds, with varying degrees of comfort characterizing the process. Like other people, lesbians and gay men identify themselves along a number of axes, and while sexual orientation is often a salient dimension of their identification, other personal and social characteristics also feed into how they view themselves.

This perspective is vital to taking up the opposition between "resistance" and "accommodation." "Resistance," as feminist anthropologist Lila Abu-Lughod has pointed out, has become a romanticized concept in recent years, as many of us who study subordinated peoples strive to replace a focus on victimization with an understanding of agency and rebellion.[5] We are eager to locate what James Scott has called "weapons of the weak" in the cultural repertoires of the peoples we study;[6] we are comfortable with narratives that reassure us that acquiescence is not the necessary consequence of subordination.

Ritual is a particularly rich arena for examining the interplay of resistance and accommodation. This is a domain in which anthropologists have been particularly active, having documented a seemingly limitless array of rituals, ceremonials, performances, and other formulaic events that occur outside of ordinary time. While much of the literature on ritual details how these events reinforce traditional values and reinvigorate commitment to the status quo, if you will, other work has demonstrated that rituals can also dramatize rebellion and resistance to the established order and offer a controlled environment for expressing disaffection with things as they are.[7]

I came to this investigation of gay and lesbian commitment rituals from previous work on lesbian motherhood.[8] In both research ventures my focus has been on the changing shape of gay/lesbian identity in American culture, particularly on the often paradoxical interrelationships among ideas and behaviors that seem to represent resistance to the established sex/gender system and those that appear to express a yearning for conformity and acceptance. In simplest terms, my work challenges the notion that homosexuality is intrinsically subversive of the sex/gender system, but instead focuses on the more complicated, contradictory relationships between the ways gays and lesbians organize their lives and their views of their places in the wider society.

In my book on lesbian mothers, I argue that they confront the traditional notion that only heterosexual women can be mothers and at the same time reinscribe and strengthen the longstanding conflation, or assumed sameness, of womanhood and motherhood. On the one hand, the existence of lesbian mothers challenges the assumption that procreation and sexuality are necessarily connected, but at the same time, lesbian mothers' constructions of their identities point to a belief that mothers and non-mothers are different from each other in fundamental, natural ways. In my earlier work, I found that lesbian mothers constantly crossed boundaries to interact with other mothers (regardless of their sexuality) and, in fact, to constitute their sense of self. Studying gay/lesbian weddings has led me to examine points of overlap between gay and straight social worlds and to look at how these worlds can be both bounded and permeable as values and aspirations merge and diverge.

The interconnectedness and inseparability of resistance to the larger society and accommodation to social and cultural norms are more sharply etched in the wedding ceremonies I discuss below. Lesbians incorporate both elements into these rituals so that contradictory claims are often central both to the texts and the performances that constitute these ceremonial occasions.

"JUST AN ORDINARY JEWISH WEDDING"—JEWISH WEDDINGS AND CLAIMS TO COMMUNITY

In December 1993 I attended a formal lesbian wedding at an elegant downtown hotel in San Francisco. Both in terms of liturgy and performance, the ceremony was virtually indistinguishable from a traditional Jewish wedding. Attendants dressed in tuxedos or long, pastel gowns escorted the couple to the *chuppah* (the traditional canopy), followed by a flower girl strewing rose petals. One woman wore a long white bridal dress and carried a bouquet, her face covered by a veil. The other wore a tuxedo with a white rose in her lapel.

The rabbi led the couple through complicated movements of "circling" each other and explained the origins of the custom. He said a blessing over the wine and directed them to drink the wine from a cup which we were told was an heirloom from the wedding of one of their grandmothers. The rings were exchanged, and the couple said traditional vows in Hebrew, with a more updated version following in English. The rabbi then spoke about the couple and the beginning of their life together, emphasizing the complementary nature of their personalities and the ways in which their union would create a kind of wholeness. He read the *ketubah*, the marriage contract, in Hebrew and English, again explaining its ancient origins. After the *ketubah*, the rabbi chanted in Hebrew and repeated in English the Seven Blessings, which puts marriage in the context of the seven days of biblical creation. Finally, he led the couple to the breaking of the glass, which he explained as representing their ability to carry on through hard times that will undoubtedly come. The sound of breaking glass was greeted by cries of "Mazel Tov!" (congratulations) and enthusiastic applause.

The wedding party then moved to another room in the hotel for a formal sit-down dinner. A band played, toasts were offered, the couple and guests danced the hora and various ballroom dances, and the newlyweds, seated on chairs, were lifted high over the heads of the guests and bounced around to the klezmer tunes of traditional eastern European Jewish folk music. After dinner, the three-tier white wedding cake was cut, and the couple fed each other pieces of cake, taking care to smear each other's faces with icing. Later in the party, the bridal bouquet and the garter were thrown to the eager guests, who were dressed (as instructed in the invitation) in tuxedos or cocktail dresses.

When it was time for me to leave, I thanked the couple and complimented them on their beautiful wedding. They thanked me for coming, but pointedly reminded me that it was "just an ordinary Jewish wedding."

In many ways, this wedding *was* ordinary. It included the principal ritual elements of a traditional Jewish wedding and most of the informal features (some not of Jewish origin, such as speaking individual vows and throwing the bouquet) associated with such ceremonies among American Jews of eastern European extraction. The text emphasized the importance of the couple establishing a "Jewish home" and family, the significance of marriage as a fundamental creative moment in the Jewish community, and the centrality of lifelong commitment to meaningful social existence.[9]

But this was a wedding that joined two women. The two attendants in long dresses were both women, as were the "groom" (or as she called herself, the "groomette") and her two tuxedoed attendants. And although the rabbi emphasized the gendered complementarity he perceived between them—he described one of them as "soft and compassionate," the other as "strong in her convictions"—the vows the couple had written focused on their "sameness" as two women and the mutual understanding this would foster in their life together.

In our earlier conversations, this couple, who I will call Rachel Goldberg and Nancy Weinstein,[10] expressed a commitment to many of the goals expected of couples embarking on marriage: They wanted to have children in a family context and they wanted their relationship to be recognized by family and friends. But although, and perhaps because, their marriage could not be legally sanctioned by the state, they also wanted something else: to have their religion support it, to be legitimized by the Jewish community. Nancy explained to me how the public nature of the event was important to her. "It makes our relationship valid. It's before God and everybody saying we pledge to be together for the rest of our lives." Rachel felt it would be particularly important to be married by a rabbi who shares her conservative Jewish values. "I just wanted it to *mean* something. You know, it doesn't mean anything when it's not recognized by the religion." And they explicitly wanted to express their appreciation and support for the traditional nuclear family. Nancy plans to get pregnant by donor insemination but said Rachel felt they should be married "before I even get pregnant." Rachel explained her strong views on premarital pregnancy as follows:

> You see, a lot of people see being gay as this really weird thing. And for me, I've always been gay. I mean, I was gay when I was a kid. I've just always been gay and for me, it's just a part of me and more and more evidence is that it's biological and genetic. And I feel like just because I'm gay, that doesn't mean that all the other things that govern the world that I live in and the values that I have and the values that I grew up with and the society that we live in all of a sudden go out the window, just because my . . . interest is in women.

Rachel's understanding of "the progression of things" is that parents should first date, then get married, and then have children. "I just sort of always carried that idea [that] things should go along in a certain way. And I don't see just because I'm gay why that should be any different."

From this perspective, Rachel and Nancy understood the wedding as something that would be "ordinary" except for the fact that the state restricts legal marriage to heterosexual couples. They followed traditional Jewish custom to the letter, rejecting all suggestions by the rabbi for even slightly innovative readings, and explained emphatically that this ritual was a *wedding*, not a "commitment ceremony," which they described as a counter-cultural concoction not recognized by the Conservative movement in Judaism. Thus while their union cannot now be sanctioned by the state, it is, in their view, legitimated by institutional Judaism. They point out that Conservative Judaism strongly opposes marriages between Jews and non-Jews but that their wedding unites two Jewish women committed to creating a "Jewish home." While the Conservative movement, according to them, does not condone same-sex unions, their interpretation is that it has not gotten around to explicitly forbidding such rituals when they are called "weddings," as opposed to "commitment ceremonies."[11]

However, although the couple viewed their wedding as "ordinary"—a mark, on one hand, of their solidity as citizens and as Jews, and on the other hand, of their repudiation of the association of being "gay" and being "queer" (in the sense of 'nonconformist' or aggressively different)—the rabbi saw their desire to publicly celebrate their relationship as a courageous rebellion against the injustice done to them both by mainstream Judaism and by civil society. In his comments during the ceremony, the rabbi, a heterosexual Conservative Jew, remarked that they were bravely demanding the right to have their marriage sanctified by Jewish law and tradition despite the fact that "not all of Jewish society," as he put it, was ready to support a marriage of two women. He was impressed by what he saw as "their courage" and by the fact that they did not face any of the pressures to marry that heterosexual couples do. Because their decision to marry within Jewish tradition was freely chosen, in his view their commitment was all the more significant and worthy of support.

Rachel and Nancy defined their ceremony as a demonstration of their commitment to mainstream social values—a ritual of conformity, if you will. But they spent nearly ten thousand dollars to put on the ceremony (invitations, flowers, clothing, engagement and wedding rings, custom-made *ketubah*, hotel, photographer, band, food, alcohol, and honeymoon) with no expectation of reaping any of the material or social benefits heterosexual couples receive as a matter of course when they marry. Rachel and Nancy believed, they explained, in marriage and in the goal of establishing a "Jewish home" and raising children, and they contrasted their situation as two Jews to what they consider truly reprehensible—a marriage between a Jew and a non-Jew.

But to realize their objectives they would have to confront a central requirement of traditional marriage—that it be a union of two persons of different sexes. At the same time that the wedding appeared to include both "feminine" and "masculine" actors, the "masculine" actors—those wearing tuxedos—were not men but women. What we might consider their resistance to the opposite-sex requirement was carried out, paradoxically, in an attempt to approximate its form in the performance of the wedding ritual, most evidently in their choice of clothing. Interestingly, this was the one element of the ceremony that the rabbi, who had never before performed such a ceremony, told me he found unsettling and confusing.

As we have seen, Rachel and Nancy used their wedding to emphasize that they shared the concerns and beliefs of other Jewish couples; they took pains throughout the ceremony to highlight the ways in which they were *not* different from heterosexuals. But for other Jewish lesbian couples, an acknowledgment of difference is more central to the rituals they devise, as revealed both in their statements about their aims and in their wedding ceremonies.

Miriam Kaplan and Hannah Levine, like Rachel and Nancy, San Francisco residents in their early thirties, also went to great lengths to use traditional Jewish elements in devising their wedding. Miriam said:

> Especially because it wasn't legally recognized, this was our opportunity to create something that was exactly what we needed. You know, that was really a gathering in of all the support that we had in the world. And something that for the rest of our lives we would look back on when we needed strength.

Jewish culture, and connectedness with their families of origin, is of tremendous importance to both Miriam and Hannah, who met each other through their mutual interest in klezmer music. Once they fell in love, they felt strongly that their relationship would be permanent, that marriage was "right," the direction they were both moving in even before meeting each other. As Miriam put it, "We were both looking for the partner for a lifetime. We both felt that like mallards, you know, we just mate for life." Miriam explained:

> We're pretty traditional. And I think in a lot of ways we wanted, to the extent that the traditions made sense to us, we wanted to stay as close to a traditional wedding ceremony as we could, a traditional *Jewish* wed-

ding ceremony. And I think in terms of being in the world, too, it's nice to have something that's sort of universally recognized. And then people can make assumptions [that we're married to men], and if they do, they can be corrected.

Both Miriam and Hannah felt that it was important to draw on Jewish tradition in designing their wedding. As Miriam put it:

[This] was one of several occasions in life where you feel drawn to the tradition, that the collective wisdom of centuries has something to offer us. We pretty much wanted it to be as close to traditional as it could be. And make whatever few changes were necessary to accommodate the fact that we were both women. We also felt, since we had been living together for a while, and since we had a [private] commitment to each other that we considered to be binding, that the ceremony was also for us a ceremony through which we entered the Jewish community as a family, and that linked us to the Jewish people, as people. So we wanted it to be traditional, and we felt entitled to the same words and wisdom and everything that any other Jewish couple who was making this commitment both to each other and to the community would have.

What this meant for Miriam and Hannah was adhering to the traditional form of a Jewish wedding as much as possible, but also consciously departing from these forms when they felt it necessary to make a point about the ceremony united not a man and a woman, but two women. They had a *chuppah* and a *ketubah*, and they followed the same liturgical form used by Rachel and Nancy. They viewed their choice to each wear a white dress as a way to assert that this was a lesbian ceremony, but they also decided to have traditional Jewish wedding rings, unbroken bands without stones, made for the ceremony. And although the gay, Reform rabbi who officiated provided a traditional translation of the Seven Blessings, they added an eighth blessing (placed between the fourth and fifth blessings), one they described as "explicitly gay": "Blessed is Ha Shem, source of All Creation, creator of love and passion between woman and woman, man and man, woman and man. Blessed are you, Adonai our God, You open our hearts to love, and strengthen us to walk with dignity among those who are different from us."[12]

On one hand, getting married itself is something Miriam and Hannah viewed in the context of Jewish history: "This idea of marriage . . . is part of a "continuum of thousands of years" that links their relationship to the ongoing history of Jewish life. At the same time, both women were acutely aware of the difference between their situation and that of a heterosexual couple, particularly since their marriage would not be legally recognized. Miriam explained:

> We wanted to have a traditional Jewish wedding, but we didn't want to pretend that we weren't gay. And so, we wanted to acknowledge the fact that the marriage wasn't going to be legally recognized. And we thought about doing it in the ceremony, and we thought that it would be inappropriate to sort of turn it into a political thing. So what we decided was to include it in the invitation, and to have this postcard to the governor urging legalization of gay marriage. . . . It was hard to find the right place to do that. Not to ignore it, and also not to let it take away from what we were doing.

Miriam and Hannah acknowledged the contradiction their marriage presented both to Jewish tradition and to the wider society and built it into the heart of the ceremony. But their articulation of gay/lesbian marriage as a potentially controversial political issue was kept at the margin of their ceremony, so they could focus on the ways their goals corresponded to the historical concerns of the Jewish people.

Clearly, these two weddings vary in the degree to which they stress the couples' differentness from heterosexual couples. Rachel and Nancy tried to highlight similarity by making their wedding, as much as possible, a replica of a heterosexual wedding. Miriam and Hannah briefly noted the differences between themselves and straight couples in the liturgy (the "eighth blessing"), but were more explicit about difference in decisions about nonliturgical aspects of the wedding, such as their clothing and the postcards to the governor.

Despite these distinctions, both weddings make similar claims on tradition, and by extension, on the concept of (Jewish) community. They symbolize both the importance of the tie being solemnized but also assert a relationship to the thousands of years of Jewish history that are virtually always at the heart of Jewish ritual. To the extent that the essence of being Jewish is encapsulated in notions of community and collective history, these ceremonies are as much about being Jewish as they are about being lesbian.

''WHO COULD OBJECT TO SUCH A BORING AND CONVENTIONAL LIFE?'' USING CHRISTIAN TRADITIONS TO CLAIM COMMUNITY

On a sunny Saturday afternoon in September, 1994, Bonnie Martin and Barbara Johnson spoke their vows to one another in the presence of about one hundred family and friends. The ceremony was presided over by two ministers, a Methodist pastor whose church Bonnie's family had attended for many years, and a Presbyterian minister whose openly lesbian stance has stimulated tremendous controversy within her church locally and nationally. The outdoor ceremony, held on the lush grounds of a northern California conference center, was followed by cocktails, a sit-down dinner, and music and dancing in a romantic poolside setting. As the guests arrived and found their way to the glade where the ceremony was to be held, musician colleagues of Barbara's played chamber music. During the ceremony, other music was provided by friends of the couple, one of whom had written a humorous song about them and their relationship specifically for the occasion.

Bonnie, thirty-two, and Barbara, thirty-seven, both have small-town Midwestern roots, though Bonnie's family moved to the Bay Area, where she grew up, when Bonnie was young. In describing the process through which they decided to have a ceremony, both women stress having been raised by parents who had long-term, stable marriages.

> It's kind of like Bonnie says. Her parents have been together for a long time. My parents were. So that's what I got used to, this thing that had been publicly acknowledged, this thing had been recognized, and I don't know why it is, but I think that sometimes going against the grain of the societal norms and the societal rituals is not as empowering as just *doing* them. So for me, to actually go through the process of having the marriage, because that's what society knows, then that gets a whole 'nother echelon of approval that it wouldn't get otherwise.

Bonnie shares Barbara's desire to replicate the stability of her natal family and sees the urge to make a strong commitment as a significant part of her personal identity:

I really feel that that's the kind of person I am. That I make a commitment
to one person and get past all the surface stuff and make a deeper connected relationship. That's always been my goal, to find a person that
would be willing to kind of wade through all the shit with me and go forward. So that was much more important to me than dating or doing a two
year relationship, breaking up, two years, breaking up. I could see myself
going through life changing jobs and doing things, but I didn't want to
keep changing relationships.

The decision to have two ministers perform their wedding had
less to do with each woman's attachment to the denomination she
grew up in than a desire to bring together elements of their past and
present. The Methodist minister who officiated had known Bonnie's
family for years. She explains:

He was a good friend of my parents. So he was a good friend of our family.
He had participated in family events like baptisms and weddings. I had a
good feeling from him. And I wanted somebody that represented my
faith and my family.

Barbara had known Janie Spahr, a Presbyterian minister whose
business cards identify her as a "Lesbian Evangelist," for some years
and felt that her presence would be essential—because she would
bring such a strong spiritual element to the ceremony, her participation would be a "blessing."

George, the Methodist minister, started the ceremony, by talking
about family. He invited Bonnie's parents to the front and quoted
comments Bonnie has made about the "abiding love" she grew up
with and the "kindness, courage, and strength" she learned from her
parents. Following this, Janie invoked the spirit of Barbara's deceased
parents, in her words "on the other side," inviting them to join "this
circle of family" and reading from letters they had written that indicated their approval of and support for Bonnie and Barbara's relationship. She also read a selection of sayings that Barbara's mother had assembled as a wedding gift for her older daughter, along with words of
wisdom from Barbara's father, explaining that they are "really here in
spirit," and pleased that their daughter is truly loved by another person. This was an emotional moment in the proceedings; Barbara began to cry, as did some of the members of her family seated in the front.

George then talked about marriage as a holy covenant, a celebration of the mystery of great love. He said that marriage and love are not always easy and that a couple has a responsibility to grow, have a sense of humor, and be flexible. From individual love, he concluded, flows love for all creation.

Bonnie and Barbara then talked to the congregation about "love." They described the process that led to the ceremony—the months of meeting with Janie and George, and the "homework" Janie assigned them to prepare for the ceremony and for their future together. Janie spoke about her own observations of their growing spirituality during the process, marked especially by the way their dogs sat nearby during their sessions, listening attentively—in other words, invoking the naturalness of their love. With Bonnie and Barbara looking slightly embarrassed, Janie mentioned some of the things they had written about in their diaries that are important in their relationship—their walks with their dogs, hikes, the process by which they "let each other in," making a place for each other in their lives, becoming increasingly intimate, and "learning not to be afraid." Janie asked, rhetorically, "Why marriage, holy union?" The answer, she explained, is about respect, sharing values, and the desire to share family—she reminded the congregation, "These are Midwest people with Midwest backgrounds." (At this, the crowd broke into applause and laughter.) "What is wonderful about being in a lesbian relationship?" Janie asked, and added as an aside, "I want you to know they are lesbians!" Lesbian relationships, she explained, benefit from the likeness of two women, their softness, the fact that their similarities limit the need for explanations.

Bonnie and Barbara then spoke of their spiritual balance, inspiration, strength, mutual support to be themselves, and their efforts to create a synthesis, to combine their love to make a new entity, "us." Janie acknowledged their comments, reminding the congregation that they were there to "witness their love." The two women spoke their vows in unison, exchanged rings, and kissed.

The next part of the ceremony was announced as a time for sharing. Family members and friends stood up to make comments, some clearly prepared in advance, others off the cuff. The first to speak was Bonnie's mother, who read a poem she wrote. It spoke of love and support, blessings from god, and welcomed Barbara to the family, saying that she fits right in because her name starts with *B* (like all the names in their family) and she is from Iowa.

At the end of the ceremony, Bonnie and Barbara carried out a ritual they explained as a symbol of the unification of their two families. Each of the family members held two roses—Bonnie's family's flowers were dark pink, and Barbara's family's were light pink. The couple walked through the front rows where family members were seated, speaking briefly to and embracing each person, who gave each of them a rose. At the end of the process, they each held a mixed bouquet of dark and light pink roses tied with purple ribbons, symbolizing the new family the ceremony would create—a combination of two, formerly separate units.

Margaret Barnes and Lisa Howard also held their wedding in a luxurious outdoor setting, a historic Victorian inn in California's wine country. The springtime ceremony was held on a veranda overlooking a formal garden, with both women wearing subdued pastel dresses in delicate shades of pink and green. Margaret and Lisa had begun their relationship some ten years earlier when they were business students. They share similar backgrounds, coming from well-off families on the East Coast, and both had attended elite colleges and graduate schools. Now working for conservative investment firms, the two women present themselves as anything but "queer." Their comfortable San Francisco home is far from the gay ghetto, and their demanding work schedules leave little time for participation in gay community events.

Margaret and Lisa's decision to have a wedding was largely inspired by their friends Jeff and Paul, who had held a rather elaborate party a year or two earlier to celebrate their domestic partner registration.[13] The two women were coming close to the tenth anniversary of their relationship and wanted to celebrate their having endured many challenges to its survival, particularly those posed by years of conflicting professional obligations. A close friend of theirs, actually the man who had introduced them, died of AIDS shortly before they began planning the ceremony; this experience convinced them they didn't want to wait until the end of their lives for their families and friends to meet. Their conception of their wedding, then, was not only an occasion for their families and their large circle of friends to support and celebrate their relationship, but an opportunity for all of the important people in their lives to get to know each other and form lasting connections.

Margaret's family had a difficult time accepting her lesbianism when she revealed it to them some years earlier, and she was concerned they might not participate. Long before plans were final or formal invitations had been sent, she wrote them a letter describing the kind of event they were planning and why their involvement was essential.

> I really hope that you will be there too, and to the extent that you feel comfortable, will participate in our celebration. For Lisa and me, this is as close as we can come to a wedding, so it is terrifically important that all our loved ones are there for this once-in-a-lifetime occasion. You know I have always loved weddings because I love the gathering together of all the people who have been really close to the couples over the years.... It's a really joyous occasion, and it seems appropriate to gather together all the really important people in your life to witness your commitment and to express their support for you as a couple.

In an effort to acknowledge the problems she felt her family would have with the ceremony, Margaret added:

> I know that it has been hard for you to become comfortable with my being gay and not following the path you had always expected for me. But I also know that you are fond of Lisa, and I believe that at some level you realize that our path is not really so very different from yours, or from that of my sister and brothers. A year from now Lisa and I will have been together for ten years, and our lives are pretty much like that of our married friends—we work hard, we pay lots of taxes, we entertain some, we give as much time as we can to volunteer work, we're faithful to each other, and we take care of each other. Under the circumstances it is sometimes amazing to us to think that we can't be married legally; who could object to such a boring and conventional life?

To facilitate socializing among guests, Lisa and Margaret planned the wedding to include a weekend of activities in the vicinity of the inn where the ceremony was held. In addition to attending the ceremony on Saturday afternoon, those who came for the weekend arrived Thursday night, spent Friday together, shared an informal dinner on Friday, and took an excursion to local wineries on Sunday.

Their simple Protestant wedding was led by a Unitarian minister (the same minister who officiated at Jeff and Paul's ceremony). Lisa and Margaret exchanged nonmatching rings, chosen to not look like wedding rings, which might stimulate questions at work about "husbands."

Lisa and Margaret modeled their vows on those used by two lesbian friends whose wedding they attended the previous summer. Each read the following statement:

On this day before God and our family and friends, I reaffirm the commitment I have made to you. I join your life with mine in righteousness and justice, in love and compassion. I will be your loving friend as you are mine. Set me as a seal upon your heart, like the seal upon your hand. For love is stronger than death; it is the flame of God. I will cherish you, honor you, uphold and sustain you in all truth and sincerity. I will respect you, and I will love you with all my being.

The ceremony was followed by a dinner and toasts from family and friends. The two brides took a short trip afterward and returned to their jobs a week later. Though Margaret's firm offers an extra week of vacation to employees who get married, Margaret had not requested this time off, instead taking regular vacation time. In other words, everything about this wedding was calculated to be compatible with family standards of good taste on such occasions, and also was intentionally discreet and low-key. At the same time that they wanted very much to celebrate their relationship in a public manner, both were apprehensive about drawing attention to themselves and about coming out to nongay colleagues. Only a few carefully selected coworkers were invited to the ceremony.

About a month after the ceremony, I settled into a lounge chair in Margaret and Lisa's garden. Over iced tea and cookies, they showed me their photo album and, with much laughter, recounted various odd happenings over the wedding weekend. Beyond the humor, however, their description was intense; they perceived the ceremony as having deepened their relationship in ways they had not anticipated. Even more startling, they had decided to come out at work and to become much more public than they ever had about being gay. When Margaret returned to work after her week off, she responded to her colleagues' casual questions about her vacation by announcing that she and her partner of ten years had gotten married. The responses she received seemed to be warm, for the most part, but she said that even if they weren't, she now felt it was her responsibility to let her coworkers see that gay life is not only represented by the Sisters of Perpetual Indulgence.[14] The wedding led her to see her relationship as the core of her life in a way that disguising it would be betrayal.

A few months later, I spoke with Margaret on the phone, and she described an adventure she and Lisa had at an elegant Peninsula restaurant with close friends, a straight married couple. The couples, who met one another at business school, share an anniversary and have celebrated the date together for many years. This year, for the tenth anniversary of their relationships, they went out to dinner. During the dinner, the waiters overheard their talk of an anniversary, and when they served dessert, they decorated a small cake with a candle and presented it, with much ceremony, to the straight couple. At that point, the straight couple pointed to Lisa and Margaret and said, "But what about them?" When the confused waiter said, "But they're not married," Margaret and Lisa immediately answered, "Yes, we are," holding out their left hands and displaying the very nonmatching rings they had chosen so they would not resemble wedding rings. A second cake was brought to the table in minutes.

"IT WAS LIKE THE EARTH BEING RAISED UP": A PAGAN RITUAL

Muriel Parker, fifty-four, and Carol Lang, thirty-seven, held their commitment ceremony in the spring of 1993 in a San Francisco redwood grove. What they had originally planned as a party to celebrate their having registered as domestic partners some months earlier gradually evolved into a wedding as they expanded their guest list, and they finally decided to have it catered. Since Muriel is active in goddess-worship activities and is a member of a crone circle—a support group of women over fifty who get together to perform pagan rituals—there was little question that the ritual would need to be constructed on a pagan model. But Carol identifies as a Roman Catholic, and wanted some touches in the ceremony that would recall "traditional" Christianity.

The ritual was performed around an altar set up in the middle of the redwood grove that represented the four directions and their four associated elements, with four candles and four symbols. The officiant, a woman minister who is heavily involved in the feminist spirituality movement, introduced herself as one of the celebrants as she welcomed the participants to the ritual. She began:

It was Jesus who said that wherever two or three are gathered, there will spirit be also. Let us acknowledge the sacred circle we create. Let us recognize that this space is holy and that our intentions are good. Let us look around the circle of those who are gathered and let us say in one voice: Peace and greetings to all.

She continued by invoking the spirit:

Oh, Holy One, wise and loving nurturer, be present for us today. Bless this circle we have created and make it sacred to you. Hecate, Mother of our souls, destiny caller, come to us today, share your wisdom as we celebrate. We come in celebration and thanksgiving for this gift of love which you have given Muriel and Carol. Help us to love as courageously. Help us to live as boldly. Help us to be as unwilling to sacrifice our happiness to convention. Dwell in us and expand our vision to see your endless possibilities and our hearts to encompass your boundless opportunities. We ask you to bless this ceremony of heart as it unfolds today and the life these two women will live together. Be with us, share with us. Come, holy spirit, come. Blessed be.

North, which stands for earth in pagan practice, was symbolized on the altar with a crystal globe and a green candle; east (air) was represented by a feather and a yellow candle, south (fire) was symbolized by two dragons and a red candle, and a container of water represented west, with a blue candle. The seventy guests sat in a circle around the altar, and the minister had everyone stand to "call the directions," which Muriel and Carol said is the start of all pagan rituals. After invoking blessings from east, south, west, and north, the minister said:

Sky above and earth below, we acknowledge the power that you share with us. We open ourselves to the lessons you will teach us. Bless us, guide us, strengthen us as we gather to celebrate this union and our love for these two women. Blessed be.

Because the two women frequently attend drumming workshops, they brought drums and rattles to the ceremony, and had a well-known local drummer participate. At one point in the ceremony, the drummer and her assistant picked up their drums and sat behind Muriel and Carol, inviting the guests to circle the couple while drumming and shaking rattles. Muriel describes "everyone rattling and shaking and drumming and banging. Oh, my god, it went on and on and on. It was like the earth was being raised up."

The symbolic focus of the ceremony was the word "namaste," which has become a kind of totem for the couple. Though they don't know exactly what it means, suspecting that it comes from "some eastern tradition, Hindu or Buddhist,"[15] they found it written in a picture of a rainbow on a trip to Hawaii and decided that their finding it was fateful and that it contained "the spirit of what we wanted to say to each other." Carol explains that it means to them, " 'I honor the place in you in which the entire universe dwells. I honor the place in you which is of love, of truth, and life, and of peace. When you are in that place in you and I am in that place in me, we are one.' What 'namaste' really means is mutual respect for where you are." After she repeated the word with various permutations, the minister talked about the importance of friends and family supporting the couple and asked them to chant, "Namaste, we hear you. Namaste, we see you. Namaste, we celebrate your love."

This part of the ceremony was followed by a "handfasting," a ritual in which the couple join hands in a way that suggests the infinity of a circle, symbolizing "the entirety of the universe as represented in relationship." In explaining this part of the ceremony, the minister alluded to evidence that women's unions were once celebrated in Europe in the same way that the unions of heterosexual couples were.[16]

Muriel and Carol talked with me at length about the shape the ceremony eventually took and the "organic" process by which it was created. To demonstrate, they presented me with a copy of the book they used to record all the ritual elements, pointing out the corrections they made as the ceremony evolved. Some of Muriel's changes had to do with cutting anything that seemed "too political." She explained, "There was mention made of 'I'm a lesbian' and some political statement about justifying the fact that it's okay. I didn't want that in there. Because I didn't feel it was necessary to acknowledge that I'm taking a political stand as a woman loving a woman. I was acknowledging publicly my love for this person. Not because I'm a lesbian, not because she's a lesbian, but because we are one and we love each other. And that's purely and simply what I wanted to say."

While the process of creating the ceremony helped Muriel and

Carol define their relationship and what was important to them, many of their negotiations with family members over who would attend the ritual were acrimonious. Muriel, who had been married to a man for some twenty years, has three grown children, two sons and a daughter, and six grandchildren. She said:

> About a week before the ceremony, my oldest son called and said he and his wife didn't feel that their children should be exposed to that kind of thing. But he himself would be glad to come because I'm his mother and he would like to honor me that way. And then followed an hour or so later by my other son with a similar story. And so I thought about it over night. And I called them both back the next day and told both of them that I didn't want either one of them at the ceremony if that's the way they felt. They were going to come by themselves without their wives and more particularly, without their children.

Muriel reminded her sons that she did not need social approval to follow her conscience. As a young white woman marrying a black man in the 1950s, she had endured the hostility of her family and community and had not given in. She had raised her mixed-race children under tremendous adversity; thus she found her sons' conventional attitudes particularly ironic.

> At one point my daughter, who did come with her two oldest children, didn't want to come for the same reasons. And I just told her, "What the hell do you think we *do* at home? Roll around on the floor naked in front of your children, or something? You think that sex governs our lives, that's all we're about, is sex? You know, we live a normal life. We want to make a public statement of our love." She capitulated. And did come. And participated.

Muriel's daughter and her foster daughter both attended and sang a song during the ceremony. On the morning of the ceremony, this daughter, accompanied by her own teenage daughters, arrived early to give them "something old, something new, something borrowed, something blue." She then told Carol, "You're now part of our family," which left everyone in tears.

Carol also had problems with her family. An only child, her widowed mother is remarried, and travels around the country in a mobile home. They are not close. Carol explained,

> My mother and I have a very complicated relationship about me being gay. What I decided to do was send her the invitation with a letter ex-

plaining that this was a really important step in my life and this was
something I wanted to do. And she called me from somewhere and said,
"How could you do this to me?" basically. . . . And I tried to explain to her
how important this was for me and that I was only planning on doing this
once and how there were a lot of other people that she knew that would
be there. All the straight people that she knew that would be there. You
know, sort of like, they can support me and you can't. And her whole
thing was about how this was so terrible and her husband is very religious
and how immoral this is. All this stuff. And so that was the end of that.
My fourth grade teacher and her husband who I've stayed in contact with
all these years came as my surrogate parents for me.

The group of people that came together at the ceremony was diverse, including Muriel and Carol's lesbian friends, their friends from
other times in their lives (including one of Carol's childhood friends),
and a few coworkers.

One of the things that we wanted since we were having such an eclectic
group of people coming—we had straight folks, we had gay folks, we had
folks that had never heard of a ceremony between women, we had radical lesbians that probably this was the first time they had been in the
same room with men for a while. We had a lot of different folks together.

It was particularly significant to the two women that there were a
number of children in attendance, and that many of the guests later
described the ritual as the most moving and meaningful one anyone
could recall. Carol sums up her feelings: "It was like being in a cocoon
of love and excitement and joy."

DISCUSSION

The growing frequency of commitment ceremonies can be perplexing
both for the gay or lesbian individual and for the scholar of gender and
sexuality. Does it constitute courageous repudiation of the notion that
only persons of different sexes may marry, and as such can it be con-
strued as outright resistance to heterosexism? Or does it represent instead simple accommodation to the norms of the straight world, a calculated effort to win acceptance by somehow fitting in? I suggest that a
more radical conclusion would be that the complex symbolic strategies

played out in these ceremonies indicate that resistance and accommo-dation are neither distinct nor mutually exclusive, and that cultural creations emerging from gay/lesbian life have much to teach us about how to theorize social process. The elaboration of a separate lesbian culture can be achieved through the intensification of ties that go be-yond the lesbian community; this apparent paradox forces us to under-stand the interrelationship of lesbian and straight cultures in a more dynamic way than models of separation will permit.

The five weddings described here represent anything but a cul-tural unity, drawing their ritual content from distinct sources and having different, explicit ceremonial agendas. The Jewish weddings draw on Jewish tradition, and in doing so place the commitment that is, in each case, the focus of the celebration in a historical and commu-nity context. The effect of this emphasis is to inform the audience (the couple and the guests—in all cases, both gay and straight, friends and family) that gay/lesbian marriage is not really anything astonishing or a departure from tradition—that it is, rather, natural and congruent with the past.

Using different ritual strategies, the two Christian weddings do much the same thing. Rather than explicitly invoking historical depth, however, they rely on a more diffuse sort of nostalgia, by using a series of familiar symbols and the language commonly associated with getting married. They also elaborate and celebrate the participation of family in specific, ritual moves. In Bonnie and Barbara's wedding, the participation of Bonnie's parents and the invitation extended to Bar-bara's deceased parents to join the ceremony spiritually, and the for-mation of bouquets made of roses given by both families, highlighted the significance of the ceremony as an event that unified two families. At the same time, the participation of friends, and particularly the minister's reading of the women's diaries, made clear that these two women were lesbians and that their relationship was a sexual union.

The traditional style of Margaret and Lisa's wedding and its orga-nization as a weekend event also served to highlight the significance of family. At the same time, however, the effect of the ritual was to break down their long-term reticence and to create a context for talk-ing about their relationship in public. That is, by making their rela-tionship more like that of heterosexuals, they were freed to reveal their differentness. This was dramatically demonstrated at the anniversary dinner that took place several months after the wedding, and in Margaret's change of heart about coming out at work.

Finally, the pagan ceremony, although designed to emphasize the ties of the two brides to a feminist spiritual tradition that differs from the religious affiliations of their families, also defined the couple as entitled to community acceptance equivalent to that extended to heterosexual couples. Although Carol's mother refused to attend the event or to respond to the invitation, a childhood friend and teacher were present and symbolized the integration of her past and present. Muriel's sons did not attend, prompting her angry response, but her daughter, granddaughters, and her foster daughter were present and played a central role in the proceedings. The song sung by her daughter and foster daughter symbolized the coming together of her old life as mother and her new life as lesbian; her angry response to her son's bias reminded him, as well, that this was not her first courageous act.

Like other rituals anthropologists have examined, these events are dramatic occasions that, to paraphrase the anthropologist Barbara Myerhoff, employ sacred symbols to cope with paradox, creating the belief that things are simply as they are portrayed and that their portrayal is proper, true, inevitable, and natural.[17] In that rituals stand outside the routine of normal events, they can more readily dispel contradictions and embrace incongruity.[18] Just as heterosexual weddings convey to couples their place in the history of their families and remind them of the contribution they will make to the continuation of tradition, so lesbian weddings symbolically claim that lesbian couples are not estranged from the values of the wider community, and that they are, in fact, part of that community. Even as they also celebrate their involvement in a lesbian subculture, each of these weddings, then, makes the claim that the marrying couple are members of the wider community. But in view of the unwillingness of that community to acknowledge their presence, all of the rituals also address refusal of their claims. They cannot simply ask for what Bruce Bawer calls their "place at the table," they must *demand* it.[19]

What does the emerging visibility of lesbian motherhood and the increasingly common phenomenon of lesbian wedding ceremonies tell us about how lesbian cultures are constituted in America? As I have mentioned, in my earlier research I found that lesbian

mothers make claims to the symbolic accouterments of motherhood
—constructing motherhood and womanhood as naturally linked, and
thereby reinscribing a conflation that has tended to be used to understand the devalued status of women, and also to celebrate what have
been seen as distinctly maternal moral attributes. The emphasis they
tend to place on the salience of ties with their blood relatives, particularly with their parents and siblings, as they constitute their families
points to a concern with ties to blood relatives as a source of reliability
and stability that will in turn define their ties with their own children.
Like heterosexual single mothers, whom I also studied, lesbian mothers constructed an ideal image of a kinship system they saw as extend-
ing from their parents through themselves and their children. Not the
least of the benefits described as coming from motherhood, then, was
the closeness it promoted with families of origin; some of their expectations were material, but even when such instrumental rewards were
mentioned, it was the closeness of the tie and its naturalness that was
most emphasized.

In much the same way, lesbian weddings seem to make conservative statements about kinship, if not about gender. Individual relationships are understood to be grounded in a web of relationships based on
marriage and biology. The group assembled to witness and participate
in the ceremony tends to be defined as "community," without whose
support the relationship being celebrated would be far more vulnerable to a variety of pressures. The content of the ritual focuses on the
naturalness and inevitability of these connections, tracing their roots
in history and tradition. Central as well is the tendency to draw participants from both within the gay community and beyond it; virtually
all of the couples I interviewed emphasized the participation of both
gay and straight people in their ceremonies, particularly relatives.
Those couples whose families did not attend gave lengthy explanations and, sometimes, excuses for their absence, often grieving over
such slights for years after the event.

But both lesbian motherhood and weddings also disrupt conventional claims about gender and kinship, to the extent that they define
the right to share in the moral domain of family. Lesbian mothers, particularly those who entered into parenthood as lesbians, rather than
during heterosexual marriages, may be seen to be insistent on their
right to share in the emotional and spiritual rewards of motherhood,

and to be demanding their places in groups of blood relatives despite the "unsuitability" of their sexual orientation. The varied ways in which lesbians can become parents—donor insemination, adoption, surrogacy, second-parent adoption, or comothering, as well as instrumental sexual encounters of various kinds—challenge the assumption that sexual intercourse and procreation are synonymous, generating a notion of reproductive choice that goes far beyond the questions of contraception and abortion that usually frame that issue.

Lesbian couples who marry in some ways make even sharper demands on the conventional intersections between kinship and gender. In insisting upon public recognition of their relationships, lesbians assert that the marital tie is not the "natural" preserve of heterosexual couples—that marriage need not institutionalize gender. But even in this respect, lesbian and gay weddings make ambiguous, shifting, symbolic statements: The wedding that was most outwardly conventional perhaps most directly challenged the naturalness of gender; recreating a "traditional" Jewish wedding depended on staging what the bride feared the heterosexual guests might take as a drag parody. Lesbian ceremonies seem to demand recognition of the couple as a key symbol of difference from the mainstream (think of how loaded the image of the same-sex kiss has been in media representations) at the same time that they claim membership in the seemingly mainstream institution of marriage. Their resistance is to the monopoly heterosexuals have long held on weddings as public proclamations of relationships, not to the idea that such celebrations might be important. When I asked couples how they would respond to those who would accuse them of mimicking a heterosexual institution, most denied that marriage and commitment *were* intrinsically heterosexual; they saw their rituals as an effort to reclaim something that was theirs all along, by virtue of their membership in the wider community.

CHAPTER 6

Requiem for a Street Fighter

KATH WESTON

À mon Requiem, peut-être ai-je aussi, d'instinct, cher-
ché à sortir du convenu. Voilà si longtemps que j'ac-
compagne à l'orgue des services d'enterrements! J'en
ai par-dessus la tête. J'ai voulu faire autre chose.

GABRIEL FAURÉ

INTROÏT

"Who was Julie Cordell?" That's the question I encountered again
and again after the publication of my book on lesbians, gay men, and
kinship.[1] I had expected perhaps, "Are mothers really easier to come
out to than fathers?" or "What do you think of gay marriage?" In-

stead, "Who was Julie . . . ?" echoed off the walls and wound its way through the telephone lines to my home in Arizona. Behind that simple question lay the difficult, unspoken ones: Was she your girlfriend? Your friend? What happened to her? Why did she die so young?

It all started with a dedication. Not the kind required to make it through the seven years it took to research and write the book. No, this dedication was spartan in comparison, three lines sandwiched between the title page and the contents:

In memory of Julie Cordell
1960–1983
who came looking for community

Like many gay people of my generation, I had attended far too many funerals by the time I reached my late twenties. For San Francisco's "gay community," the 1980s was a decade that witnessed the explosion of the AIDS pandemic, the exacerbation of racial and class tensions, and worsening economic conditions for people caught in the undertow of the wave of financial speculation sweeping the city. As an ethnographer trained to read up on my subject, I knew full well that topics such as class, death, and sexuality would merit attention "in the field." As someone who claimed membership in the community I studied, I knew too well the subtle but no less debilitating effects of living in a society where heterosexuality remains a pervasive assumption.

As long as I restricted my voice to that of the researcher, I could not adequately communicate the experience of living under siege in a subaltern population, regardless of how explicitly I brought myself into the text. Claiming "insider" status by coming out in print did not solve my dilemma. A single body cannot bridge that mythical divide between insider and outsider, researcher and researched. I am neither, in any simple way, and yet I am both.

When I write, I can call myself a gay anthropologist or an anthropologist who is gay; a lesbian; queer; or a human being who has foregrounded homoeroticism in her life for almost two decades now. I can hold class relations constant by introducing myself as a woman from a working-class background, or emphasize the ways that professional employment has repositioned me in the class hierarchy. I can highlight or downplay the contradictions that face an Anglo writer who sets out to research a multiethnic "gay community" that includes people of color who may or may not call themselves gay. Because my subjectivity is neither seamless nor fixed, the queering of my own identity has not always translated into feelings of closeness or identification with the people I study.[2] An ever-shifting self-as-subject has shaped my work in ways that can never be confined to field encounter or text.

In the charged context of analyzing as I live a stigmatized existence, composing a book has meant writing not only between the lines but also behind the lines. What follows does not fall neatly into any one of the established anthropological genres of ethnography, reflections on fieldwork, or literary critique of a monograph already produced. To address that deceptively straightforward question—"Who was Julie?"—I needed new ways to link observation to participation and context to contemplation. Only then would I begin to convey the effects of a kind of engagement with my research topic that cannot be neatly packaged into a field study of limited duration. Julie Cordell could have been—in some sense, was—my "best informant." Even though, by the time I taped my first interview, she was already dead.

KYRIE

As gay writers have experienced increasing success in getting their work published, many have paused to take a closer look at the place of writing in queer lives. In recent years anthropologists, too, have scrutinized, in minute detail, what they write, how they write, and the political implications of both. This process of self-examination (some would say obsession) has raised a host of stylistic and ethical issues for the would-be writer. But in the midst of all this discussion, few have stopped to wonder how a writer arrives at the dedications that stand like sentinels at the gates to a book or a poem.

When it comes to the front matter of books, there seem to be two kinds of readers: the ones who skip over the acknowledgments and dedication to "get to the good stuff," and the ones who consider the first few pages of a book part of the good stuff, a place to get the dirt on who's who and who knows who. With the passing years, I must confess that I find myself in the latter group. So I suppose I should not have been surprised when people started asking about Julie.

If a book is dedicated to someone who does not share the author's surname, speculation provides a handy tool for filling in the gaps. Perhaps the person mentioned is a spouse, child, or lover. Perhaps she represents the mythical woman-behind-the-woman, the one who stood by the author through the long hours of writing and revisions. The limited, almost stereotypical character of the images that come to mind suggests just how little an author customarily reveals regarding the events that led to a particular book's dedication.

More than a few writers dedicate their books to relatives. Who can forget *Lesbian Nation*, which Jill Johnston claimed she wrote "for my mother, who should've been a lesbian, and for my daughter, in hopes she will be"? Like many authors, the anthropologist Lila Abu-Lughod dedicated one volume to her parents; Richard Handler presented *Nationalism and the Politics of Culture in Quebec* to "my father's sisters Gertrude, Esther, Mary, and Talie." Occasionally a lyric touch breathes life, along with mystery, into these concise formulations, as in the poet Audre Lorde's preface to *The Black Unicorn*, which reads, "For Linda Gertrude Belmar Lorde and Frederick Byron Lorde. The Face Has Many Seasons."[3]

Some dedications embrace (as they construct) entire communities, like the one in Gloria Anzaldúa's *Borderlands/La Frontera*, "*a todos mexicanos* on both sides of the border," or the one in the Gay American Indians anthology, *Living the Spirit*, to "our ancestors and the memory of our fallen warriors." More obliquely, David Bergman, editor of *Camp Grounds: Style and Homosexuality*, incorporates a quotation from a "gay" poet: "In Memory of Karl Keller: 'Do you think the friendship of me would be unalloy'd satisfaction?'—Walt Whitman."[4]

The most common dedications are brief and cryptic: for "Wendy," "Yangitelig," "The 36 Sexual Rebels," even "Susan Louise and the Voice Dolls."[5] These allusions may or may not become decipherable once a reader has turned the pages. Sometimes they resonate with the book's topic or hint at some aspect of the fieldwork situation. In a twist on the ubiquitous invocation of kin, Robert Alvarez Jr. offers *Familia*, in part, to the memory of his grandparents, who double as subjects of his study. More solemn, but no less restrained, are the inscriptions that open Vincent Crapanzano's *Waiting: The Whites of South Africa* ("For Tesgemariam Abebe and Rudolph Schmidt, Who Died") and Jonathan Boyarin's *Storm from Paradise: The Politics of Jew-*

ish Memory ("For Aaron, the brother whom I never knew"). I suspect that behind many dedications are attachments laden with a feeling and a fierceness that seldom come across in the text that follows.[6]

When it comes to my dedication of *Families We Choose* to Julie Cordell, there are many possible stories I could tell by way of explanation.[7] Julie was not my inspiration for writing the book, although she had labored long hours on her own account of the women's music industry, a project I greatly respected. Julie was not my lover, although she was certainly my friend, and I would be lying to say we never stole a kiss in the back of the clubs when we went to hear jazz and salsa.

Because Julie met her death two years before my formal research project got under way, she technically was not a participant in the field study that provided material for the book. Her name appears at the beginning of *Families We Choose* due to a different sort of connection: an interpretive link between the narratives I constructed of Julie's life and the experiences of an entire generation of lesbians and gay men, a link I made only in retrospect, after the manuscript was drafted and ready to be sent to the publisher. To understand this connection, you need to know something more about the way Julie Cordell lived and about the way she died.

OFFERTOIRE

I first met Julie at a gathering of women who played conga drums. Although she was younger than I, she had moved to the Bay Area from New Mexico at about the same age I had been when I left the Midwest behind for an unseen city, eager to explore gay San Francisco. Like me, she had grown up white and working-class. At the time of her death, after three years on the West Coast, Julie was twenty-three.

Except for a stint working as a typesetter for local newspapers, Julie found only marginal, dead-end jobs waiting for her in the Bay Area. At times she worked in the underground economy to make ends meet. Julie was one of the few lesbians I've known who lived in a literal closet. The walk-in closet in the Oakland apartment she shared with roommates was just large enough to contain a full-size mattress; it was all she could afford. I remember that apartment well because it had a staircase leading up to the roof, where we would go with friends to enjoy the spectacular view of the bay and play drums until the sun dipped below the horizon.

In her struggles for survival, Julie was far from alone, although she felt alone with her "money troubles" much of the time. During those years many young lesbians, gay men, and bisexuals had difficulty getting by on the modest income derived from service-sector jobs in an urban landscape being radically altered by gentrification. Twice roommates kicked Julie out for being late with her share of the rent. After one of these incidents, which left her homeless on the eve of her birthday, Julie camped out in my studio apartment for a month until she was able to locate work and move on. Her parents were Christian fundamentalists who rejected her lesbian identification and called her up on the phone every so often to urge her to resist the devil's influence by leaving San Francisco, that legendary city of vice and iniquity. In any case, they were not wealthy people, and could not have offered much in the way of financial assistance even if Julie had been willing to ask.

"The edge" is not a comfortable place to live. Tired of moving from household to household and job to job, Julie found herself locked into a serious depression. After months of battling the condition on her own, she decided to check herself into a psychiatric hospital. Like many queers, she had first encountered the mental health system when she was coming out, grappling with desires she didn't understand. This time she turned to psychiatry with a sort of desperation, only to find herself further marginalized among her gay friends and in society at large.

LIBERA ME

The last time I spoke with Julie, she told me she felt the gay community had let her down. In retrospect, her dream of finding a harmonious community that had learned to cope with differences of class, race, gender, age, ability, and sexuality seems naive. At the time, however, many queer migrants to the Bay Area subscribed to similarly utopian visions. When Julie had begun the research for her own book on women's music, she had been dismayed to discover not just a creative endeavor but a business, its stars no more than human. The roommates who had kicked her out were both lesbians. She had expected them to be more understanding, based upon a shared sexual identity.

While Julie was hospitalized, yet another gay roommate attempted to steal all her possessions and refused to return the keys to her car until I leaned on the doorbell for a solid ten minutes. After Julie's release from the psychiatric facility, it took police intervention and an escort by a few concerned friends to get Julie back into her own apartment to gather up her few belongings. As the police officer stood by looking bored and impatient, Julie's former roommate began to taunt her, removing items from boxes as quickly as Julie could pack them, until the two eventually came to blows. Of the friends who offered their assistance on this occasion, I was the only one who identified as gay. This rueful observation was Julie's, not mine. In my preoccupation with keeping the interchange between Julie and her roommate from escalating into a full-scale brawl, I had set aside any inclination to operate as the note-taking anthropologist.

By the fall of 1983 Julie had made a decision to leave San Francisco for the southwestern city in which she had come of age. Her options were limited: She had little income, no savings, and no confidence that she could hold down a job in her depressed and medicated state. Although Julie had turned to friends in the past for help during emergencies, she did not feel she could rely on them for the basic necessities of life. Instead, she turned to the only people she could name as family: relatives by "blood" and adoption. Her stepfather agreed to drive to California to pick her up from the hospital where she had undergone a second round of psychiatric treatment. She would be allowed back "home," provided she agreed to leave behind the corrupting influence of "homosexual companions" and return to her parents' version of faith in a Christian god.

The day before her stepfather was scheduled to arrive, Julie and I had planned to meet to say goodbye. When I called that morning to let her know I was running late, the receptionist told me the hospital had released her to her stepfather's custody the previous afternoon. Disheartened at the lost opportunity to say our farewells, and suspicious of her stepfather's motives, I resolved to call Julie at her parents' house later in the month.

A few weeks later I did call, hoping to reconnect with Julie and to offer her support in what to me looked like extremely adverse circumstances in which to come to terms with her needs, her desires, her depression, and her future. After a long pause, her stepfather informed me, "Julie is no longer with us." I asked for her phone number, supposing she had found some way to gain a measure of independence with a room or an apartment of her own. "I mean she is no longer *with* us," he repeated. He went on: "After I picked her up from the hospital, she suddenly leaped out of the car as we were driving through the city. We never made it out of San Francisco. The next thing I knew, they told me she had jumped off the Golden Gate Bridge."

What happened in the car that late autumn day only Julie's stepfather knows. The report filed by the Coast Guard crew that picked her up off Baker's Beach said she was still alive when they hauled her aboard the boat. Even as she hit the water, her body fought to live, to draw in one more breath. It was to be her last battle.

IN PARADISUM

Why did I dedicate *Families We Choose* to Julie Cordell? One reason is thoroughly embedded in desires that spring from my own cultural context: a wish to restore to Julie her chosen name, coupled with a determination that her memory endure at least a few years beyond a life that was much too short. When all is said and done, I miss her deeply, and I still rage at the way she died. Read another way, the story behind my dedication bears a message and a moral. In what has often been characterized as a "post-AIDS" and "new gay" era, queers are still dying of some very old-fashioned causes. We still grapple with pervasive heterosexism in our encounters with employers, religious institutions, medical providers, and members of our straight families. Despite the visibility of gay organizations in urban areas, many of us still struggle to gain a modicum of self-acceptance. Suicide rates remain disproportionately high among gay and lesbian youth.[8] Class conflict and racism cut a wide swath through "our" communities.

As the writing and rewriting of the manuscript for *Families We Choose* progressed, the prospect of opening the book with a reference to Julie acquired new significance for me. I began to rework my interpretations of what had happened to Julie in light of what I had learned while I was officially studying the gay community in the Bay Area. It was this back-and-forth movement between the stories of Julie I had told since her death and the stories of lesbians and gay men who had never met my friend that finally convinced me to dedicate the work to her.

Families We Choose chronicles the historical emergence of the concept of gay families, a category that scarcely existed when Julie jumped from that bridge in 1983. Before the 1980s, "gay people" and "family" tended to appear as mutually exclusive categories in the United States. Lesbians and gay men were supposed to represent either an ominous threat to "the family" (in New Right rhetoric), or a group capable of creating exciting new alternatives to "the family" (in the rhetoric of many gay liberationists). Both formulations located queers somewhere outside kinship. To speak of gay families, lesbian families, chosen families, and families of friends was not the commonplace then that it has since become.

In the book I trace the appearance of gay families to two related developments of the 1970s and 1980s. The first was the unprecedented impact of the gay movement's call for all gay people to come out to heterosexuals, including relatives by "blood" and adoption. Within a matter of a decade it became customary for self-identified gay men and lesbians at least to consider disclosing their sexual identities to parents and other close kin. But did coming out necessarily imply membership in something called a gay community? Disillusionment set in as queers began to recognize what later seemed obvious: their different positioning within a population defined in terms of sexuality, but crosscut by lines of race, ethnicity, gender, age, ability, and class. More and more people dissociated themselves from the sanitized and masculinized gayness represented by the image of the "Castro clone." Some even questioned whether the concept of coming out applied in the same way to people of color and working-class whites.

Julie was not the only one in the early 1980s who had sought acceptance from parents, only to be told to fend for herself unless she was prepared to "go straight." And Julie was far from the only one who had failed to find, in the gay mecca that was supposed to be San Francisco, the vision of community that had originally brought her to the Bay Area. For Julie, as for many others, "community" turned out to be an entity too abstract, too encompassing, and too homogenizing to provide the face-to-face relationships, the tolerance for conflict, and the emotional sustenance that could have seen her through a difficult life transition. In Julie's eyes, neither the gay community nor the women's community had ever come to terms with the class differences that had contributed to her precarious financial condition, or with the stigmatizing label of mental illness.

What would have happened if Julie had been born a few years later, or held on until there was a cultural construct—a "family of friends"—that might have allowed her to turn to her peers for the validation and material support that her parents were never able to provide? Sometimes I tell myself it's wishful thinking to believe that a simple category like "family" could have carried the weight of the problems and oppression that Julie faced at that point in her life. Other times I tell myself to have more faith in the power of human creativity. I remember all the days when Julie discovered whatever intangible resources she needed to bounce back from seemingly overwhelming chaos and despair.

Julie Cordell was not a working-class hero; neither was she a passive victim of circumstances. She could be demanding. From time to time, as she put it, she "got on people's nerves." Then again, in a culture that values the trappings of self-sufficiency, it's not easy to have to ask for the things you need to live. Sometimes Julie tripped over her own stubbornness and insecurities, only to pick herself back up and try again. Sometimes she stayed down for the count. More than once, friends stepped in to help. After a while, some of them grew tired of helping and left her lying there in the mess that she and society had made. No, Julie was nothing like a working-class hero. There was a time when she fought, she danced, she ate, she kissed, she breathed. She doesn't do those things any more.

Would a chosen family have given Julie the support she needed to bounce back one more time? Would "once more" have been enough, in the absence of a meaningful job and adequate mental health care services? I've often wondered, though I'll never know. What I do know is that Julie's parents took her ravaged body back to New Mexico without consulting her friends about the disposition of her remains or even informing us of her death. Under prevailing statutes, which grant great powers to relatives narrowly defined through marriage or "blood," they had every legal right to do so.

Today Julie's ashes lie in a vault under a surname she rejected as a young adult. Julie chose for herself the name "Cordell," and this was the name under which her friends marked her passing when we gathered to beat drums and read poetry at the ocean's edge. It took me a long time after the ritual to feel anything but anger and pain and loss whenever I looked at the Golden Gate Bridge. It has taken even longer to remember the unparalleled beauty of that bridge against the setting sun the evening Julie and I played congas on a rooftop in Oakland.

PART THREE

·

REINVENTIONS

CHAPTER 7

Club Q:
Dancing with (a) Difference

DEBORAH P. AMORY

SAN FRANCISCO, EARLY 1989

It's twenty years after Stonewall, and the Reagan-Bush era has a few more years left in it. George Bush has just chosen everyone's favorite joke as his running mate, and government scandals are rife: HUD, Wedtech, the Iran-Contra affair. It is the age of microchips and multi-national capitalism; Third World women work in factories to produce everyone's favorite consumer goods. "Cosby" is the No. 1 show on television. Soul II Soul, a black collective band from Britain, is changing the beat of funk. No new public housing has been built in the United States for ten years; the rich have gotten richer, the poor, poorer, and some say the middle class has all but disappeared. The AIDS pandemic has brought issues of sex and sexuality to a new place of prominence in American life; ACT UP has elevated civil disobedience to an art form. As lesbian and gay visibility has increased, so has violence directed against us; queer bashing is on the rise, but rarely recorded as a hate crime. Everyone is in therapy; twelve-step programs abound. Music videos have changed the way America looks—at TV, at itself: Style is in fashion, attitude is in fashion, shopping has become a way of life. And Club Q is happening.

OCTOBER 29, 1989: HALLOWEEN AT CLUB Q

Imagine yourself entering a different world. You pay six dollars at the door, five dollars with a "Q card"; as part of the price of admission, you receive a little plastic bag of party favors—a spider ring, a tiny rubber rat. You move from the dark, hard street into a huge room that is also dark, and sharp in places, but filled with hundreds of beautiful women, all sizes, colors, shapes: women in tuxes, women in leather, pretty, soft femmes with long hair. Butches with impassive faces lean against the wall, and k.d. lang look-alikes sport bolo ties. Black lace bras abound, athletic underwear becomes outerwear. Women of many colors inhabit this magical space. You see tall dark women with dreds, many shades of blond (bottled and born), straight black hair, and sedate perms. Sweat glistens off of light skin and dark skin. Everyone looks beautiful.

Screens scattered about the walls project an endless stream of tantalizing images that flash by: psychedelic colors and patterns; still shots of movie stars and famous personalities; videos of YOU as you dance below; an old movie of a train speeding through a tunnel and emerging out the other side. The bar is in the center of the room, slightly back from the main dance floor, and a few booths line the walls. A slow pattern of bodies winds its way around the periphery; the room's so crowded you have to brush against everyone, or touch them lightly on the shoulder to get by. "There's a lot of unnecessary touching going on," someone wryly observes. Knots of women congregate here and there, but most are dancing to the beat that's pounding through your temples. And you can tell who's from out of town: They're the ones standing in the middle of the room, with their mouths hanging open.

As midnight approaches the crowd starts to anticipate the appearance of the Club Q dancers. One or two have been performing, intermittently, on the small platform above the entrance, but now attention turns toward the big center stage, four feet or so above the dance floor. The stage is set with stark, white tombstones, marked with names, dates, "RIQ" (Rest In Q). The recesses of the room are cloaked in spider webs and skeletons; some of the crowd is in costume.

Just before midnight, the music pauses, lights dim, and smoke starts to seep from the edges of the stage. The crowd reacts by backing away from the smoke, and then there's a surge forward as everyone realizes it's not fire but dry ice, a cue that the dancers are about to appear. In the darkness the dancers have taken up their places among the tombstones; each one is bound in white paper bandages. The lights go up, and you hear the first strains of a song: "BACK TO LIFE, BACK TO REALITY, BACK TO THE HERE AND NOW . . ." With the first note, the first word, the crowd roars, and as the song unfurls so do the dancers. Their first pose is frozen in time, dead to life, so many mummies trapped in a graveyard. They are constrained by the wrappings, but start to move to the music; some seductively unravel their bonds, others punch their way through to freedom with the beat. BACK TO LIFE, BACK TO THE PRESENT TENSE . . . The wrappings fall to the floor to reveal twelve beautiful women, mostly dressed in skimpy black Club Q T-shirts. There are ten women of color and two white women. The appreciative spectators below whistle, shout and roar their admiration and lust. When the song is over, another begins and then the dancers invite the crowd onto the stage. Innumerable wannabes reach up for the beckoning hands, take center stage and join in the fun.

WHAT'S HAPPENING HERE?

During 1988 and 1989, Club Q exploded onto the San Francisco dance scene as a monthly party for women. For two years, Club Q met only one Friday a month; by 1990, Club Q was happening every Friday, and

two years later it was gone.[1] Founded together with The Box (a club
for lesbians and gay men together, meeting in the same place but on
different days), Club Q enjoyed amazing success in the easy come, easy
go world of lesbian dance clubs. Other clubs in the Bay Area started
to offer similar entertainment packages: dancers on stage, door prizes,
performance art in progress. But Club Q was held up as the standard,
and is even memorialized in Karen Everett's video, *Framing Lesbian
Fashion*.[2] Why was Club Q so wildly successful in those early years?
That is one of the questions that prompted this article.[3]

I will argue that Club Q represents a particular moment in lesbian
history, a moment belonging to the hot young urban woman: a
younger (in her twenties) member of the lesbian community, marked
most conspicuously by a celebration of sexuality, style and attitude,
and a relative position of privilege in terms of money and education.
Some critics have called this young woman the "lipstick lesbian," and
in these accounts she is assumed to be white.[4] But the fact of the matter
is that the hot young urban woman who stood on center stage at Club
Q was more likely to be black, Latina, or Asian. The women at Club
Q took the notion of the lipstick lesbian and worked it, right across the
color spectrum.

Recent accounts of lesbian identity have focused largely on the
"rebirth" of lesbian sexuality that followed the sex wars of the early
eighties.[5] Less successful, I think, has been the effort to integrate issues of race and class into feminist and lesbian analyses.[6] The general
failure of theorists, particularly white women, to explore the ways in
which race, gender, class and sexuality are interconnected is most obviously due to the "racial blindness" that the privileges of whiteness
afford.[7] As Norma Alarcón argues, white women all too often appropriate and then negate the differences insisted upon by women of
color.[8] In this article, I'm the next big white girl who will grapple with
some of these issues. In my attempt to avoid the pitfalls of simultaneously invoking and erasing the importance of race, I will emphasize
identity as a practice situated in specific historical contexts, a complex
intertwining of sameness and difference, heated up by desire and
played out across those chain link fences that mark socio-economic in-
equalities.[9]

In the funny way that theory often seems to follow practice, feminist theorists were hotly debating issues of race, class, and gender just as Club Q was happening. By the end of the 1980s, Club Q served as a meeting place for a broad range of Bay Area women. The clientele was mostly lesbian, with some bisexuals and a few straight women. The crowd was young, in their 20s, but also included women in their 30s and 40s. White women thought the place was racially mixed; enough women of color attended to create a critical mass amidst the whiteness. The crowd also included working class as well as middle and upper class women. Club Q provides a unique lens into the politics of identity and style both because of the women who gathered there, and because it constituted a cultural institution that celebrated many different aspects of lesbian culture in a self-conscious way.

The lesbian identity being forged at Club Q revolved around an open celebration of sexuality, expressed through dance and cruising, built around the power of the lesbian gaze.[10] At stake in this drama was a sense of legitimacy in a hostile world, a sense of the power articulated by women's bodies in motion. Moreover, expressions of lesbian identity drew on a number of historical motifs. While definitely part of the eighties repudiation of lesbian-feminist politics and style, Club Q also demonstrates the impact of black popular culture on mainstream lesbian culture. Just as racism erases the contributions of black artists and musicians to mainstream white culture, lesbian history has all too often been written only in terms of its white (and middle-class) participants.[11] In this article, I hope to do otherwise, demonstrating how the celebration of style, sexuality and cruising at Club Q enabled women to experiment with different senses of themselves, to look and/or venture across racial and class borders, and to recreate themselves within and against those lines.

PRACTICING THEORY

During two years of my graduate school education, I spent a significant number of Friday nights at Club Q.[12] While some of my peers were studying, I was dancing, and Club Q gave me new ways to think about what I was supposed to be learning in school. In particular, it provided a detailed example and localized site of identity formation in that complicated realm at the margins of societies and cultures that Gloria Anzaldúa has named "the borderlands."[13] Hopefully, this article will provide some insight into the ways in which we who inhabit a specific borderland think about ourselves, our identities and our lives.

In feminist theory, people talk about the "multiply-positioned subject," a lesbian (in this case) who stands at the intersection of various discourses on race and ethnicity, class, gender and sexual orientation. In other words, we are talking about a brave girl who lives in a world where the color of her skin, eyes and hair; who she sleeps with, and how; the amount of money she carries in her pocket (or purse); the language(s) she speaks and the music she listens to all make a profound difference in her life. This girl has emerged from the infamous "demise" of the unified Enlightenment subject, i.e., the dead white man of Western civilization fame.[14] The multiple differences in this postmodern subject's life (i.e., her race, her class, her gender, her sexuality) are described as "multiple subject positions," positions that are often contradictory, always complex, and that are created by ideologies of race, class, gender and sexual orientation.[15] Not incidentally, the theorization of this postmodern subject grew out of women of color's cogent critiques of Anglo-American feminist movements.[16] These accounts insist on the specificities of differences between women as one way of accounting for the complexities of all women's lives and countering the racism of too many feminist theories and practices.

Recent analyses of gender and sexuality also confront the assumption that sex and sexuality constitute the simple biological basis for gender, the "natural" facts underlying cultural constructions of gender. Instead, sexuality as well as gender are seen as cultural constructs. The heterosexual social contract (which depends on notions of heterosexuality as a "natural" act) becomes the glue that holds our ideological system of gender together. As Judith Butler has pointed out, gender becomes the performative act whereby sex is "naturalized," that is, made to appear natural.[17]

The notion of gender as a performative act emphasizes the constructedness both of gender and of sexuality; it challenges essentialist theories of identity. But what are some of the implications of thinking of gender as a performative act? Is there some balance to be struck between structure and agency, essentialism and performance, especially for those multiply positioned subjects of postmodernist feminist theory? And how can we ensure that feminist theory attends to issues of race and class as well as gender and sexuality? I will address these questions after describing more of the event that was Club Q and how it got to be that way.

HISTORY OF CLUB Q

Club Q was the brainchild of Page Hodel, local DJ and mixtress[18] extraordinaire. The club grew out of and reflects Page's many years of experience as a DJ in the Bay Area. In an interview, Page explained that she used to put on huge birthday bashes that gained her a reputation for throwing a good party. When she decided to open her own club, she conceptualized it as a monthly party for women, a place where everyone would be made to feel welcome, where everyone could dance. For Page, getting clean and sober[19] also involved the realization that music makes you high, and it's an even better high than the one that comes from drugs or alcohol. Thus Club Q could be a place where music and dancing provided that necessary sense of escape and release from a sometimes overwhelming world.

Based on her experiences over the years, Page included the best of what a club experience could offer. She featured dancers at her club; not just go-go dancers on pedestals or in a cage, but a whole group of dancers like the performers in Janet Jackson or Paula Abdul videos. The party atmosphere was also enhanced by decorations and door prizes. Perhaps best of all, having her own club meant that Page could play the music she loves best, which is funk.[20] Page attributes her success as a DJ to the fact that she likes to watch and listen to the crowd; rather than working a standard play list, she gauges the mood and makeup of the crowd by the requests she gets, what she sees happening on the floor; she spins the discs accordingly.

Page's predilection for funk influenced the music she played, but the Q's extraordinary popularity in 1989 and 1990 was also due, I think, to a particular historical juncture. Black women artists (like Paula Abdul, Whitney Houston, Janet Jackson) crossed over into the white mainstream at about that time; they (and others) often sampled off of funk greats like George Clinton. Page's familiarity with black musical forms proved serendipitous for Q-goers precisely because of the larger historical context. The Q dancers recreated the energy and drama found in music videos like Janet Jackson's "Rhythm Nation"; Jackson, in turn, was sampling off of Sly and the Family Stone.[21] In this complicated realm of cultural borrowings and border crossings, diverse trajectories of history, music, and people all converged on the Q.

Mrs. Gigi L'Amoure, local anthropologist, has also observed that the relative demise of the club scene in San Francisco by the mid-nineties highlights the intertwined fortunes of music and politics.[22] Club Q and other popular dance sites (for boys as well as girls) emerged just as Queer Nation was organizing in San Francisco, and as a new generation of political activists were getting their feet good and wet (and sometimes slimy). Queer Nation, and other groups, all too soon ran aground on the rocks of racism and sexism among lesbians and gays. Mrs. L'Amoure maintains that inspired political activism constitutes part of the necessary historical context for an inspired club scene. Clearly, both the political and the musical moments that gave birth to Club Q have changed.

Given the specificity of Club Q's time and place in history, we might ask why it proved to be such a rich site of cultural production. Renato Rosaldo points out that if we think of ritual as a busy intersection, a complicated processual convergence in time and space, we have to rethink the concept of culture. For example, lesbian culture (and, by extension, lesbian identity) can no longer stand as a carefully circumscribed, monolithic whole. Instead, "Culture can arguably be conceived as a more porous array of intersections where distinct processes crisscross from within and beyond its borders. Such heterogeneous processes often derive from differences of age, gender, class, race, and sexual orientation."[23] It was precisely these "differences" that arrived at the Q, paid their money at the door, and then danced their way through to new notions of lesbian identity.

PUMP UP THE JAM

Club Q evolved from a birthday party to a monthly party and became a major phenomenon among San Francisco dance clubs in 1988 and 1989. The Club stood out as a favorite among other dance clubs because it reflected the needs and desires of certain lesbians at a particular point. In interviews conducted with club-goers, everyone cited the dancing and the dancers as their favorite part of the Q experience. Going to Club Q was about going dancing: dancing with friends, asking another woman to dance, dancing by yourself, watching the dancers do it. The dancing was high quality, high energy, the best of the latest moves from music videos.

The dancing at Club Q celebrated women's bodies and women's sexualities. The Q dancers epitomized this fact as they moved, individually and collectively, across the stage. Each dancer looked different, moved differently, but each one was strikingly beautiful and some of us dreamed of becoming one. The only restriction on their dress was that they wear a Club Q T-shirt (a black T-shirt with a large pink *Q* on the front). They danced in torn jeans, bicycle shorts, a little leather, a few chains. Some of the dancing was highly erotic; others punched out short, sharp moves to the pounding bass; one woman managed an accelerated tap dancing to the beat. Two or more dancers would come together to grind out a soul train of ecstasy; they danced hips to mouth, reaching from behind to touch another's breast or grip her thighs. The energy was wild and catching, and inspired club-goers on the dance floor to their own versions of physical delight.

An important part of this celebration of sexuality involved cruising for girls, cruising other women's bodies and striking a pose while others cruised you. Most women wore clothing that was comfortable for heavy dancing, and just about every fashion sensibility was represented. There were some signs of S/M—leather collars, chains, little signals here and there—that mixed with chinos and floral print dresses on the same dance floor. Fashion and attitude were commented upon perhaps simply because everyone was looking everywhere, at everything; the dancers on stage, the light show, the slide and video screens flashing images overhead, the club-goers dancing everywhere in every which way. One Q-goer tried to explain exactly what was so exciting about the club for her. Yes, it's the dancing, the excitement of all those women together in one place, she said, but it's more: "It's a feast, really. A visual feast."

In interviews I have repeatedly asked women what it means to be looking at other women dancing on a stage. Just about everyone maintained that what they saw at Club Q was not degrading or oppressive.

While some of the dancing was erotic and suggestive, more of it was purely physical, athletic action. Others remarked that it's not the same as a straight club, obviously, because at the Q women were watching women. There was not the same threat of force behind the lesbian gaze that lies behind straight men scoping women. There was certainly a sense of playfulness about it when the act of flirtation took place in a less violent and safer place. The flirtation revolved around an appreciation of each other's bodies, for each other's sexualities, a heightened sense of sameness and difference. That's why it was so fun to go to Club Q and watch girls.

Not to overstate the case, attitude and cruising were also the most commonly cited reasons that women did not like Club Q. "Those girls are too young to have that much attitude," commented one lesbian in her thirties who only occasionally frequented the club. Needless to say, some women felt uncomfortable and judged by all those watchful eyes. Clearly, it seemed that Club Q catered to a new generation of lesbians, and their sexual boldness could be intimidating, or perhaps simply annoying.

Many women also commented on the diversity of the crowd. For a big club run by a white woman, women of color made up a significant part of the clientele. Thirty-five percent of two hundred women surveyed on an August night in 1990 identified themselves as women of color—black, Latina, Asian, Native American. The diversity was no accident; Page hired women of color to work at the club, and prefers to play funk. The club itself demonstrated a commitment to African-American culture and women of color, and local women responded positively to that commitment.

Club Q presented a formidable exception to the rule of racial segregation in straight and gay clubs alike. In subtle and not-so-subtle ways, racism structures the types of people who walk through club doors. Page pointed out that until recently, most lesbian clubs didn't play funk, house[24] or rap, except on isolated nights set aside for women of color. And most owners also hire white people to work those clubs.

Historically, lesbian bars have been predominantly working class spaces, but the dance clubs that emerged in the late eighties often drew a more affluent crowd. Twenty-five percent of the women surveyed at Club Q identified themselves as working class, fifty-two percent as middle class, twenty-one percent as upper class.[25] The price of admission to Club Q—five or six dollars—was not overwhelming, but also not insignificant. The presence of butch/femme style and S/M style at the club seemed to indicate working class influences,[26] although the more recent butch/femme revival has muted those class connotations. By the late 1980s, black-leather motorcycle jackets had become a standard fashion accessory for many different girls.

Q-goers often described the club as a *safe* place. Women who are survivors of violence and abuse remarked that they felt comfortable and protected at Club Q, because the women who worked the doors and the floor kept a friendly and watchful eye on things. Women in a program (any twelve-step program, but particularly Alcoholics Anonymous) regularly attended; they commented, "You don't see sloppy drunks there." At the Q, there was a conspicuous absence of drunken behavior and brawls. People went to the Q to dance, above all else, not just to drink.

Finally, the one major controversy surrounding Club Q centered on whether or not men would be allowed in. Soon after the club started meeting regularly, a battle over the apparent exclusion of men erupted at Club Q and in the local gay press. But it proved to be a minor incident; men in fact were admitted and made occasional appearances at the club, either as friends of women dancing there or as uninformed tourists.

PERFORMING IDENTITIES AT CLUB Q

Clearly, Club Q was all about performance. The dancers performed on stage, and many of the women on the packed dance floor below performed their own dramas of seduction, dance and delight. It seems important to point out that in a room full of women from all different walks of life, what feels natural to some looks like performance to others. And this is where two different arguments meet: essentialism versus constructionism, the "natural" facts of life versus the drama of the dance.

If gender is a complex performative act, what does that mean in a world where many genders and many sexualities exist? Straight gender—what straight women and men believe and do every day of their lives, and not just in bed—highlights the "naturalness" of heterosexuality, and labels homosexuality "unnatural." Coming out as a lesbian or gay man tends to throw that world into chaos—and, I would argue, can lead to some very unpopular conclusions. Heterosexuality can become the unnatural act, and a weird performance in and of itself. Homosexuality—what you do in bed with another girl, for example—thus seems eminently natural.

My point is that essentialism and constructionism—the Truth of nature and the truths of the performance—coexist, to varying degrees, in that thing we call lesbian identity.[27] A Q-goer who identifies as butch stated, "I was born this way. For years I thought I was a boy. Now I know I'm a butch." Another patron of Club Q, who similarly believes and experiences her identity as natural and quite essential, also demonstrated the performative aspects of being a butch when she took me out "butchbonding."[28] Sam, a working-class butch, knew she had a lot to teach me. (Too ruling class to be considered a real butch, I have been described as a "classic coed" by others.) We went out and shot pool, cruised girls, got tattoos together; all the while, she instructed me on the finer points of being a butch. I got lessons in how to walk, how to talk, how to wear those handcuffs. Yes, gender and sexuality are both performative acts and something experienced as an essential, natural part of lesbian identity.

Clearly, the either/or approach (it's all performance, it's all biology as destiny) obscures the complexity of what happens as we become ourselves, as we enact our lesbian identities. My point is simply that it can take stepping outside the mainstream and landing in a place like Club Q to appreciate these complexities, precisely because it's here that dominant ideologies lose their otherwise transparent quality.[29] The walls of naturalness come tumbling down under such persistent attacks by the unmentionable and the unthinkable, all dressed up, finally, with someplace to go.

As Stuart Hall points out, popular culture and the places that produce it, like Club Q, do not represent a transparent reality or truth but a "profoundly mythic experience,"[30] particularly for those of us who live our lives as marginalized peoples. It is where we go to imagine and create ourselves, and to see ourselves in new ways for the first time. Identity practices are especially performative at a place like Club Q,

but that fact doesn't need to obscure the realities of other easily essentialized structures like race and class.

Ann Cvetkovich focuses on identity performances in her comparison of Madonna's autobiographical flick, *Truth or Dare* (1991) and
Jennie Livingston's film about drag balls in New York, *Paris Is Burning*
(1991).[31] Madonna, as a white woman with money, has a lot more
power and resources with which to "perform" her identity than do the
black and Latino drag queens who are struggling to make ends meet
in between balls. Nonetheless, the performers in *Paris Is Burning* reveal both the power and the artifice of race and class through their
stylized enactments of whiteness and class privilege. Moreover, the
importance of sex-change operations to some of these men, of passing
as white or middle-class during the day (as well as at night), suggests
that this performance is not simply a frivolous game.[32] The point to
remember is that performances of identity take place within very real
(though not natural) structures of inequality.

IDENTIFYING (WITH) NARRATIVES OF THE PAST

So what about Club Q and the lesbian identities being forged there?[33]
Perhaps the problem is that gay, lesbian, and feminist theorizing of
identity as a thing in and of itself has prevented us from moving beyond the essentialist-vs.-constructionist debate. For even those scholars who argue for a social constructionist perspective treat identity as
if it were a static object of analysis, an implicitly essential "thing." Perhaps this is because some of us experience our identities as essential
even as we theorize them as constructed.[34] In any event, I would side
with those theorists who describe identity not as a "thing" that we
"have" but a process of becoming, a practice that is rooted in enactments of sameness and difference, a potentially liberatory practice.[35]
Identity formation thus describes the ways we experiment with different visions of ourselves in the world, particularly at places like Club Q.

As for lesbian identities in the late eighties, there certainly occurred a rebirth of lesbian sexuality, apparent both at Club Q and
other sites of cultural production articulating a pro-sex sensibility. But

there is no sexuality without race and class; for example, the late nineteenth-century romantic friendship model may be described as a white upper-class form of gender identity, while the butch/femme style and erotics of the fifties grew out of a mixed-race and specifically working-class context.[36] What's going on at Club Q? How are the women at Q positioning themselves and being positioned within various narratives of the past?

For lesbian identity in the late eighties, one of the most important historical contexts to consider is that of black popular culture. Stuart Hall has identified style, music and the body as three central components of that hotly contested realm of culture.[37] The music of Club Q comes out of that artistic tradition, and more specifically out of the black gay artistic tradition, as Anthony Thomas has pointed out.[38] Disco, house, and club music all originated in black gay communities, and subsequently crossed over into mainstream white culture where their "roots" became invisible.[39] And as most of us are aware by now, voguing (the style of dance that imitates models on a runway and is featured in *Paris Is Burning*) originated in the black and Latino drag culture of New York City. In short, the women of Club Q were drawing on these traditions in the process of transforming lesbian identities.

Butch/femme style also made a comeback in the late eighties, and was much in evidence at Club Q. The lipstick lesbian of late eighties fame represents a refashioning and rearticulation of classic femme sensibilities. For the first time in a long while, femmes are actively taking center stage in lesbian contexts, or perhaps more accurately they are simply becoming more visible in our representations of ourselves. The current refashioning of butch/femme style also occurs with an awareness of the outlaw status of that sensibility in the past, both in the fifties and in the lesbian-feminist seventies.[40] Invoking these traditions helps to position current "wild women" outside the boundaries of dominant lesbian as well as American culture.

Women of color were also visible at Club Q in new ways for a "mainstream" lesbian context. In the early eighties, lesbians of color produced not only critiques of white feminism but also courageous and empowering articulations of what it is like and what it means to be a lesbian of color in a racist and homophobic society. Gloria Anzaldúa, Cherríe Moraga, Audre Lorde, June Jordan and Pat Parker, to name just a few, have all helped to articulate bold new possibilities for another generation of lesbians. The women of color at Club Q are heirs to this legacy, even as white women struggle (or pretend) to understand it, and as some of us struggle to build a politics that fundamentally challenges these structures of inequality.

Finally, the world of Club Q articulates many of the contradictions facing us in the 1990s. These contradictions include increasing economic hardship for the majority of Americans, a fact that only heightens racial and class tensions. Gay and lesbian activists are striving to consolidate gains made since Stonewall and to challenge the backlash that inevitably accompanies economic recession. Much attention has been focused on building an inclusive community for all, even as the daily affronts of racism, classism, and other forms of discrimination maintain those old hierarchies of inequality among lesbians and gays.

At Club Q, these contradictions revolved around the simultaneous invocation of sameness (we're all girls lusting after each other, after all) and difference (how race and class structure our lives) in a very specific historical context. The club self-consciously celebrated African-American music and dance; working class butches and femmes cruised the same dance floor as sedate professional girls. On the one hand, the cruising and celebrations of style at the Q provided the possibility, at least, of establishing cross-racial and cross-class relationships, from sexual liaisons to friendships and alliances. It also provided the opportunity for women of color to meet and mingle with each other in a "mainstream" lesbian context. As one black woman put it, "I guess I was totally turned on by seeing other women of color, Asian, Latina, as well as black . . . they were all totally HOT. You know, it makes me realize; attitude looks sorta good on *everybody*."

As history spirals around us, questions of cultural appropriation also become important. White people have always appropriated black culture (Elvis Presley is a case in point), middle-class lipstick lesbians play with working-class butch/femme culture; some argue that the recent rise of the bisexual rights movement involves appropriations of gay culture.[41] In all of these instances, histories and experiences of oppression have been erased through selective celebration of styles. Crossing aesthetic boundaries that are also boundaries of race and class can serve to position white folks outside the mainstream of domi-

nant culture, in a conscious move of alliance with marginalized others.[42] There are ever-present dangers of fetishizing those others, however, a fact that helps to highlight how Club Q was as much a site of
cultural contestation as of celebration.

Those heady nights at Club Q have already receded into the past
tense, and hard times are upon us. There are no jobs, there's still no
justice, and there's just no good dancing to be found in San Francisco
these days. Now that I'm spending a lot more time at home, I've tried
not to be too nostalgic about those delicious, sweaty nights at Club Q.
But perhaps more to the point, I hope that the writing of the story will
help to make that particular historical moment yet another of those
always proliferating, always important narratives about the past.

CHAPTER 8

"Dick(less) Tracy" and the Homecoming Queen: Lesbian Power and Representation in Gay-Male Cherry Grove

ESTHER NEWTON

Dedicated to our young artists and intellectuals: breathless, beautiful and brilliant

Sometimes our theatre is really rough. But the audience we play for needs us. Lesbians never see themselves represented. And seeing yourself represented is what makes you feel you have a place in the world.

LISA KRON, a professionally trained actress and longtime WOW director and performer

1

In the twenty-three years since the publication of my work on professional female impersonators, I have often been asked if lesbians also did drag, and if not, why not?[1] The drag show scene I had written about in the 1960s was a world of gay men, in which the ten or so lesbian "drag kings" competing against each other in a Chicago drag ball seemed almost an oddity among hundreds of drag-queen contestants. When the touring Jewel Box Review advertised twenty-five men and a girl, I spent the evening checking out the gowned and feathered female impersonators to find out who the "real girl" was without ever considering that the self-assured tuxedo-clad male emcee would turn out to be Storme DeLarverie, a lesbian performer.[2] The general gasps of wonder that greeted Storme's revelation of her gender at the finale were certainly a tribute to her adept drag performance, but also exposed a certain void of expectation. Did lesbians do drag? Yes, but not as often as gay men did, and with far less impact.[3] Two stimulating essays and a controversial event in the recent community life of Cherry Grove, a gay and lesbian resort, got me to thinking again about why this might be.

While doing a book tour in the summer of 1993, I met a young graduate student in anthropology at Berkeley who was doubling as a reporter for the *Seattle Gay News*. In exchange for an interview, Sarah Murray shyly gave me a paper she had written on "lesbians and drag." "Drag has not developed into an autonomous theatrical genre within the lesbian community," Murray argued, pointing toward "the heart of the differences between lesbian and gay male subcultures in the United States" for answers.[4]

Murray's (and my own) sense of a profound and significant asymmetry between gay men's and lesbians' relation to drag clashed with the audacious proposition put forward by Sue-Ellen Case in "Toward a Butch/Femme Aesthetic."[5] "The butch-femme couple," she writes, "[are] playfully inhabiting the camp space of irony and wit, free from biological determinism, elitist essentialism, and the heterosexist cleavage of sexual difference" (305). Case's association of butch-femme with camp seems predicated on the assumption that butch clothing, whether on-stage or off, equals drag, in her reference to "the cross-dressed butch" and her assertion that the butch represents and bears the stigma of lesbian desire because of her [masculine?] clothing (302).[6]

Butch-femme as camp? Case's notion was an irritant—exciting and disturbing, suggestive but hard to pin down. What butch-femme couple was she talking about, and just where exactly, beyond the printed page, was to be found this "camp space" they inhabited? On the stage, apparently, since Case's only exemplars are lesbian performers Lois Weaver and Peggy Shaw, who played the Beauty and the Beast, respectively, in the Split Britches production. "The portrayal is faithful to the historical situation of the butch role" (302), Case adds, but nothing in Joan Nestle's appended statement indicates that butch-femme was ever a camp in the fifties and sixties. The significance of Weaver and Shaw's performances, it seems to me, has much more to do with the recent past and the future, and despite Case's proviso that to recuperate butch-femme for a feminist aesthetic one would have to "[develop] an understanding of the function of roles in the homosexual lifestyle . . . particularly in relation to the historical class and racial relations embedded in such a project" (295), her construction of butch-femme as a form of drag/camp seemed a provocative and flip abstraction, ungrounded in history—the opposite of Sarah Murray's judicious social theories exploring the marginal role of theatrical drag in lesbian culture.

Gay male camp culture of the 1960s, I had argued, was self-consciously theatrical, played on incongruity, and had to be funny.[7] My own experience of butch-femme bar culture in the late fifties and sixties told me that butch-femme was not, as Case asserted, ironic, not a camp, and certainly not, as Judith Butler had suggested, a parody, at least not then.[8] It was utterly serious, always "for real," completely different in feeling and tone from the fabulous and bittersweet excesses of the camp drag queen. But before I could send Case's argument packing, I had to agree with certain implications of her essay. First, bar life *had* had a dramatic side—fist and knife fights, jealous passions, the erotic bravura of "the fish"—a coupled slow dance—and the striking entrances that certain lesbians achieved. In 1959 my juvenile brain was imprinted by the panache of a curly haired blond butch, debonair and assured in beautifully cut men's sportswear, who dismounted from an ordinary yellow cab as if from a chauffeured Cadillac, sweeping into a smoky New York City dive called the Seven Steps and intentionally turning every head. And yes, the spectacular gender effects and contrasts achieved by many butch-femme couples—then as now—seem more related, certainly aesthetically, to gay male drag/camp than to the plain and androgynous lesbian-feminist look that displaced it in the 1970s and 1980s.

But is the assimilation of butch-femme with gay male drag/camp an accurate description, or rather a cultural manifesto and political maneuver? In my view there have been two major themes of gay male sensibility and political action: one is drag queen-centered camp that highlights theatricality and humor, and the other is an egalitarian anarchism that foregrounds authenticity and realism. That lesbians, like gay men, have been drawn to egalitarianism is obvious, from the days of the Daughters of Bilitis in the 1950s through lesbian-feminism and twelve-step programs. But the other gay male sensibility, camp style, has always centered around the figure of the queen; as such it is not easily appropriated by lesbians.[9] And until the performance theorists came along, no one positioned lesbian butch-femme as comparable to drag queen-centered camp, primarily because it had so lacked the element of humor and light theatricality, the self-conscious play with which Case endowed it.[10]

Conflations of butch with drag (queen) and butch-femme with camp obliterate several critical distinctions.[11] From the perspective of cultural history, the lesbian relationship to drag and to camp sensibility has been and continues to be mediated through the fact of its primary production in the particular suffering and creativity, and in the social networks, of gay men. The tendency of some male and female queer theorists and writers to describe "queers" (Case reverts to the older term "homosexual") as if gender were no longer a relevant or important difference deletes just what, in my view, we should be highlighting: the appropriation of gay male practices and culture by lesbians.[12]

Drag and camp are not simply antiessentialist performances that somehow undermine traditional gender dichotomy, nor are they to be diluted into the broader concept of transvestism or cross-dressing without first specifying how they function ethnographically.[13] (Not coincidentally, drag's detractors commit the opposite error, that drag per se reinforces traditional gender.) For one thing, it is not even clear when and under what conditions lesbians consider butch appearance and clothing to *be* drag.[14] Most drag performances I have seen, and I have seen many, usually build on and even reinforce what are taken to be stable (essential) selves and concepts of authenticity rather than destabilizing or abolishing them, even as they may flirt with such possibilities.

Both mundane and theatrical drag and camp are signification practices that cannot be separated from material conditions or from the intentions of actors and audiences who embody and interpret them.[15] They are always what philosopher Kenneth Burke called "a [symbolic] strategy for a situation," that is, drag as performance and camp as a sensibility are cultural schema used by individuals and by collectivities to signify, constitute, and advance particular agendas in specific situations. This is not to advocate observation *instead* of social theory, but rather to insist that social theory emerge from and be considered in the frame of social behavior and belief, not just in relation to other theories.

The most important historical situation in which drag and camp have been implicated has been the greater power of gay men than lesbians within every socioeconomic class and ethnic group. After a brief review of this power imbalance, I will show how lesbians have (and have not) been able to use drag and camp in a dense site of gay and lesbian culture production. In the resort community of Cherry Grove, lesbians have attempted to modify or interrupt the customary deployment of traditional symbols—not to destabilize gender categories as such, but rather to destabilize male monopolies and to symbolize and constitute the power of the lesbian minority. Finally I suggest that the proposition that lesbian butch-femme and female impersonation have an equivalent relation to the drag/camp system should itself be understood as a sign and a strategy of emerging lesbian empowerment rather than as history or social theory. Drag and camp are embedded in histories and power relations, including when they are deployed in the theatrical venues so beloved in Cherry Grove, in the lesbian theatrical and film productions studied by performance theorists, or on the pages of academic journals.

2

I think of myself as a queer first, a woman second. ACT UP New York is my political home. Despite gay male sexism, I could not survive without gay male camp, aesthetics, humor and sexuality. I would go crazy. To me, gay men are family, straight feminists merely allies.   IRENE ELIZABETH STROUD

Since the early 1980s there has been an apparent convergence between lesbians and gay men that is reflected in the revalorization of the genderless term "queer." I write "apparent convergence" because much of the movement has resulted from lesbians moving closer to gay men and gay male culture than the reverse. Widespread dissatisfaction with the excesses of lesbian feminism and heterosexism in mainstream feminism caused many lesbians to look toward gay male culture for alternatives and to be attracted to male-dominated groups like ACT UP.[16] Indeed, Sue-Ellen Case's stated purpose in revalorizing the concept of the butch-femme couple was to chastise both straight feminism (for its homophobic theories) and lesbian-feminism (for its class prejudice, "antipornography crusade and its alliance with the right").[17]

But lesbians who swallow the queer concept whole, without qualification, risk indigestion. When Maria Maggenti worked with ACT UP and Queer Nation, she

believe[d], like many women before me, that with hard work, enthusiasm, knowledge, and skill, not to mention the sheer force of personality, I will somehow be exempted from my status as girl, outsider, woman,

bitch, cunt, other . . . [although] . . . in fact, it is nearly impossible to cross the million-year-old canyons that make men men and women women. I avoid my own late-night questions about what it means to be a lesbian in a gay male universe and prefer to believe in the united colors of the Queer Nation.[18]

No matter how much distinctions between lesbians and gay men remain unproblematized, they cannot remain unproblematic because gay men belong to the dominant gender. Holding race and class constant, gay men have more power and money than lesbians do.[19] Their history as a distinct social entity is longer, their institutions are more numerous and developed, and they take up much more symbolic and actual public space, both in relation to dominant society and within most, if not all institutions termed "gay and lesbian."

Turn to the Stonewall issue of the *Advocate*. In a long article on the Stonewall celebrations of June 1994 in New York City, Chris Bull allots only one phrase to the Dyke March organized by the direct-action group the Lesbian Avengers. A large, boisterous, and highly successful takeover of Fifth Avenue, it was likely the largest public gathering of lesbians in history, but one would never know from the *Advocate*. Bull writes, "The proliferation of splinter marches mirrored larger disagreement over the political significance of the Stonewall riots."[20] Almost as if responding, the lesbian magazine *Deneuve* writes in its Stonewall issue,

Why should a woman read today's *Advocate*? Well, as the mag's *woman-oriented* pitch letter puts it, it's "significantly redefined and expanded to include better coverage of lesbian news and interests than ever before." Translation: They axed or alienated most of their female staff. But the mag also features "a new balance in our coverage of lesbian and gay men's issues." From here, that looks a lot like the old "balance." Boys, boys, boys—and the occasional fag hag.[21]

In citing the resentment of some lesbians all of the time, and many lesbians some of the time, toward gay male power and entitlement, my intent is not to provoke, much less enlarge that anger. Both before and after my separatist mood in the 1970s, gay men have been near and usually dear to me—as subjects of inquiry, friends, and political allies. In fact, the lesbian relation to gay men, both within gay life and through gay men to the dominant culture, has been underdescribed and undertheorized. As a group, and often as individuals, they are there on our lesbian horizon, and because of their historic predominance, gay men occupy both object (as *other* to straight America) and subject positions in American life whenever homosexuality comes up, a near-hegemony which, despite the efforts and effects of separatism, lesbians have not been able to elude or entirely escape anywhere.[22]

What do these generalizations mean in people's lives? How do lesbians use drag and camp in the context of gay male predominance? Events I witnessed during the summer of 1994 in Cherry Grove surrounding the election of the first-ever lesbian Homecoming Queen, the most important ceremonial role in Grove life, provide some answers.

3

A "camp" *herself* is a queen who sits and starts entertaining a group of people at a bar around her. They all start listening to what she's got to say. . . . A camp is a flip person who has declared emotional freedom. She is going to say to the world, "I'm queer." SKIP ARNOLD, Female impersonator, 1966

In Cherry Grove, a summer resort community of about 275 houses in the New York metropolitan area, gay men used their greater socioeconomic power as *men* (not as patriarchs or lovers) to discriminate against lesbians (for example, in buying and renting houses and in access to leading community roles). They also assumed a hegemonic subject position in which both straight people and lesbians, albeit for different reasons, were cast as the *other*. Gay men's subject position was effected through that central Grove persona, the queen, embedded in a camp sensibility.[23]

The early years of Grove history, from about 1932 to 1960, were dominated by what might be called queenly figures, who most often were middle-aged heterosexual or bisexual women of a definite flamboyance, referred to by gay men as "fag hags."[24] Mrs. Helen Ely, the alpha of the species, used her ample liquor cabinet and big beach house to host theme parties (at which she would appear in her own grand dresses and costumes), helped found and dominated the most impor-

tant community organization, the Arts Project, and frequently represented Grove interests to the outside world when legal and political
issues arose.

The term "queen," however, was usually restricted to gay men,
some of whom hosted theme parties, but whose principal roles were
played out in everyday social interaction, at parties and on the stage
of the Community Theater. They didn't need wealth: Theatrical flair,
quick repartee, and a talent for campy drag performance were enough.
Designer Arthur Brill came to one of the first gay parties in the mid
1930s as the Statue of Liberty. Drag queen Dicki Martini wowed
Grove audiences in gay revues featuring female impersonation that
signified the gay (and lesbian) collectivity. Men dressed as men were
relegated to escorting or supporting these larger-than-life figures.
Even when male "beauties" were of great erotic interest to other men;
they were not often center stage. When the Queen of the Night made
her grand entrance from the ocean to the Heavenly Bodies Party of
1957, she was carried by muscular bearers in loin cloths in that recurring and central trope of Grove celebrations: young men elevating her
royal highness, a drag Salome, Cleopatra, or Marilyn Monroe, figura-
tively (and sometimes literally) over their heads.

During the 1960s and 1970s, gay men gradually appropriated and
inhabited all the queenly roles. On stage, Irish, Jewish, and Italian gay
men like Thom *Panzi* Hansen, Dickie Addison, and *Rose* Levine
brought a new glamour and dedication to queenly performances.[25]
Teri Warren, a hairdresser from the Bronx who rose to be not only a
star Grove performer but also president of the Arts Project, told me
frankly, "I want to be the Helen Ely of my generation." In 1976 the
Grove formalized the position of the queen by instituting the Homecoming Queen contest—the winner being picked by a panel of local
notables. The Homecoming Queen had no formal power. *Her* duty
was to represent the Grove at Arts Project events such as fund raisers,
bingo night, and elections, but her most visible and important ceremonial moment occurred as leader of the Invasion of the neighboring upscale gay resort, Fire Island Pines. On Fourth of July weekend every
year, cross-dressed Grovers—mostly men, with always a sprinkling of
women—ferried down the Great South Bay to bless the glitzy Pines
harbor, thereby reasserting both gay [male] commonality and gay
[male] conflicts over class and age difference. The requirement to

cross-dress for getting on the ferry provided a very loose community standard as to what could constitute drag for both women and men.

The idea of wearing one of Martin's dresses to compete in the homecoming queen contest as Scarlett Ooh came to Joan Van Ness as she woke up on the morning of May 30, 1994. She was missing her *sister* Martin, who had died of AIDS two years before: "I was feeling sort of campy, you know, in the mood to do something outrageous." Though two friends, Donald and Evan, "were immediately excited by the idea," they were not impressed by how Joan looked in Martin's dress. Known locally themselves as the *Shapiro Sisters*, Donald and Evan offered to dress Joan and make her up for the contest to be held that night as a benefit for the Arts Project of Cherry Grove. She accepted gladly, even though "According to Van Ness, those who would have thought of her in drag, would have imagined her in butch-drag tux, not as the unlikely female-female impersonator complete with bouffant blond wig, and feather boa that she donned to compete."[26] Actually, Joan, dressed in a tux, had accompanied her late "sister" Martin on the Invasion of the Pines several times, once as a groom to Martin's bride.

By the time the ten drag queen contestants took the stage that night, word had spread through the exited crowd that among them was Joan in a dress, heels, wig, and pancake make-up. According to Panzi and *Bella*, two former winners who monitored the applause for each contestant, Joan was the clear winner, elected Queen Scarlett Ooh, symbolic representative for the 1994 season.

Taken out of context Joan's election might appear to validate theories that treat lesbian and gay male drag as equivalent forms of camp. Joan, embodying in herself a butch/femme gemini, if not the butch-femme couple invoked by Case, since she was a butch in drag queen's (if not exactly femme's) clothing, certainly could be described as "playfully inhabiting the camp space of irony and wit, free from biological determinism" (305).[27] But in fact it is impossible to understand what Joan's candidacy or victory meant to Grovers without knowing the history of lesbian/gay male relations in the community and beyond. If the goal is to theorize how representational strategies work, how can intellectuals skip over this ethnographic step to broad abstractions and generalities without being guilty of a misleading (and reprehensible) imperialism ("Who cares what you think your representations mean, they mean what we say they do"). There is a balance to be struck between accepting the "natives'" accounts at face value with no analysis, and discounting them completely as "fictions" or useful only to our already determined theoretical agenda. In any case, many queer theorists never even consider ethnography or history. Are academic intellectuals only interested in theorizing each others' representations?[28]

4

While presenting a slide history of the Grove in the community theater I showed a picture of a former resident, a lesbian private detective. Panzi shouted out, "Oh yes, we used to call her 'Dickless Tracy.'"

Lesbian numbers and power in the gay Grove had fluctuated. From the 1930s to the 1960s a distinguished and well-off group of lesbians known as "ladies" were outnumbered by men of similar upper-middle-class backgrounds by at least five to one, yet they still played important roles as hostesses and in the community theater. Both genders shared a common identification with the theater, but women were jokingly referred to (and referred to themselves) as "Lithuanians" suggesting an exotic group from some faraway land.

As capital and infrastructure made the Grove a more accessible resort, a diverse population of gay men flooded in. The "ladies" retreated, and a new group of working class "dykes" and their femmes constituted a small and rather beleaguered minority from 1960 to about 1973. During this period of growing gay nationalism, promiscuous and ubiquitous male-male sexual desire was increasingly seen as the common bond between gays, a formulation that excluded lesbians far more than their being "Lithuanians" had done. Yet during the seventies and eighties lesbians gained footholds, and by 1987, in a gritty, gradual, and individual process, they had become business owners and homeowners, theater technicians and actors, and leaders in the volunteer fire department—without, as a group, ever directly challenging gay male predominance as expressed through queen-centered camp.

For instance, in Amelia Migliaccio's recounting of a "fabulous"

story that "just kind of depicts what Cherry Grove is," all the parts
were played by men. Back in the early 1970s, in the period of greatest
male hegemony, Amelia lived in a mixed-gender household that became friendly with an all-male "royal family" living next door. When
a man in Amelia's household named Eric was tapped to become a viscount, Amelia got into the spirit by baking ziti and all kinds of Italian
food for the coronation ceremony. The day of the coronation,

> **We thought, well, we really should dress for the occasion. So I wore a**
> **gown and [her butch lover] Babe wore a tuxedo. And of course we had to**
> **dress Eric, who was now going to be the new viscount, so I put a wig and**
> **makeup and eyelashes and a dress on him.**

After a public procession led by the central figure—a large man
known as the *Infanta* dressed in red velvet robes and red velvet hat and
sporting a huge Papal-type ring—the begowned Eric was subjected to
various tests to see "if he was truly gay," including taking "a sample
from his toenail to see if it was really Meat Rack soil."

Amelia made food for the protagonists, dressed the prospective
gay viscount (as a femme she was perfectly capable with using make-
up) and helped arrange the *mise-en-scene*. She and her butch lover
dressed as extras and didn't question the exclusionary criteria for being
"truly gay," (e.g., soil from the outdoor male cruising area that lesbians
never frequented). Amelia assessed the lesbian situation at the end of
her narrative matter-of-factly, stressing, "It was an all male family. I
want you to understand that."

> **E N**: Were there any duchesses?
> **Amelia**: Well there may have been, but they were still of the
> male gender.
> **E N**: There were no women at all?
> **Amelia**: No women at all. In fact Babe was invited to be-
> come a baron or a baroness, I'm not sure, and that never hap-
> pened. It never happened, but she was being considered.

As queens, gay men assumed the subject position in a coherent camp
sensibility that acted to marginalize, or even obliterate, lesbians as
iconic. By this I mean both that lesbians were rarely allowed any representation as a group within the community, *and* that lesbians were virtually never allowed to represent the community as a whole. This ex-

clusion was effected by gay men's far greater numbers and power, by social pressure, and by outright discrimination. Given the overwhelming hostility of the surrounding straight world and, during the 1970s and 1980s, of lesbian-feminism toward the butch-femme system that predominated in the Grove, lesbians were glad to be tolerated in a physically safe space that supported the existence of same-gender love, and accepted playing second fiddle.

Although the camp system helped lesbians imagine other narratives about gender, elements of its internal logic also marginalized them. First, since drag was defined in the first instance as the clothing of the "other" gender, lesbians, as women, could not easily embody queens. (Even the word "drag" has its probable historical origin in the long gowns males wore playing female parts on stage). Though a few of the "ladies" had been wealthy and confident enough to be queenly hostesses, or even portray queenly figures on stage, they were considered to be dressing grandly or in costume rather than to be in drag.[29] By the sixties lesbian femmes were implicitly barred from dressing up in any context that could be interpreted as competing with gay male queens.[30] Amelia could dress up in a gown to witness Eric's *rite de passage*, but she could not be part of it.

Second, by its overwhelming emphasis on the queen, the camp system has acted to disempower the "king" role that butch gay men or lesbians might have logically played (in this key respect camp is deliberately and devastatingly subversive of masculine power). As Babe's bit part in Amelia's narrative implies, the role of drag butch was not well defined.

In narrators' accounts of the past or in daily life during the eighties, I hardly ever heard the term "drag butch," much less drag king, and there was no distinction between "real boys" and drag butches to parallel the well-known one of r.g. [real girl] and drag queen. In the exception that proved the rule, a Jock of the Year contest was held in the late seventies to pick a consort for the Homecoming Queen. Most of the lesbian contestants dressed in black leather pants, jackets, and caps (the insignia of gay male leathermen) but the judges picked a very butch woman who was wearing a black tee-shirt with the words "Keep Cherry Grove Gay," bright red shorts rolled up to reveal a girdle, and a tiara. The lesbians present were strongly divided over this representation—some found it trivializing, others said it was an appropriate camp—and the contest was not repeated. (Years later a Grove man dismissed the jock contest as having excited "less interest than an outdoor barbecue in January.")

However, by the early eighties, leading butch Lyn Hutton, dressed one year in black leather pants, jacket, and motorcycle cap, and the next year in a tux, became the customary, though title-less escort of the Queen during the Invasion of the Pines. (In the late eighties, I asked Lyn Hutton why, although she had dressed splendidly in a tux and red bowtie to attend an "Italian wedding," she wasn't playing a part in the ceremony. "No, I've spent ten years clearing the aisles," she said with mild bitterness. "That's my role.")

Although lesbians were severely limited in how they could participate in drag events, which meant virtually all Grove events, through the medium of camp they could imaginatively enter the system, especially on less formal levels. All Grovers were familiar with camp humor, and some lesbians could employ it, as in this boardwalk exchange on a summer morning in the 1980s. I was chatting with Lynne, a feminine lesbian with long curly hair, who was wearing a mismatched outfit of flowered Bermuda shorts, socks of a different color, sneakers of yet another:

Lynne: [*taking my arm*]: I love these butch numbers!
EN: You pretend like you don't but I knew.
Lynne: Oh, exposed!
Passing gay man to Lynne: *Love* your outfit.
Lynne: Like it? $2.99 on 14th St.
Man: Liar. You paid at least $3.99.
Lynne: I see you know my routine.
   Ted Drach approaches, wrapped in a sheet like a toga. A wreath in his hair, drink in a plastic glass; obviously returning from an all-night party.
Ted: They stole my underwear.
Lynne: Now here comes a *real* man.
Ted: Oh God, what I wouldn't *give* for a real man.
Lynne: [*taking his arm and walking off*]: Let's go, honey.

Of particular significance for understanding Joan as the Homecoming Queen is the interplay between and among dominant gender categories (man/woman) and gay gender categories (queen-butch, "real" man, femme-butch). Lynne contrasts the "real man," Ted Drach, with the clothes-conscious queen who inquired about her outfit and with my (butch) self. Ted demurs. He is a queen, not a "real" man, because he *wants* a "real" man. Lynne trumps us all on exiting—she, the femme, is the "real" man.[31]

Years before Joan's exploits, others had experimented successfully with what I have referred to as "compound drag"—representations of conventional masculinity by a "nellie" gay man or femme lesbian or of femininity or nellieness by a "butch" lesbian. A butch lesbian named Cris described how, back in the fifties, she tried to impersonate a gay man on stage by doing a "real drag number":

> I played Carole Channing. I got in drag, fell down the steps in my high heels [she laughs], the whole place broke up. . . . Oh, I was trying to be so [makes a feminine gesture of twirling her hair] you know, cause I didn't want them to know who I was, and I had this wig, I really did it, and I thought, "Now I'm really going to get away with this, they're gonna think I'm one of the guys." And the guys of course can walk in heels, and I couldn't.

In the 1970s a fondly remembered production of Little Mary Sunshine in the Grove theater had featured a chorus of the butchest lesbians, like Lyn Hutton, in gowns and makeup that had been a big hit and had also successfully featured nellie queens as princes and bandits. As lesbians were gradually becoming more of a presence in the Grove, a group of dykes and femmes entered the Arts Project's thirtieth anniversary ball as "Sisters of the Sand." The central figure, played by Grove homeowner Jan Felshin, was the "sheiksa" dressed as a sultan— carried by solemn butch litter-bearers, and surrounded by skimpily clad dancing girls, thus refiguring the central trope of the queen and splitting her erotic bearers/admirers into butch and femme elements. In contrast to the jock contest, this representation was universally applauded; yet like the jock contest, it was not repeated. The women felt they had proved their point—they could bend the rules just enough to play by them. None of these representations took root to grow into recurring traditions.

By the mid-eighties, the representational possibilities had not changed that much, even though the lesbian presence was increasing. Revues in the Grove's theater from that period featured a parade of older but flashy drag queens, so well known they were referred to affectionately as "the Golden Girls." The lesbians who ventured on stage were usually dressed in tuxes as male-looking props to escort the Golden Girls to center stage. Lesbians never sang sexy or funny love songs to each other or to drag queens—whereas straight women and gay men together often represented heterosexual couples in singing duets.[32] When I questioned the lack of lesbian representation in the revues, other lesbians professed not to have noticed. Butch-femme duos were not represented, in part because only butches seemed to want to participate. No femmes volunteer, I was also told, in a reference to the implicit ban on femme performance that might upstage drag queens. But in any case, all the shows of the era were written by gay men, who apparently had little or no interest in giving lesbians onstage roles.

Only on one evening in 1986 at Drag Search, an open talent night at the hotel disco modeled after Star Search—the Ed McMahon TV talent show of the era—did I see an indication of the more daring and confident lesbian attitude that was to emerge later. (Significantly, this popular commercial event never had the symbolic weight of theatrical productions or even theme parties, and most contestants were from outside the Grove).[33] The drag queen emcee, *Electra*, explained that he'd always encouraged people to perform and had been disturbed all summer that no "ladies" were performing. The girls liked to get out and shake their tits by the pool in the wet tee-shirt contest, he remarked dryly, but this afternoon three girls had approached him and said they wanted to perform, and here they were, the Jersey Girls.

The three "girls," in their twenties, wearing shorts and no make-up, proceeded to lip synch an upbeat neo-Andrews Sisters style song with the recurring line, "It's not the meat, it's the motion." Their coordinated dance steps showed they had taken their performance seriously enough to rehearse a bit. "It's not the meat"—they pointed to their crotches—"it's the motion. . . ." They swiveled their hips energetically. Each performer took a turn in the spotlight. When the most butch of the three came forward, the crowd went wild. After admonishing, "It *is* the meat *and* the motion," Electra came out and let them do an encore. When he said the Jersey Girls couldn't compete in the *Miss* Ice Palace competition, their pals, a claque of energetic young lesbians, set up a prolonged howl. "I'm glad they don't know where I live," quipped Electra. "Miss Ice Palace has to be a male in drag," he continued over the hoots of the lesbians. "But listen, maybe next year we'll have a new category, '*Mr.* Ice Palace.' Let's have an *Elvis Presley* up here, a *Frank Sinatra*, why not?" But it didn't happen.[34]

As a rule, lesbians either found a way to participate on the edges of queen-centered camp or they could appreciate it as spectators; they could not alter the basic schema. The more public the event, the more central to Grove self-definition, the more lesbians were relegated to walk-on parts or pushed backstage.

In retrospect, 1988 was the year when, as one older Grove lesbian said with a sly grin, "they [gay men] first began to get real nervous." At the same time as gay male predominance was being undermined by ill-nesses and deaths from aging and from AIDS, lesbians began going there in very large numbers.[35] The word was out, another lesbian told me then, that the Grove was a good place for lesbians. In general, these newer arrivals were younger and took certain 1970s attitude changes for granted: I refer to them as post-feminists in this sense.

More and more comments were heard from gay men about "those pushy dykes" who made too much noise, hogged the boardwalks, and generally took up too much space. At the annual Art Show, the 1988 Homecoming Queen, *Vera*, out of drag and rather drab, wore a black tee-shirt emblazoned with the crisp white letters: "What Becomes a Lesbian Most?" across his chest. When Lynne commented on it he said, laughing sarcastically, "You notice there's nothing written on the back." Lynne, my lover, and I all made disapproving faces, which Vera ignored.

At Bella's Dish, a weekly late-night event at the hotel, a group of visiting queens from the Pines put on a "fashion show" wearing tram-pish outfits they apparently thought appropriate for a Grove venue. As the lead queen mounted the stage she declaimed, "My name is Tawana Schwartz, and this is what I was wearing the night I was raped by six white lesbians in Cherry Grove" [a reference to an infamous New York case in which a young black woman named Tawana Brawley claimed she was raped by some white men]. My (white) lesbian friends were looking at each other, and I made a slitting motion across my throat.

As in the Vera incident, we just sat there fuming. We all knew that the Grove, like America, had a history of sexist, racist, and anti-Semitic representations, but did that excuse doing them in 1988?[36]

In 1991 tensions surfaced again over gender, race, and representation issues. A lesbian named April (who is black) objected to *Miss Stephanie* from the Pines (who is white) doing a blackface version of Diana Ross in one of the Grove theatrical revues. April "was not any kind of revolutionary," I was told, but she quietly went to the director and said that if Stephanie did blackface, she, April, couldn't participate. The director held a meeting with Stephanie and some others from the cast, all of whom tried to talk April out of her objections—It didn't mean anything, wasn't racist, just for fun, etc., etc. Meanwhile, some of the men were heard to say If we let these dykes tell us not to do blackface, next they'll be telling us not to do drag, and we can't let them tell us what to do. The women involved were split on the issue, vaguely along dyke versus post-feminist lines. In the end, Stephanie did Diana Ross in "brown face," and April and other feminists silently boycotted the show. The director let it be known that if lesbians didn't like the shows they could damn well write their own (a challenge that was taken up in 1993 by a woman who produced a mildly successful first-ever lesbian-written revue in the light, campy Grove style).

At the very end of the 1991 season, people began to see publicity for a planned "Women's Weekend" in the Grove in September organized by a Long Island lesbian newspaper. Someone made and distributed a leaflet to every house in the Grove and Pines, with the bold words "Do We Need This?" printed across the Women's Weekend ads. Local lesbians were upset, but nothing came of it. Every succeeding year the number of lesbians grew. By 1994 Grovers generally agreed that while gay men and straight people together still owned around 75 percent of the houses, lesbian home ownership was slowly growing, and—most dramatically and visibly—lesbians comprised over half of day-trippers and renters.

Alongside the grousing and resentment, some male Grovers were trying accommodation. At a meeting of the property owners association at the beginning of the 1994 season, someone proposed putting two benches at the end of the walk leading to the Meat Rack, the gay male outdoor cruising area. The head of the newly established memorial fund, a highly respected elder male home owner, objected that it would be inappropriate to pay for something from the memorial fund that would not be used by the whole community. Apparently it was understood that it was women who don't use the Meat Rack and so shouldn't have their contributions used to pay for Meat Rack amenities. In the event, another prominent male Grover raised the money privately, i.e., only among men. It was in this precarious balance of changing demographics and power that Joan ran for and won the homecoming-queen contest.

5

[L]esbians . . . suffer from an odd invisibility in our society. This invisibility allows us to see both how the masculine and the feminine are defined in opposition to each other, and how relationships to men function as the critical factor in gaining social visibility and cultural power.

Reaction to Joan's victory was immediate. Thom Hansen (Panzi) joked next morning, "I'm afraid to walk down to my house." As president of the Arts Project, he—aided by Bella—had judged the applause meter and Joan had clearly won. (Sometime around 1990 the old system of picking the queen by local notables had been replaced by an applause meter, since there had been many complaints of cronyism—another barrier to lesbians). Panzi had thought Joan's entry was funny (though he told a newspaper interviewer he had not approved of having a woman Homecoming Queen), but he was amazed at not only the hurt egos but "also, I'm afraid, the outright misogyny of some of these queens." Some had turned in their Arts Project membership cards and others were flying their Arts Project flags upside down. And, he added, "We all said Too bad Esther's already written her book, this would have been a great chapter." After Panzi, who was clearly both ruffled and amused, had walked off, a lesbian friend with whom I was sitting remarked, "This is a terrible year for some of these guys. First a lesbian writes the definitive book on the Grove's history, then a lesbian becomes Homecoming Queen," jarring me into a consideration of how my recent book might have figured into the tensions.[37]

Considering the number of young lesbians I was seeing all around

me, the queens might have considered themselves lucky that some lesbians cared enough to crash the contest on gay male terms, for Joan's
victory was both subversive of *and* submissive to male power. As such,
though, it was the perfect challenge to the "old boy" system of the
Grove. The contest was rarely about "beauty"; usually the Queen was
a middle-aged community booster. Joan had been around since 1979.
She had appeared in numerous Arts Project shows, gone on the Invasion in a tux, and volunteered for every cause and committee: the
Dunes project, the memorial fund, the doctor's fund had all received
her checks. A volunteer firefighter for over a decade, she owned a
house that she was constantly improving, encircled by a well-tended
garden. She was the perfect Shannon Faulkner at the Citadel—soldier
of the year, boy scout of the decade. There was only one reason why
Joan should not be Homecoming Queen, and everybody knew it—she
was an r.g., a real girl.

In the first days after Joan's election, the dyke versus post-feminist
split among community-involved lesbians evident in the April/Miss
Stephanie affair surfaced again. Indeed, my most feminist Grove
friends decried Joan's having entered the contest, which one described
as "patriarchal stuff," adding, "She wants to be accepted by the men
so badly she'll do anything." In contrast, most dykes professed to be
shocked by the male reaction, since it was all just a camp and in fun,
while obviously relishing Joan's victory. Lynne gloated that "the dykes
elected [Joan]" by clapping extra loud at the contest, and added that
Joan's new lover, Lorraine, who was quite butch, was going to make a
great [cross-dressed] escort for Queen Scarlett Ooh at the Invasion.[38]
Joan left no doubt she was utterly determined to exercise her
queenship. When I later asked her if it was a real pain to dress up like
this, she said "no, because the community elected me and I'm very
proud of it. It's an honor. And there's no question but that I won. Sure
the dykes clapped loudest, but without the men I couldn't have won."
"It wasn't even close," Lorraine added. "And so of course I'm going to
do it," Joan said. Lyn Hutton looked me straight in the eye and dead-
panned, "It's a camp. That's my only comment." Meanwhile, Panzi
was advising Joan that if she was going to be the Homecoming Queen
she had to appear at every public event, every weekend.

The controversy neared its peak the weekend of June 11–12, with
Joan's first scheduled public appearance as queen to hostess tea at

Cherry's bar.[39] On the appointed day a couple of fliers proclaiming "Boycott Dyke Tea," were quickly torn down. Initially sparse attendance ultimately swelled to a good-size crowd, with a much larger than usual lesbian presence. "Joan looked great" in drag, one lesbian acquaintance who had initially scoffed said, and watching the normally short-haired, no-makeup, preppie-looking Joan on videotape later, I would never have recognized her, so heavy was her drag queen makeup, so voluminous her gown, so Hello-Dollyish her wig. Adding to the theatrical effect was Lorraine at her side—taller, butch and good looking—wearing a well-fitting suit and tie.

Fred, an older male friend, told me that the Joan affair was the talk of the Grove from the moment he got on the ferry that weekend until he left. He couldn't understand why Joan would do such a thing, she seemed "such a sensitive person." A charming man with many female friends, Fred seemed impervious to my argument that Joan was the victim of unreasoning prejudice. Other men insinuated that Donald and Evan, the Shapiro Sisters, had put Joan up to it to get revenge on the Arts Project because Donald had lost the contest the previous year. Or that Panzi had fixed the contest somehow, since he had been heard to remark before Joan came on-stage, "History will be made tonight." There were male slurs against Joan: How could she fulfill the Queen role? She had no personality and didn't know how to pose for a camera; she must have been put up to it, she didn't have the brains to think it up herself, and so on.

The next weekend the controversy overflowed the Grove. Two big New York City newspapers wrote features on it, without taking sides.[40] But the boil burst with the publication of *Patti Ann's* weekly "Talk of the Grove" column in the local *Fire Island Tide*:

> Joan Van Ness accepted the "Cat calls" or whatever and allowed herself to become "Homecoming" for 1994. I would like to add that this was a 25 year tradition of males cross dressing as a female that was swept aside, and pushed into the sewer . . . I had thought Joan was more sophisticated than to embroil herself into this controversy. However! On with the "Invasion in Exile."[41]

Not only did Patti Ann call for an alternative Invasion to be led by *Vicki*, whom he referred to as "the real 'Queen,'" he appealed traitorously to the men of the Pines ("Do you want a woman 'Queen' blessing your harbor?") . . . and to "the intelligent, sophisticated women of

Joan as "Queen Scarlett Ooh" escorted by two prominent Grove lesbians, at the Invasion of the Pines, July 4, 1994. Photo by Esther Newton.

Joan as "Queen Scarlett Ooh" (left) mugs for the camera with her girl-friend. Photo by Esther Newton.

Cherry Grove, thank you for your support of the tradition. You know who you are, and hopeful you'll make your voices heard." Finally he shot his most poisonous arrow past the signifier of Joan's victory toward the signified—the social change sweeping Cherry Grove: "(Quote from a former professional 'Drag Queen') 'First the boys got sick, they died, their houses sold and now kicked in the ass and their tradition is taken away. P.A. it is time to sell.'"

Patti Ann's article backfired. All the lesbians and many men joined in opposition to this divisive provocation. Calls for unity, references to the lesbian contributions in the AIDS crisis, and appeals to the camp tradition flew thick and fast. One prominent lesbian wrote in response: "P.A., How dare you? It was evil and cruel. I know I speak for myself and all of the so-called unintelligent and unsophisticated women of the Grove in saying to you, unequivocally, 'take it back.'"[42]

Another long-time lesbian homeowner, arguing that it was the American way to accept changing values, went so far as appealing to our revolutionary history that was indirectly commemorated by the July 4 Invasion, and observing pointedly,

> [Lesbians] cannot (and should not) be relegated to the permanent role of supporting and applauding the men. Joan Van Ness won the title in a fair election, cheered by members of both sexes. Perhaps her victory represents the evolution of a new tradition—one that allows men and women to share equally in all that this wonderful community has to offer. What a great tradition that would be![43]

One of the few remaining "ladies" weighed in, too, writing a letter to the rival local paper decrying Patti Ann's column in the most sarcastic terms and reminding readers that in the old days men and women had gotten along. Echoing Lyn Hutton's remark, she asserted that the Homecoming Queen was about camp, not about drag per se, a point to which I will return later. Privately she castigated Patti Ann and his followers as "illiterates" and "not the most popular in Cherry Grove," a reference to lingering class resentment toward the working-class parvenus like Patti Ann who had come to dominate the Grove in the 1970s.

Even feminist lesbians fell in line, though one remarked (probably accurately) that the younger lesbian renters we were seeing all around us "didn't give a rat's ass" about the Homecoming Queen contest. When I mentioned that Joan's Queendom had united all the community-involved women for the first time in an explicitly feminist cause, this friend commented:

> At least half the women on the island think drag is disgusting. . . . Drag is a men's thing, and there are areas that we are concerned with that we don't want them mixing into, and women shouldn't mix into this. But then when there was such immediate opposition from some men, then everybody had to swing behind Joan. Otherwise it would never have been a feminist issue.

Most of the male establishment also firmed up against Patti Ann and his band of naysayers. Rose Levine, who had once gotten himself in trouble with disparaging remarks in his gossip column about "chubby lesbians" taking over the fire department, wrote an approving and supportive article about Joan in the rival *Fire Island News*. Thom's long-time friend Max said that although the head of the Grove could not be a "king," Joan's drag was high camp, and he couldn't understand what all the fuss was about. Max wasn't going to go on the Invasion itself [in the end he did], but he would go down to support "the Empress," who would lead the procession to the boat. I had never heard of an Empress, so he explained that Thom (Panzi) was the Empress of the Invasion, he thought he owned it. (I wondered then if Thom as the empress could be seen to trump Joan as the Queen, and I was later to witness a number of attempts to upstage Joan.)

David, the owner of one of the Grove's most beautiful houses on the bay, explained that he had decided to be more open toward women after his lover's death. He approved of Joan as Queen. Why shouldn't she be Queen? Only the men who just couldn't change were still disgruntled. And it was only for one year, after all. If those men didn't like it they could go down and try to win it back next year. Joan had breathed life into what was perhaps a dying institution. And it *was* camp. David and his new lover were the only men I talked to who suggested, hesitantly, that Joan's being Queen was appropriate because there were more women in the Grove now.

The day of the Invasion a crowd ten deep lined all approaches to the deck of the Ice Palace and all the way down to the ferry, including a large number of women, perhaps a third of the total of several thousand spectators—not only Grovers but many visitors from Long Is-

land. By noon the usual kinds of mostly middle-aged Grove drag
queens—trampish, showy, French maids, queens with gowns made
cleverly out of garbage bags, and one who was wearing and showing a
large realistic dildo under his dress—were being introduced by Sal the
emcee and milling around having their photos taken. There were
fewer male group entries and more women entrants (though not even
a quarter of the total) than in the past, including a campy and confident Elvis imitator with a drag queen show girl on *his* arm who did
a funny little well-rehearsed song-and-dance number together. Sal
made quite a few references to there being a woman Queen this year,
lightly sarcastic, but nothing really mean. One contestant who was
wearing fishnet stockings but also a leather motorcycle cap announced
that he didn't know what his drag name was, that his drag was confused: "Since this year our drag queen is a woman, this proves we are
all confused in Cherry Grove."

Several people remarked that as usual Panzi's drag was cleverest of
all. He had always led the Invasion in glamour drag, but this year he
came as a "firedyke" (lesbians had long been prominent in the volunteer fire department), complete with big rubber boots, official lettered
firefighting coat, and black fire hat. His make-up was relatively understated, and he wore an earlobe-length red wig—nothing glamorous
but not ugly, either—thus avoiding the stereotype of lesbians being
ugly that Queen Vera had invoked. He announced over his bullhorn
that if a dyke could be the Queen then he could be in the fire department. From time to time to the delight of the crowd, he flipped up his
short skirt to show his "vagina," represented by false pubic hair (he
later explained sheepishly that after shortening the wig he needed
something to do with the leftover hair).

Aiding Panzi in maintaining order and "in keeping with the
theme," as Grovers say, there were two male marshals dressed in short
wigs and black leather pants, jackets, and caps. For the knowledgeable
Grove audience these two were impersonating the two lesbians who
for years had served as marshals in male leather drag. Grove regulars
and the public roles they play are so well-known among residents that
it is easy to portray them through several transformations of gender.
From this perspective people understood that Joan, as Queen Scarlett
Ooh, was also portraying her dead friend Martin.

Finally some coronation music began blaring over the loudspeak-

ers. Preceded by the marshals and then by an honor guard of two socially prominent Grove lesbians dressed as naval officers, came Queen
Scarlett Ooh, smiling and waving to the crowd, escorted by Lyn Hutton in dazzling white tails. Bullhorn blaring, Panzi urged the spectators to welcome the new Queen, who was making history for Cherry
Grove—the first Homecoming Queen ever to be a woman! There was
applause and ooohs and ahhs. Joan, Lyn, and their dyke naval escorts
willingly posed for lots of photographs, and then Joan was escorted to
the boat by Lyn, followed by all the other queens and dykes through
the excited crowd. As the cross-dressers embarked, Panzi shouted
through his bullhorn, "Ladies and Gentlemen, I am proud to announce that this is the most successful Invasion, ever!"[44]

Nevertheless, I did overhear male grumblings in the crowd that
faded to murmurs as soon as they realized I could hear—"It's just un-
believable!!!" in an aggrieved, complaining tone—but there was no
sign of any protest or alternative invasion, and several people said there
were only three men who went over by water taxi, in what was effectively an invisible protest.

Every boat in the Pines harbor was decorated in welcome, including one yacht filled with cheering women that sported a banner
reading "Women of the Pines Welcome the Grove's First Woman
Queen." The gay rainbow flag was flying everywhere, as it had during
the Gay Games and Stonewall 25 celebrations that just a month before
had brought millions of gays and lesbians to New York. Panzi had
draped the prow of our ferry with a piece of the mile-long flag that
had been carried by hundreds in the official Stonewall 25 march, and
I marveled again at his clever leadership in making such a prominent
appeal to gay and lesbian unity.

Queen Scarlett Ooh and her naval escort were first off the boat.
There was polite applause from the overwhelmingly young, white
male crowd. Then, one by one, other queens and dykes got off, the
showiest eliciting the biggest cheers, as usual. Again I overheard a few
fragments of complaints about Joan, such as "They should have said it
had to be a female *impersonator*."

Back in the Grove at Cherry's bar, Queen Scarlett Ooh was holding court in her platinum wig and low-cut red gown slit up the side,
now escorted by Lorraine (who had said that her job in the public sec-
tor precluded participation in the Invasion) in a man's suit and mus-

tache. In response to my friendly "How's it goin'?" Joan said firmly, "Great. There is no controversy. The only controversy is those sour grapes over there," pointing toward four or five middle-aged drag queens sitting glumly along the bar. "You know what it is, they're all sour old drunks. Everyone else has been very supportive."

A month later my friend Fred told me that Joan as the Homecoming Queen was "incredibly campy" and completely okay. I reminded him how he had said she shouldn't have run for Queen because it was "insensitive" to the feelings of the boys. He said he'd changed his mind after thinking it over and almost didn't own up to his original position, stressing how, the previous season, when Fred's ailing companion had to be taken by fire department wagon to the police helicopter, Joan was the one who came, and she was "absolutely marvelous" with them both.

Through the medium of such longstanding personal and professional interdependency, the Grove's wounds began to close. My feminist friend Lucy was running into male opposition to her authority over an important local committee. Some women sitting around at Lucy's house commented that the men just hated dykes, you felt it all the time. But even if the men hated you, they were not going to hit you or hit on you. Lucy sighed that the Grove was like family. She couldn't believe the support of *everyone* in the Grove at the time of her son's premature death. People just hung out, they brought food, whatever they could do or contribute. But just like family, too, you can't scratch too deep below the surface, Lucy laughed.

Meanwhile, Patti Ann, the leader of the male resistors, had bought into one of the Grove's most successful restaurants, which was owned by a powerful local lesbian. Lesbians thought he would have to mute his male supremacist stance to get along with his new co-owner and not alienate the many women patrons. The whole controversy died down, but behind the scenes Arts Project membership for the summer of 1994 dropped by almost a third. Panzi and others thought disgruntled men were "voting with their feet."

At the opening of the 1995 season, one of the Shapiro Sisters was elected Homecoming Queen. But the changes signaled by Joan's Queenship were still at work. Of the three shows scheduled for the theater, one was written and directed by Lynne Tunderman, and Panzi had convinced the leadership of the Arts Project to break with almost a half century of precedent—that all talent must be local, by hiring Lea Delaria, a prominent lesbian comic from outside the Grove, to perform for the second show. In spite of this, membership in the Arts Project was back up to over three hundred, to levels before the rumpus over Queen Scarlett Ooh.

6

This notion of being "locked out" is a compelling one; it signals the lesbian's sociosymbolic status as one of not being in the game or even in the room where the game repeatedly and perpetually plays itself out. The lesbian's distance from the symbolic order is so great, her status as empty signifier so decisive, that she is effectively erased in the psychosocial register of the visible.

Cherry Grove is too white, too middle-class and too middle-aged to be a microcosm of America's diverse lesbian and gay communities. In any case, it is more of a hothouse than a laboratory, with gays and lesbians living in unusual proximity and interdependence, a situation that made lesbian erasure from "the register of the visible" both more acute and perhaps more changeable than in America's big cities or rural areas. It is just this hothouse closeness that magnifies and reveals the fundamental asymmetry between lesbians and gay men, and thus of lesbians to drag and camp. As a group, Grove men always had more money than lesbians, owned more houses, took up the most public space and wielded hegemonic (though usually comically inflected) symbolic power through the system of queen-centered camp. While lesbians could and did deploy camp humor informally, they could not be queens and so could never have center stage. Lesbian butches, the queens' theoretical complement, were not persecuted, but they were not celebrated either, and played only marginal roles in Grove public life.

This is a version of the problem of lesbian "visibility" that lesbian performance theorists are now so usefully preoccupied with.[45] Certainly Grove lesbians were "empty signifiers," lacking social power to be instruments of representation. It was only in the context of the larger and more powerful lesbian presence, hence audience, of the 1990s that Joan Van Ness was able to redress the lack of lesbian visibility brilliantly (though unconsciously, since she maintained in private that had she known what a furor her candidacy would cause she would never have competed) by executing three strategic moves. First, she placed herself squarely in the Grove male tradition by appealing to the memory of her dead sister, Martin, who had died of AIDS (from one perspective she *became* Martin), and she went to the local drag queens, the Shapiro Sisters, to have herself transformed into a queen.[46] Second, she framed her Queendom within the more gender-neutral category of camp, rather than the more male-specific drag. This framing of Joan's intervention as camp or even high camp, and so irreproachable, was repeated and validated by influential Grovers like Lyn Hutton, Max Killingsworth, and Panzi. Third, Joan reached back to a secondary but legitimate possibility within what can only be called gay gender (since through historical elaboration it has established partial autonomy from the heterosexual system)—that of compound drag, whereby queens could parody (an appropriate word here, because it was always done for laughs) "real men" or butches, and butches could parody either "real women" or drag queens.[47]

Contrary to assertions that drag subverts *any* gender position, or gender as a system, for many Grovers, certainly for the major actors in this narrative, drag becomes a performance in relation to what is subjectively experienced and socially accepted as an authentic self, defined by more or less coherent gay gender positions: butch (for masculine gay women and men), femme (primarily for feminine gay women), and queen (only for effeminate men).[48]

Lyn told me she had felt "awkward as hell" going to a relative's wedding in a dress to please her mother. "Well, that *was* drag for me. This"—her tux and tie—"isn't drag for me, it's getting dressed up." For Lyn, the clothing of her gay (true/butch) gender—the tux—is not a costume, but a sign of her true self. At the same time, on July 4 she wears the tux to comply with the rules of the Invasion, that participants must show both gay and straight spectators that they are gay by wearing drag. Does drag cover or reveal the true self, express or obscure it? That depends, but without concepts of authenticity, the transformations drag performs are meaningless.

What made Joan's portrayal of Queen Scarlett Ooh drag? For one thing, because she looked like a drag queen (rather than, say, a housewife or waitress). But for another, because she wore the clothes of her opposite gay gender. When I asked Joan what made her performance drag, she looked at me blankly, and so I rephrased, "Is being on the butch side what makes what you are doing 'drag'? Like if you were more feminine," I explain, when she still seems uncomprehending, "and got into this gown, would people accept it?" "No," she replied, seemingly on firm ground. "My being the way I am is what makes the whole thing camp." This simple statement contains the proposition that her "real self" is butch; that therefore her wearing a dress is a drag performance, a "camp." Or, as the Jersey Girls had put it eight years before, "It's not the meat, it's the motion"—that is, lesbians don't need a penis to be sexy, campy performers, to wear drag, hold the attention of an audience, to be as gay as a gay man and so represent gayness—in short, to be what the performance theorists call "phallic."

Performance theorists are on to something about the decentering of gender, including gay gender, in postmodern society, but they are wrong to propose that gay male or lesbian representations are taking place in a hypothetical "camp space of irony and wit, free from biological determinism, elitist essentialism, and the heterosexist cleavage of sexual difference." Even if we ignore the differences between performance spaces—the WOW Cafe (the all-women theater space and company that nurtured many of the lesbian performers mentioned here), the Cherry Grove theater, or the Invasion—and mundane gay life, even in these creative spaces performers are working under material conditions to specific audiences. Both camp and butch-femme do tend to dislodge gender from biology, but the purpose and effect are not to eliminate gender—a hopeless project, in any case—but rather to multiply and elaborate gender's meanings. Butch-femme and camp are not demolishing essentialism and the idea that there is an authentic (gay) self; rather, that is their foundation.[49] Nor are these creative spaces at all free from the many power imbalances between gay men and lesbians that the term *queer* papers over—quite the contrary. Grovers *are* redeploying elements of gay gender, but less in the service of shifting and self-reflective styles than that of shifting collective power.

Joan's victory in the Homecoming Queen contest, the burgeoning of camp in lesbian theater, and the work of the performance theorists are situated ethnographically within the historical frame of (gay) male dominance, in Cherry Grove, in off-Broadway theater, and in academia. Everyone in the Grove accepted that Joan Van Ness's running for and winning the title of Homecoming Queen in a male-dominated public venue and arguably within the queen-centered camp tradition constituted a subversive bid for inclusion and for lesbian visibility within the landscape of gay male symbolic and social power.

Although nineties butch drag has its own tradition in butch-femme sensibility and practice, and queer theory likewise has roots in feminism, for lesbians to name themselves as bearers and creators of camp on the stages of drag contests or of off-Broadway theaters and in the pages of academic journals *constitutes and reflects* a significant and wide-ranging change in lesbian/gay life, a change in which lesbians are aspiring to more power and representation through gay men and through the appropriation of gay male culture. Camille Paglia credits three gay men with helping create "the campy, semimythic diva and deranged gender-neutral entity" she proclaims herself to be.[50] The same process is evident in the off-Broadway lesbian theater originating in the WOW cafe, like the plays of Split Britches, the Five Lesbian Brothers, Holly Hughes, and Carmelita Tropicana, that have inspired performance theorists. Kate Davy cites Holly Hughes as locating her inspiration in "the queer theatrical tradition in the gay male drag performances of Charles Ludlam, Jack Smith, and Ethyl Eichelberger."[51] Lynda Hart recounts the story, enacted in Peggy Shaw and Lois Weaver's performance piece "Anniversary Waltz," of how the two actors who figure so centrally in Case's butch-femme camp scenario met:

> Shaw was traveling with "Hot Peaches," a gay theater group consisting mostly of drag queens. Weaver was traveling with the feminist theater group Spiderwoman. They met on tour in Berlin. Spiderwoman had arrived without their costumes; feminists at the time were busy, as Weaver says, "deconstructing the feminine image," hence they were accustomed to wearing old clothes, "rags with baby's toys tied around their belts." That night, however, they went on stage wearing the resplendent gowns and sequined accessories of the drag queens, and Weaver "knew that somehow they would never be the same again." And, indeed, before the tour was over Weaver would be transformed from a drag feminist into a sexy femme, playing to Shaw's butch.[52]

Hart concludes, "This representation points to sexual preference as a choice that is not bound to a gendered object"—in other words, drag/camp can serve lesbians as well as gay men. Kate Davy has a more ambivalent attitude toward the fact that "as the notion of camp has circulated among WOW practitioners in recent years, it has garnered a certain currency that has noticeably influenced the work."[53] It has done so because camp as a representational system is more developed than butch-femme, and *also* because of the social and economic successes of gay male theater. WOW performers were sick of being poor and performing only in a lesbian ghetto while gay male theater was gaining acceptance and success in mainstream venues.[54]

When Peggy Shaw, Lois Weaver, Holly Hughes, Carmelita Tropicana, and the women at the WOW Cafe were looking for theatrical alternatives to the earnestness of lesbian-feminist political theater and the realism of Jane Chambers, they reached back into the gendered and dramatic world of butch-femme and across to the camp theater of artists like Charles Ludlam with which butch-femme was most compatible. Why hadn't lesbians developed a theatrical drag tradition? Sarah Murray's essay asked. Alongside her sophisticated arguments about psychological and symbolic differences between gay men and lesbians, she should have placed more emphasis on the lack of opportunity, confidence, and clout that goes a long long way toward explaining why "the power of women, lesbian and straight, to create distinctive and persuasive images of women that break with conventional mainstream images *and are taken up by others and culturally reproduced* has been and continues to be weak, despite our abundance of creative expression."[55] It is a sign of change that Case's essay was able to do just that: take up and culturally reproduce a butch-femme image based on her reading of Lois Weaver and Peggy Shaw's performance of *Beauty and the Beast*. That is why "Towards a Butch-Femme Aesthetic" is more of a cultural manifesto than a cultural analysis, much more of a "historical reenactment" than a history.

What I see happening, at least among white urban lesbians (whose influence among lesbians in general is not to be lightly dismissed), is a creative ferment arising from the synthesis of lesbian traditions—butch-femme and feminism—with gay male culture (queer identity, camp theatricality, and modes of sexual behavior and imagery)—in the context of *modestly expanding lesbian power*.[56] Can it be a coincidence that this unprecedented outpouring of sophisticated work on lesbian signification and visibility that focuses, whether wholeheartedly or with reservations, on butch-femme as camp or queer, comes at the same time as Judith Butler, Teresa de Lauretis, Sue-Ellen Case, Lynda Hart, Jill Dolan, Peggy Phelan, and others have ascended to tenured positions at research universities and attained a critical mass within the queer theory or performance studies domains unheard of for lesbians in other intellectual disciplines? (Perhaps we need our own *Patti Ann* to make us appreciate the significance of these accomplishments). My purpose is not to denounce successful lesbian intellectuals—quite the opposite—but to issue this cautionary note on behalf of ethnographically grounded social theory: In the long run what we see in the mirror we hold up to lesbian signification practices will be distorted, unless it shows us the tangle of power and precedent in which even our own faces will be seen, acting in and upon our moment in history.

NOTES

INTRODUCTION

1   The Radicalesbians tract "The Woman-Identified Woman" probably offers the classic statement of this position. In Anne Koedt, Ellen Levine, Anita Rapone, eds., *Radical Feminism* (New York: Quadrangle Books, 1972, pp. 240–245).

2   Marilyn Frye, "Lesbian 'Sex,'" in *An Intimate Wilderness: Lesbian Writers on Sexuality*, ed. Judith Barrington (Portland, OR: Eighth Mountain Press, 1991, pp. 1–8).

3   Elizabeth Lapovsky Kennedy and Madeline D. Davis, *Boots of Leather, Slippers of Gold: The History of a Lesbian Community* (New York: Routledge, 1993).

4   Shane Phelan, *Identity Politics: Lesbian Feminism and the Limits of Community* (Philadelphia: Temple University Press, 1989).

5   Adrienne Rich, "Compulsory Heterosexuality and Lesbian Existence," *Signs* 5 (4) (1980): 631–660.

6   Lillian Faderman, *Surpassing the Love of Men: Romantic Friendship and Love Between Women from the Renaissance to the Present* (New York: William Morrow, 1981). See also Carroll Smith-Rosenberg, "The Female World of Love and Ritual: Relations between Women in Nineteenth Century America," *Signs* 1 (1) (1975): 1–29.

7   For a perceptive account of how this view of lesbianism was framed by radical feminist politics, see Alice Echols, *Daring to be Bad: Radical Feminism in America 1967–1975* (Minneapolis: University of Minnesota Press, 1989).

8   Similar debates are taking place about women and feminism in general. See, for example, various works by bell hooks; Alice Walker's concept of "womanism" (*In Search of Our Mothers' Gardens*. [San Diego: Harcourt Brace Jovanovich, 1984]); Patricia Hill Collins, *Black Feminist Thought: Knowledge, Consciousness, and the Politics of Empowerment* (New York: Routledge, 1991); and Chandra Talpade Mohanty, Ann Russo, and Lourdes Torres, eds., *Third World Women and the Politics of Feminism* (Bloomington: Indiana University Press, 1991).

9   Cherríe Moraga and Gloria Anzaldúa, eds., *This Bridge Called My Back: Writings by Radical Women of Color* (New York: Kitchen Table: Women of Color Press, 1981).

10   Barbara Smith, ed., *Home Girls: A Black Feminist Anthology* (New York: Kitchen Table Press, 1983); Evelyn Torton Beck, ed., *Nice Jewish Girls: A Lesbian Anthology* (Boston: Beacon Press, 1989 [1982]); Carla Trujillo, ed., *Chicana Lesbians: The Girls Our Mothers Warned Us About* (Berkeley: Third Woman Press, 1991); Gloria Anzaldúa, ed., *Making Face, Making Soul—Haciendo Caras: Creative and Critical Perspectives by Women of Color* (San Francisco: Aunt Lute Foundation Books, 1990); Juanita Ramos, ed., *Compañeras: Latina Lesbians* (New York: Latina Lesbian History Project, 1987); Makeda Silvera, ed., *Piece of my Heart: A Lesbian of Colour Anthology* (Toronto: Sister Vision Press, 1991); Asian Women United of California, eds., *Making Waves: An Anthology of Writings By and About Asian American Women* (Boston: Beacon Press, 1989); Catherine E. McKinley and L. Joyce DeLaney, eds., *Afrekete: An Anthology of Black Lesbian Writing* (New York: Anchor Books, 1995).

11   See, for example, Deborah Abbott and Ellen Farmer, eds., *From Wedded Wife to Lesbian Life: Stories of Transformation* (Freedom, CA: Crossing Press, 1995); Marcy Adelman, ed., *Long Time Passing: Lives of Older Lesbians* (Boston: Alyson Publications, 1986); Joan Nestle, ed., *The Persistent Desire: A Femme-Butch Reader* (Boston: Alyson Publications, 1992); Lesléa Newman, ed., *The Femme Mystique* (Boston: Alyson Publications, 1995); and Mark Thompson, ed., *Leather Folk: Radical Sex, People, Politics, and Practice* (Boston: Alyson Publications, 1991). I suppose a recent volume by gay and lesbian anthropologists (Ellen Lewin and William Leap, eds., *Out In the Field: Reflections of Lesbian and Gay Anthropologists* [Urbana: University of Illinois Press, 1996]) might be considered yet another example of this trend!

12   Kathleen B. Jones, *Compassionate Authority: Democracy and the Representation of Women* (New York: Routledge, 1993), 194.

13   Silvera, 2–5, 38–39, 115–118.

14   Beck, 192–201, 91–99, 69–72.

15   Adelman, 177–182.

16   Trujillo, 84.

17   Phelan, 169.

18   Allan Bérubé and Jeffrey Escoffier, 1991, "Queer Nation." *Out/Look: National Lesbian and Gay Quarterly* 11 (winter 1991): 12.

19   Michael Warner, ed., *Fear of a Queer Planet: Queer Politics and Social Theory* (Minneapolis: University of Minnesota Press, 1993), xxvi–xxvii. The claims of queer theorists to oppose "normal business in the academy" is in ironic contrast to the fact that many of them publish academic books and articles prolifically and have achieved considerable success in academic employment.

20   Lisa Duggan, "Making It All Perfectly Queer," *Socialist Review* 22 (1) (1992): 20.

21   See, for instance, Judith Butler, *Gender Trouble* (New York: Routledge, 1990); Teresa de Lauretis, *Technologies of Gender* (Bloomington: Indiana University Press, 1987); Jeffrey Weeks, "History, Desire, and Identities," in *Conceiving Sexuality*, ed. Richard G. Parker and John H. Gagnon (New York: Routledge,

1995), 33−50; and Kate Bornstein, *Gender Outlaw: On Men, Women, and the Rest of Us* (New York: Routledge, 1994).

22   Michael Bronski, *Culture Clash: The Making of Gay Sensibility* (Boston: South End Press, 1984).

23   Susan Krieger, *The Mirror Dance: Identity in a Women's Community* (Philadelphia: Temple University Press, 1983).

24   Richard K. Herrell, "The Symbolic Strategies of Chicago's Gay and Lesbian Pride Day Parade," In *Gay Culture in America: Essays from the Field*, ed. Gilbert Herdt (Boston: Beacon Press, 1992), 225−252.

25   John D'Emilio, *Sexual Politics, Sexual Communities: The Making of a Homosexual Minority in the United States 1940−1970* (Chicago: University of Chicago Press, 1983); Kennedy and Davis; Esther Newton, *Cherry Grove, Fire Island: Sixty Years in America's First Gay and Lesbian Town* (Boston: Beacon Press, 1993).

26   Benedict Anderson, *Imagined Communities*. London: Verso, 1991, 143.

27   Anderson, 196.

28   The early work of Jonathan Ned Katz (*Gay American History: Lesbians and Gay Men in the U.S.A.* [New York: Avon Books, 1976]) and Lillian Faderman was followed by volumes such as Martin B. Duberman, Martha Vicinus, and George Chauncey Jr., eds., *Hidden From History: Reclaiming the Lesbian and Gay Past* (New York: New American Library, 1989) (which, perhaps not coincidentally, has the same title as an earlier work in feminist history), and an array of work by Martin Duberman, John D'Emilio, Allan Bérubé, John Boswell, George Chauncey, Lillian Faderman, Judith Brown, David Greenberg, Elizabeth Kennedy and Madeline Davis, and Esther Newton. See, for example, Allan Bérubé, *Coming Out Under Fire: The History of Gay Men and Women in World War Two* (New York: Free Press, 1990); John Boswell, *Christianity, Social Tolerance, and Homosexuality* (Chicago: University of Chicago Press, 1980), and *Same-Sex Unions in Premodern Europe* (New York: Villard, 1994); Judith Brown, *Immodest Acts: The Life of a Lesbian Nun in Renaissance Italy* (New York: Oxford University Press, 1986); George Chauncey, *Gay New York: Gender, Urban Culture, and the Making of the Gay Male World 1890−1940* (New York: Basic Books, 1994); Martin B. Duberman, *Stonewall* (New York: Plume, 1993); Lillian Faderman, *Odd Girls and Twilight Lovers: A History of Lesbian Life in Twentieth-Century America* (New York: Columbia University Press, 1991); and David F. Greenberg, *The Construction of Homosexuality* (Chicago: University of Chicago Press, 1988). John Boswell's most recent book, in particular, has been used to justify demands that gay marriages be legalized or otherwise recognized as equivalent to, and perhaps even more authentic than, heterosexual unions.

29   Bonnie Zimmerman, "The Politics of Transliteration: Lesbian Personal Narratives," *Signs* 9 (4) (1984): 663−682.

30   Kath Weston, *Families We Choose: Lesbians, Gays, Kinship* (New York: Columbia University Press, 1991).

31   Ellen Lewin, "Writing Lesbian and Gay Culture: What the Natives Have to Say for Themselves," *American Ethnologist* 18 (4) (1991): 786−792.

32   Eric Hobsbawm and Terence Ranger, eds., *The Invention of Tradition* (Cambridge: Cambridge University Press, 1983).

33   See, for example, Lila Abu-Lughod, "The Romance of Resistance: Trac-

ing Transformations of Power Through Bedouin Women," *American Ethnologist* 17 (1) (1990): 41–55; Nicholas B. Dirks, "Ritual and Resistance: Subversion as a Social Fact," in *Culture/Power/History: A Reader in Contemporary Social Theory*, Nicholas B. Dirks, Geoff Eley, and Sherry B. Ortner, eds. (Princeton: Princeton University Press, 1994), 483–503; Aihwa Ong, *Spirits of Resistance and Capitalist Discipline: Factory Women in Malaysia* (Albany: SUNY Press, 1987); James C. Scott, *Weapons of the Weak: Everyday Forms of Peasant Resistance* (New Haven: Yale University Press, 1985).

34   See, for example, many of the essays in Warner.

35   See Abu-Lughod for a cogent critique of the recent tendency to see resistance everywhere.

36   Evelyn Blackwood, "Breaking the Mirror: The Construction of Lesbianism and the Anthropological Discourse on Homosexuality," in *Anthropology and Homosexual Behavior*, ed. Evelyn Blackwood (New York: Haworth Press, 1986), 1–18; Esther Newton, "Yams, Grinders, and Gays: The Anthropology of Homosexuality," *Out/Look* 1 (1) (spring 1988): 28–37; Kath Weston, "Lesbian/Gay Studies in the House of Anthropology," *Annual Review of Anthropology* 22 (1993): 339–367.

37   Weston, "Lesbian/Gay Studies," 341.

38   "Queer theory" has been most strongly in evidence among philosophers, literary critics, and proponents of cultural studies, and less characteristic of scholars in "empirical" fields like history, sociology, and anthropology. See Lisa Duggan, "The Discipline Problem: Queer Theory Meets Lesbian and Gay History," in *Sex Wars: Sexual Dissent and Political Culture*, ed. Lisa Duggan and Nan D. Hunter (New York: Routledge, 1995): 194–206. Many would claim that queer theory faces the same problems experienced by earlier incarnations of gay and lesbian studies in regard to accessibility or relevance to the nonacademic lesbian and gay community, and especially to women, gay people of color, and independent scholars. See, for example, Jeffrey Escoffier, "Inside the Ivory Closet: The Challenges Facing Lesbian & Gay Studies," *Out/Look* 3 (2): (fall 1990): 40–48.

39   Steven Epstein, "Gay Politics, Ethnic Identity: The Limits of Social Constructionism," *Socialist Review* 17 (3–4) (1987): 9–54.

40   Beth E. Schneider and Nancy E. Stoller, eds., *Women Resisting AIDS: Feminist Strategies of Empowerment* (Philadelphia: Temple University Press, 1995); Sandra Butler and Barbara Rosenblum, *Cancer in Two Voices* (San Francisco: Spinsters Book Company, 1991).

41   See Louise Krasniewicz, *Nuclear Summer: The Clash of Communities at the Seneca Women's Peace Encampment* (Ithaca: Cornell University Press, 1992), for an example of a kind of analysis that might usefully be applied to the study of lesbian political activists in other settings. See also Urvashi Vaid, *Virtually Equal: The Mainstreaming of Gay and Lesbian Liberation* (New York: Anchor Books, 1995), for an account of gay and lesbian involvement in recent electoral politics.

42   Marcy Adelman, ed., *Long Time Passing: Lives of Older Lesbians* (Boston: Alyson Publications, 1986).

43   Lisa Duggan and Nan D. Hunter, *Sex Wars: Sexual Dissent and Political Culture* (New York: Routledge, 1995).

44   Susan K. Cahn, *Coming on Strong: Gender and Sexuality in Twentieth-Century Women's Sport* (Cambridge: Harvard University Press, 1994).

45   See Bornstein, *Gender Outlaw*, and for a fictional approach, see Leslie Feinberg, *Stone Butch Blues* (Ithaca, NY: Firebrand Books, 1993).

46   Edward Sapir, "Culture, Genuine and Spurious," in *Selected Writings of Edward Sapir in Language, Culture and Personality*, ed. David G. Mandelbaum (Berkeley: University of California Press, 1963), 308–331.

47   Sapir, 314.

48   Sapir, 325.

CHAPTER 1:
KENNEDY, "BUT WE WOULD NEVER TALK ABOUT IT"

1   The "New Woman" refers to the two generations of women involved in the transition from the nineteenth to the twentieth century. As a result of the nineteenth-century women's movement, women began to enter the public sphere during this period. The New Woman was part of the social changes that began to give women some autonomy in the public sphere. She was struggling for women's right to earn a living, gain an education, control their reproduction, and finally to vote. See, for instance, Carroll Smith-Rosenberg, "Discourses of Sexuality and Subjectivity: The New Woman, 1870–1936," in *Hidden from History: Reclaiming the Gay and Lesbian Past*, ed. Martin Bauml Duberman, Martha Vicinus, and George Chauncey (New York: New American Library, 1989), 264–281.

2   This article is part of a larger research project in which I aim to write the life story of Julia Boyer Reinstein. It is based on more than forty hours of oral history tapes I collected from 1994 to 1996. Of necessity one article can't capture the full complexity of Julia's life. Many interesting and relevant topics must be set aside to focus on the construction of discretion in a specific period of time and location.

3   Although I avoid the term "closet," my approach is influenced a great deal by the writing of Eve Kosofsky Sedgwick, who has explicated the centrality of the closet to twentieth-century culture. I particularly appreciate the subtlety with which she deconstructs the simple binarism of "in" and "out," showing the contested nature of permissible speech about gayness in American history and of the relationship between knowledge and ignorance in matters of sexuality (*The Epistemology of the Closet* [Berkeley: University of California Press, 1990]).

4   Elizabeth Lapovsky Kennedy and Madeline Davis, *Boots of Leather, Slippers of Gold: The History of a Lesbian Community* (New York: Routledge, 1993).

5   Elsa Gidlow, *Elsa: I Come with My Songs: The Autobiography of Elsa Gidlow* (San Francisco: Booklegger Press, 1986).

6   The power of the gay liberation framework to erase or to caricature as pathetic other interesting forms of lesbian and gay life is worth noting. Throughout my work in lesbian and gay history, I have encountered interesting incidents suggesting that many people who led private gay lives found them completely satisfy-

ing, not oppressive, which I puzzled over briefly, then dismissed as examples of false consciousness or lack of appreciation of the benefits of being out. I was particularly hard on middle-class or bourgeois women who had to remain closeted to keep their jobs. In the late 1970s I remember discussing with members of the San Francisco Gay and Lesbian History Project the strange responses of several older lesbians who were loathe to be interviewed. We couldn't understand their claim that they were reluctant to share memories about their lives as lesbians because the secret was part of the beauty or excitement of being lesbian. Similarly, in the early 1990s when I was part of the planning conference for the Stonewall 25 museum exhibits, I could not quite digest a conversation I heard between Martin Duberman and a curator for the theater collection at one of the museums. They were about the same age, and they were arguing about whether the thirties, forties, and fifties had been oppressive. The curator took the position that, as part of the theater world, in his experience life for gays had been fun, but Duberman viewed the period as extremely repressive, because people were stigmatized and could not be "out." At the time, I was amazed such a disagreement was possible, and I fliply decided the curator had false consciousness or that he liked his oppression.

7   See, for instance, Judith Butler, "Imitation and Gender Insubordination," in *The Lesbian and Gay Studies Reader*, ed. Henry Abelove, Michele Aina Barale, and David M. Halperin (New York: Routledge, 1993), 307–320; and Shane Phelan, "Becoming Out: Lesbian Identity and Politics," *Signs* 18 (4) (1993): 765–790.

8   Smith-Rosenberg, "Discourses of Sexuality."

9   Esther Newton, "The Mythic Mannish Woman: Radclyffe Hall and the New Woman," in *Hidden From History*, 281–293.

10   Martha Vicinus also points out the problems in this argument, noting that other forms of lesbianism clearly existed in the early twentieth century ("'They wonder to which sex I belong': The Historical Roots of the Modern Lesbian Identity," *The Lesbian and Gay Studies Reader*, 432–452).

11   Leila Rupp, "'Imagine my surprise': Women's Relationships in Mid-twentieth Century America," in *Hidden From History*, 395–410.

12   Lillian Faderman, *Odd Girls and Twilight Lovers: A History of Lesbian Life in Twentieth-Century America* (New York: Columbia University Press, 1991), 109.

13   Faderman, 109.

14   In the introduction and the conclusion of this paper I abbreviate Julia Boyer Reinstein's name as "Boyer Reinstein," but in the body of the paper I use "Julia." I discussed the issue of using first or last names with Boyer Reinstein, who said the decision was up to me. The only thing was that she wanted to be called "Boyer Reinstein," rather than "Reinstein," if I decided to use her last name. She has frequently used the double last name, at her husband's suggestion, ever since she was married. He and his mother were worried the Germans would invade the United States during World War II and that they would be high on the list of those who would likely be killed. They wanted Julia to use "Boyer Reinstein" on official documents so that, if necessary, she could take her step children, flee to Canada, and go back to using her maiden name. Boyer Reinstein also said she feels that even though she was "Mrs. Reinstein" for a long time, she never completely denied her lesbian side, so "Boyer Reinstein" is more appropriate.

I switch to "Julia" in the body of the paper which relies primarily on oral history to better capture the familiarity of that context, and because she refers to many of her friends by their first names. To use their surnames would distort the quality of her recollections (and in some cases, Julia had forgotten the last names).

15   When the company acquired local plants, the plants kept their local names, becoming subsidiaries of Consolidated Power and Light.

16   Julia also met Willa Cather through her father's acquaintances. Cather had a greater impact on Julia's life, encouraging and inspiring her in her work as an historian.

17   I probed during our interviews to determine if any of these encounters were perhaps coerced, in the sense that the partners felt obligated to be with Julia or she with them, but Julia said she was certain they were not. If there wasn't mutual interest, she slept alone or was free to decline. "If I had somebody that I didn't particularly like, I just spent the evening and came back to the hotel, and maybe I would say goodnight to my father out in the hall and walk in my room, and he and his girlfriend walked in their room." I would imagine that having a room next to her father's made it unlikely that anyone would force himself or herself on her.

18   Faderman, *Odd Girls and Twilight Lovers*, 62–93. For other information on women's willingness to explore relationships with women, see Katharine Bement Davis, *Factors in the Sex Life of Twenty-Two Hundred Women* (New York: Harper and Row, 1929).

19   At another point in the interview, Julia mentioned a variation of this arrangement. Julia and her father would leave the house with the pretext of going to some business-related meeting or weekend. Somewhere out of town, they would hook up with Dorothy and Helen. Julia would join Dorothy and Helen would join Julia's father, and they would agree to meet later to return.

20   Julia couldn't remember the name of the group, but she said she was sure it was one in which whites did support work for African Americans.

21   Gidlow, *Elsa*, 302–303.

22   The lesbians who were part of the founding of Cherry Grove, as documented by Esther Newton in *Cherry Grove, Fire Island*, are another interesting group to compare with Boyer Reinstein and her friends. The Cherry Grove women were all upper class; they emphasized discretion and were not part of the tradition of mannish lesbians (*Cherry Grove, Fire Island: Sixty Years in America's First Gay and Lesbian Town*, [New York: Beacon 1993]). They were careful not to be too obvious. Many were married and insisted on being addressed as "Mrs. So-and-so." In New York City they lived very "respectable" lives, but in Cherry Grove, a resort removed from the strictures of everyday life, they were able to live openly as lesbians. But it is possible that their lives away from the resorts were quite similar to Boyer Reinstein and her friends', a topic worth further exploration. bell hooks' discussion of the treatment of gays and lesbians in mid-century southern black communities suggests that poverty and the need for community solidarity might create structures of discretion in the rural south that are similar to those of Boyer Reinstein ("Homophobia in Black Communities," *Talking Back: Thinking Feminist, Thinking Black* [Boston: South End Press, 1989] 120–26). This phenomenon also deserves further study.

CHAPTER 2:
THORPE, "A HOUSE WHERE QUEERS GO"

1   Most of the women quoted in this study chose to use their real names, although some omitted their last names. The only pseudonyms are Brandy Maguire and Sandy. I would like to thank all these women for their time and thoughtful reflections on the past and for their courage then and today. Thanks also to Lisa Roehl, Kathy Babbitt, and Lesley Finch for their insight and support.

2   Ruth Ellis, interview by the author, 16 January 1992.

3   Lillian Faderman, *Odd Girls and Twilight Lovers: A History of Lesbian Life in Twentieth-Century America* (New York: Columbia University Press, 1991), 161.

4   Janet Kahn and Patricia Gozemba, "In and Around the Lighthouse: Working Class Lesbian Bar Culture in the 1950s and 1960s," in *Gendered Domains: Rethinking Public and Private in Women's History*, ed. Dorothy Helly and Susan Reverby (Ithaca, NY: Cornell University Press, 1992), 92.

5   Madeline Davis and Elizabeth Lapovsky Kennedy. "Oral History and the Study of Sexuality in the Lesbian Community: Buffalo, New York, 1940–1960," in *Hidden from History*, ed. Martin Duberman, et al. (New York: New American Library, 1989), 427.

6   Although Kennedy and Davis describe the desegregation of white working-class lesbian bars, the focus of their work is on these bars and the changes that took place in them. Elizabeth Lapvosky Kennedy and Madeline D. Davis, *Boots of Leather, Slippers of Gold: The History of a Lesbian Community* (New York and London: Routledge, 1993).

7   This paper is based on research for my doctoral dissertation about lesbian life in Detroit, 1940–1975. I conducted forty-eight oral history interviews—over half with women of color—for that project, which is still in progress. Most interviews took place in narrators' homes. The interviews were tape-recorded and are currently being transcribed. They will be stored for future use at the Human Sexuality Archives at Cornell University.

8   Jervis Anderson, *This Was Harlem: A Cultural Portrait, 1900–1950* (New York: Farrar, Straus, Giroux, 1982), 153.

9   Gilbert Osofsky, *Harlem: The Making of a Ghetto*, 2d ed. (New York: Harper and Row, 1971), 139.

10   Anderson, *This Was Harlem*, 153.

11   Eric Garber, "A Spectacle in Color: The Lesbian and Gay Subculture of Jazz Age Harlem," in *Hidden from History*, 321.

12   Garber, "A Spectacle in Color," 321. Joan Nestle quotes Jeanne Flash Gray, an African-American lesbian from 1920s Harlem who remembered that "Before it was discovered by others that Black Lesbians and gay men had money to spend, there were many places in Harlem run by and for Black Lesbians and gay men." In Nestle, *A Restricted Country* (Ithaca, NY: Firebrand Press, 1987), 112.

13   Garber, "A Spectacle in Color," 322.

14   Garber, "A Spectacle in Color," 323.

15   For a discussion of the role of similar house parties in Buffalo, New York, and their central role in African-American lesbian social life, see Kennedy and Davis, *Boots of Leather*, especially 123–131.

16   Ellis, interview.

17   Margaret Lorick and Alice Miller, interview by the author, 25 January 1992.

18   Before the completion of Route I-75 in the late 1950s, guests from the furthermost locations had to drive six hours or more to get to Ruth and Babe's house.

19   Ellis, interview.

20   Lorick and Miller, interview.

21   For a description of the Victory Plan adopted by activists in Detroit, see Jacqueline Jones, *Labor of Love, Labor of Sorrow: Black Women, Work, and the Family, from Slavery to the Present* (reprint, New York: Vintage Books), 239–240.

22   Sidney Fine, *Violence in the Model City: The Cavanagh Administration, Race Relations, and the Detroit Riot of 1967* (Ann Arbor: University of Michigan Press, 1989), 57.

23   Teresa L. Amott and Julie A. Matthaei, *Race, Gender, and Work: A Multicultural Economic History of Women in the United States* (Boston: South End Press, 1991), 173.

24   Judy Utley, interview by the author, 6 June 1992.

25   Brandy Maguire [pseud.], interview by the author, 23 June 1992.

26   Mable Stewart Merritt, interview by the author, 24 June 1992.

27   White lesbians who held racist beliefs in the 1950s were, I believe, reluctant to express these prejudices during interviews, for three reasons. First, white lesbians were reluctant to criticize themselves and their friends, who they believe were doing the best they could in very difficult times. Knowing, as they do, that lesbians still are subject to intense oppression on account of their sexuality, I feel certain that some women wanted to present as positive a picture as possible when discussing the past. Second, the historical period between then and now has witnessed powerful arguments for black civil rights, the result of which might be that some white lesbians have been educated about the falsity of their previous prejudices, and are therefore loathe to admit them. And third, even those white lesbians who might privately admit to animosity toward people of color have learned that to express those views today is to invite criticism and censure from other lesbians, therefore they keep those opinions to themselves.

Although lesbians of color discussed the racism of white lesbians much more freely, there is also a chance that some were wary about expressing their opinions too strongly to a white interviewer, for fear of being misunderstood or disbelieved. I also suspect that my own inability to read between the lines of interviews with African-American lesbians interferes with my understanding of the full meaning of those interviews. Despite these difficulties, considerable evidence reveals white lesbian bars to have been places fraught with racial tension and outright discrimination during this period.

28   Anita, interview by the author, 29 June 1992. Anita is a Mexican-American lesbian who socialized exclusively with African-American lesbians.
29   Ronnie, interview by the author, 5 June 1992.
30   Linda Emery, interview by the author, 23 June 1992.
31   Maguire [pseud.], interview.
32   That common ground would have had to be powerful indeed—during the 25 years this study covered, the city was a cauldron of racial tension. Major race riots in 1943 and 1967 were only the most visible signs of deep hostility between Detroit's black and white citizens. See Fine, *Violence in the Model City*; B. J. Widick, *Detroit: City of Race and Class Violence*, rev. ed. (Detroit: Wayne State University Press, 1989); Dominic J. Capeci Jr., *Race Relations in Wartime Detroit: The Sojourner Truth Housing Controversy of 1942* (Philadelphia: Temple University Press, 1984); James A. Geschwender, *Class, Race, and Worker Insurgency: The League of Revolutionary Black Workers* (Cambridge: Cambridge University Press, 1977); Dominic J. Capeci Jr. and Martha Wilkerson, *Layered Violence: The Detroit Rioters of 1943* (Jackson: University Press of Mississippi, 1991).
        African-American and white lesbians in Buffalo expressed a similar sentiment, that shared oppression as lesbians superseded racial differences between women. See Kennedy and Davis, *Boots of Leather*, 123.
33   Patricia Williams, *The Alchemy of Race and Rights* (Cambridge, MA and London: Harvard University Press, 1991), 115–130 (quote from 116). See also legal theorist Kimberle Crenshaw, who discusses the legal ramifications of what she calls "facial race-neutrality" in civil rights law, in "Race, Reform, and Retrenchment: Transformation and Legitimation in Antidiscrimination Law," *Harvard Law Review*, 101 (7) (May 1988): 1331–1387 (esp. 1378–1381).
34   Although not all the white lesbians interviewed for this study would identify themselves as politically liberal, hooks defines "liberal whites" in this context to mean white people who claim to be nonracist, "irrespective of their political leanings to the right or left." bell hooks, "Overcoming White Supremacy: A Comment," in *Talking Back: Thinking Feminist, Thinking Black* (Boston: South End Press, 1989), 113.
35   For an insightful discussion of the disbelief African Americans can encounter when pointing out racism to whites, see Derrick Bell, *Faces at the Bottom of the Well: The Permanence of Racism* (New York: Bell Books, A Division of Harper Collins, 1992), 111–113.
36   Bernice Johnson Reagon, "Coalition Politics: Turning the Century," in *Home Girls: A Black Feminist Anthology*, ed. Barbara Smith (New York: Kitchen Table, Women of Color Press, 1983), 356–368.
37   Williams, *The Alchemy of Race and Rights*, 129.
38   For a discussion of this problem in Chicago in the 1970s, see "Bars Offer Drinks, Discrimination," *Chicago Gay Life* 2, no. 4 (6 August 1976). To a significant extent, many lesbians in Detroit are still separated by race. One African-American lesbian asked me how I would find white lesbians to interview for my study. I replied that because I am white myself, it would be easy for me, because most of my social connections with lesbians were with white women. "I don't

know," she answered. "I don't think there are many white lesbians out there—there are a lot more black lesbians than white." Some white lesbians and gay men expressed equal disbelief that I would find African-American lesbians to interview.

39   Karla, interview by the author, 3 June 1992.

40   Sandy [pseud.], interview by the author, 12 June 1992.

41   For several perspectives on the importance of lynching and its justifications in race relations and in the sexual lives of African-American women, see Rennie Simson, "The Afro-American Female: The Historical Context of the Construction of Sexual Identity," Barbara Omolade, "Hearts of Darkness," and Jacquelyn Dowd Hall, " 'The Mind That Burns in Each Body': Women, Rape, and Racial Violence," in *Powers of Desire: The Politics of Sexuality*, ed. Ann Snitow, Christine Stansell, and Sharon Thompson (New York: Monthly Review Press, 1983), 229–235, 350–367, and 328–349, respectively; and Darlene Clark Hine, "Rape and the Inner Lives of Black Women in the Middle West: Preliminary Thoughts on the Culture of Dissemblance," in *Unequal Sisters: A Multi-Cultural Reader in U.S. Women's History*, ed. Ellen Carol DuBois and Vicki L. Ruiz (New York and London: Routledge, 1990), 292–297.

42   Jacquelyn Dowd Hall, "The Mind That Burns in Each Body," and *Revolt Against Chivalry: Jessie Daniel Ames and the Women's Campaign Against Lynching* (New York: Columbia University Press, 1979), especially pp. 150–157 and 194–209.

43   In their study of lesbians in Buffalo during this period, Kennedy and Davis quote one black lesbian who remembers when "black studs were coming into the bar, people [white butches] would just kind of put their arm around their women [as if] they were just coming in there to snatch up their women." Kennedy and Davis, *Boots of Leather*, 119.

44   Toni, interview by the author, 17 June 1992.

45   According to Sidney Fine, "During the 1950s Detroit lost 23.4% of its white population, while the number of nonwhites, all but about five thousand of whom were black, increased from 303,000 to 487,000 and their percentage of the total population from 16 to 29.1." *Violence in the Model City*, 3.

46   Housing in Detroit presented a mixed picture. African Americans in Detroit continued to be more likely to own their own homes and to live in sound housing than anywhere else in the nation, but compared with whites, black housing conditions in Detroit were terrible: Of 36,000 substandard households in 1966, 29,600 were black. Fine, *Violence in the Model City*, 57.

47   Fine, *Violence in the Model City*, 71.

48   Sandy described the Palais as a "family-type" bar.

49   This is in contrast to African-American lesbian house parties in Buffalo, which provided places for interracial socializing. See Kennedy and Davis, *Boots of Leather*, 117.

50   Marie White and Bev, interview by the author, 30 June 1992 and 8 February 1992, respectively.

51   Renee McCoy, interview by the author, 24 June 1992.

52   Toni, interview. Lesbians in Buffalo also remember bar owners making payoffs to police to avoid raids. Kennedy and Davis, *Boots of Leather*, 74–75.

53   White lesbians also give this reason for a scarcity of raids of lesbian bars.
54   Joan Nestle, "Lesbians and Prostitutes: An Historical Sisterhood," in *A Restricted Country*, 157–177.
55   For a description of heterosexual "blind pigs," see Fine, *Violence in the Model City*, 4.

CHAPTER 3:
KLINGER, WRITING CIVIL RIGHTS

I would like to acknowledge the generous assistance of the Mabelle McLeod Lewis Memorial Fund.
Epigraphs: Jewelle Gomez, "Black Lesbian Feminist Warrior Poet Mother: A Tribute to Audre Lorde/A Review of *Undersong*," *Lambda Book Report* 3 (9) (1993): 7; and Cherríe Moraga, quoted in Norma Alarcón, "Interview with Cherríe Moraga," *Third Woman* 3 (1 & 2) (1986): 127.
1   By using such terms as "multicultural lesbians," "lesbians of color," "Third World lesbians," and "multiethnic and multiracial lesbians," I do not want to suggest either a totalizing sameness within each group or mutually exclusive categories of identification. The most apparent common thread connecting lesbian activist writers, despite how their oppressions and experiences have been differently structured, is their sense of consistent devaluation in dominant discourses and everyday life and their shared oppositional context of struggle. When using the term "community," moreover, I am not subscribing to a stable, unified model of community comprising individuals with necessarily consistent or shared values, attitudes, expectations, beliefs, or practices. Neither a totalizing vision nor a constant core of "members" characterizes the model of community most applicable to North American lesbian cultural and political formation in the late twentieth century. For many lesbian activists, the notion of community, like the ideal of "Lesbian Nation" itself, is more of a psychically comforting, politically compelling, enabling fantasy than an accurate description of their actual experiences in movement groups. Gloria Anzaldúa captures the sentiments of lesbians whose activism is often motivated by a tantalizing desire for some kind of cultural cohesion when she notes that, imagined or real, a vision of community, or *comunidad*, "is still the carrot that I, the donkey, hunger for and seek." See "Bridge, Drawbridge, Sandbar or Island: Lesbians-of-Color *Hacienda Alianzas*," in *Bridges of Power: Women's Multicultural Alliances*, ed. Lisa Albrecht and Rose M. Brewer (Philadelphia, PA: New Society Publisher in cooperation with the National Women's Studies Association, 1990), 221. Thus, a fluid model of community accommodating the widely different levels of commitment, participation, and affiliation of individual "members," as well as the constantly changing nature of the membership itself, more aptly describes the multiethnic and multiracial lesbian critical mass that began to make its presence known in liberation politics and literary circles and to leave its mark on the alternative press in the late 1960s, 1970s, and 1980s. For a relevant and particularly compelling political conceptualization of "imag-

ined" community as an idea that "leads us away from essentialist notions of Third World feminist struggles, suggesting political rather than biological or cultural bases for alliance," see Chandra Talpade Mohanty, "Introduction: Cartographies of Struggle: Third World Women and the Politics of Feminism," in *Third World Women and the Politics of Feminism*, ed. Chandra Talpade Mohanty, Anne Russo, and Lourdes Torres (Bloomington: Indiana University Press, 1991), 4.

2   Virginia Woolf co-owned Hogarth Press from 1917 to 1937, publishing T. S. Eliot's works and those of many other writers, as well as her own. Sylvia Beach, the owner of the 1920s bookstore Shakespeare & Company and the publisher of James Joyce's *Ulysses*, was also an important figure in the history of women's publishing. For a treatment of such modernist lesbian writers as Djuna Barnes, Natalie Barney, H.D., and Gertrude Stein, see Shari Benstock, *Women of the Left Bank: Paris, 1900–1940* (Austin: University of Texas Press, 1986). For a treatment of lesbian pulp novels, see Kate Adams, "Making the World Safe for the Missionary Position: Images of the Lesbian in Post-World War II America," in *Lesbian Texts and Contexts: Radical Revisions*, ed. Karla Jay and Joanne Glasgow (New York: New York University Press, 1990), 255–274. Suzanna Danuta Walters, "As Her Hand Crept Slowly Up Her Thigh: Ann Bannon and the Politics of Pulp," *Social Text* 23 (fall–winter 1989): 83–101; Michèle Aina Barale, "When Jack Blinks: Si(gh)ting Gay Desire in Ann Bannon's *Beebo Brinker*," in *The Lesbian and Gay Studies Reader*, ed. Henry Abelove, Michèle Aina Barale, and David Halperin (New York: Routledge, 1993) 604–615; Bonnie Zimmerman, *The Safe Sea of Women: Lesbian Fiction, 1969–1989* (Boston: Beacon Press, 1990) 9, 215–216. Lesbian-pulp book covers literally come to life in a set of inventive, recuperative dramatizations of lesbian love interspersed with archival photographs, personal interviews, newspaper clippings, and documentary film footage, in Aerlyn Weissman and Lynne Fernie's *Forbidden Love: The Unashamed Stories of Lesbian Lives* (The National Film Board of Canada, 1993).

3   However, Sarah Schulman, whose trenchant collection of nonfiction essays, articles, and speeches in *My American History: Lesbian and Gay Life During the Reagan/Bush Years* (New York: Routledge, 1994) indicates that she has been and continues to be one of the most perspicacious activist consciences of the contemporary lesbian and gay liberation movement, provides justifiable cause for tempering any claims about the growing improvement in the quality of lesbian writing. Recognizing in the early 1990s that as lesbian writing becomes more proficient "lesbian writers are becoming more and more apolitical generally," she questions the integrity of lesbian literary achievements that are devoid of a politicized sensibility and that have eschewed activist issues. See Schulman, quoted in Kate Brandt, *Happy Endings: Lesbian Writers Talk About Their Lives and Work* (Tallahassee, Florida: The Naiad Press, 1993), 209.

4   Although their writing lies outside the scope of this discussion, such poets as Paula Gunn Allen, Chrystos, Cheryl Clarke, Jewelle Gomez, Judy Grahn, Irena Klepfisz, Pat Parker, Adrienne Rich, and Kitty Tsui are among the most influential and politicized, multiracial, and multiethnic lesbian voices since the 1960s.

5   Quoted in Brandt, 46.

6   Michael Bronski, *Culture Clash: The Making of Gay Sensibility* (Boston: South End Press, 1984), 144.

7   I borrow the term "paper lesbian" from Kathryn Adams' dissertation, "Paper Lesbians: Alternative Publishing and the Politics of Lesbian Representation in the United States, 1950–1990." In her introductory chapter, Adams refurbishes the metaphor "paper tiger" (*su lao fu*)—popularized when Chairman Mao used the phrase in 1946 and 1958 to emphasize "the historical dialectic of progressive and reactive forces"—by applying it to lesbians in a fashion that refuses to "sell the power of paper short."

8   Lisa Ben, quoted in Eric Marcus, *Making History: The Struggle for Gay and Lesbian Equal Rights, 1945–1990: An Oral History* (New York: HarperCollins, 1992), 9. See also segments of Brandt's interviews and correspondences with Lisa Ben in *Happy Endings* (131–139). Brandt records that Lisa Ben printed sixteen copies of each issue of *Vice Versa* (133).

9   Lee Lynch, "Cruising the Libraries," *Lesbian Texts and Contexts: Radical Revisions*, ed. Karla Jay and Joanne Glasgow (New York: New York University Press, 1990), 41–42, 45. As Barbara Smith pointed out in her groundbreaking essay, even when sociopolitical location and economic standing have not restricted one's access to print, books portraying black lesbian life have nonetheless been almost nonexistent: "I want most of all for Black women and Black lesbians somehow not to be alone. . . . Just one work to reflect the reality that I and the Black women whom I love are trying to create. When such a book exists, then each of us will not only know better how to live, but how to dream." See Barbara Smith, "Toward a Black Feminist Criticism," *All the Women Are White, All the Blacks Are Men, But Some of Us Are Brave: Black Women's Studies*, ed. Gloria T. Hull, Patricia Bell Scott, and Barbara Smith (New York: The Feminist Press, 1982), 173; reprinted in *The New Feminist Criticism: Essays on Women, Literature and Theory*, ed. Elaine Showalter (New York: Pantheon Books, 1985) 168–185.

10   The explicit connection between lesbian periodical publications and the subsequent proliferation of edited anthologies is perhaps best illustrated by such collections as Beth [Degonwadont] Brant, ed., *A Gathering of the Spirit: Writing and Art by North American Indian Women* (Ithaca: Firebrand, 1988); Melanie Kaye/Kantrowitz and Irena Klepfisz, eds., *The Tribe of Dina: A Jewish Women's Anthology* (Boston: Beacon Press, 1989); and Barbara Smith, ed., *Home Girls: A Black Feminist Anthology* (New York: Kitchen Table: Women of Color Press, 1983). Substantial portions of these lesbian-inclusive anthologies appeared previously in numbers 22/23 and 29/30 of the journal *Sinister Wisdom* and *Conditions: Five, The Black Women's Issue*.

11   The slogan was the motto of Anne Pride's KNOW, Inc., a feminist publisher of leaflets and pamphlets.

12   Bertha Harris, *Lover* (1976; reprint, with an introduction by Harris, New York: New York University Press, 1993), xxx. Taken together, the new introduction to this edition of *Lover* and the afterword to the Naiad reprint of Elana Nachman/Dykewomon's *Riverfinger Women* (Daughters, Inc., 1974; Tallahassee, Florida: The Naiad Press, 1992), provide much insight into the extratextual conditions

that produced the two novels and the deliberately male-model, capitalist manage-ment practices that guided Daughters. The 1985 *Lesbian Nuns* scandal that nearly destroyed Naiad Press—the lesbian publishing house that sold the serial rights to portions of *Lesbian Nuns* to *Forum* (a subsidiary of *Penthouse*) without the prior knowledge or consent of contributing authors—is also a flagrant example of the conflicts of interest that afflicted some of the independent lesbian presses. See Bar-bara Grier on *"Lesbian Nuns," off our backs* 15 (8) (August-September 1985): 29; Midge Stocker, "More Than a Controversy—*Lesbian Nuns*: a Brief History," *Hot Wire: The Journal of Women's Music and Culture* 2 (2) (March 1986): 52–53, 62; and Susanna J. Sturgis, "Breaking Silence, Breaking Faith: the Promotion of *Lesbian Nuns*," *Lesbian Ethics* 1 (3) (Fall 1985): 89–107.

13   Marcia Freedman, *Exile in the Promised Land: A Memoir* (Ithaca: Firebrand Books, 1990), 211.

14   Terri de la Peña, *Margins* (Seattle, Washington: Seal, 1992), 116–117.

15   Jane P. Tompkins, "Sentimental Power: Uncle Tom's Cabin and the Poli-tics of Literary History," in *The New Feminist Criticism*, 84. According to Bonnie Zimmerman, "[U]nlike the dominant culture, or even mainstream feminist cul-ture, both of which expect artists and writers to possess special talents, lesbian cul-ture operates under the assumption that if any woman can be a lesbian, then any lesbian can (and should) be a writer. . . . [Lesbian] [w]riters are more likely to be motivated by politics than by art" (*The Safe Sea of Women*, 18). See also Kate Brandt's interviews with Barbara Smith and Sarah Schulman, in which the writers discuss the issue of literary value (114, 209–210); Bonnie Zimmerman's reading of Barbara Smith's call for an ethical or political approach to literary criticism in "Lesbians Like This and That: Some Notes on Lesbian Criticism for the Nine-ties," in *New Lesbian Criticism: Literary and Cultural Readings*, ed. Sally Munt (New York: Columbia University Press, 1992), 1–15; Jewelle Gomez's discussion of po-liticized black attitudes toward and assumptions about writing, which is more util-itarian than entertaining, in "Speculative Fiction and Black Lesbians," *Signs* 18 (4) (1993): 948–955.

16   Gloria Anzaldúa, "Haciendo caras, una entrada,"in *Making Face, Making Soul/Haciendo Caras: Creative and Critical Perspectives by Women of Color*, ed. Gloria Anzaldúa (San Francisco: Aunt Lute Foundation Books, 1990), xxiv.

17   Chrystos, "Not Editable," in *Making Face, Making Soul*, 224.

18   Norma Alarcón, "The Theoretical Subject(s) of *This Bridge Called My Back* and Anglo-American Feminism," in *Criticism in the Borderlands: Studies in Chicano Literature, Culture, and Ideology*, ed. Héctor Calderón and José David Sal-dívar (Durham: Duke University Press, 1991), 28.

19   Judith Butler, *Gender Trouble: Feminism and the Subversion of Identity* (New York: Routledge, 1990), 13.

20   Jean-François Lyotard, *The Postmodern Condition: A Report on Knowledge*, trans. Geoff Bennington and Brian Massumi (Minneapolis: University of Minne-sota Press, 1984), 18.

21   Although she does not include lesbianism or homosexuality as categories of oppression in her study, Barbara Harlow provides an excellent analysis of politi-cal resistance writing in Third World and international contexts in *Resistance Lit-*

erature (New York: Methuen, 1987). See also Barbara Harlow, "Sites of Struggle: Immigration, Deportation, Prison, and Exile," in *Criticism in the Borderlands*, 149–163.

22   Lore Segal, "On the Second Book of Samuel," *Commentary: Contemporary Writers Read the Jewish Bible*, quoted in Melanie Kaye/Kantrowitz, *My Jewish Face and Other Stories* (San Francisco: Spinsters/Aunt Lute Book Company, 1990), 235.

23   Cherríe Moraga, *Loving in the War Years: lo que nunca pasó sus labios* (Boston: South End Press, 1983), iv–v. Barbara Smith's pithy comment in 1977 that she was "not convinced that one can write explicitly as a Black lesbian and live to tell about it," remains a powerful reminder that critical writing can be similarly life threatening when the writer is a lesbian of color ("Toward a Black Feminist Criticism," 172).

24   Sarah Schulman, *People In Trouble* (New York: New American Library, 1990), 1.

25   Melanie Kaye/Kantrowitz, "My Jewish Face," in *My Jewish Face and Other Stories* (San Francisco: Spinsters/Aunt Lute Book Company, 1990), 143.

26   Kaye/Kantrowitz's theoretical and political views are collected in *The Issue Is Power: Essays on Women, Jews, Violence, and Resistance* (San Francisco: Aunt Lute Foundation Books, 1992).

27   Evelyn Torton Beck dismantles the passing-privilege myth, treating candidly Jewish passing as a greatly misunderstood form of "degradation and denial," in the second edition of *Nice Jewish Girls*. See Evelyn Torton Beck, ed., *Nice Jewish Girls: A Lesbian Anthology* (Persephone Press, 1982; Boston: Beacon Press, 1989), xxvi. Beck's claim (in the first edition of her anthology) that "Jewish invisibility is a symptom of anti-Semitism as surely as lesbian invisibility is a symptom of homophobia" is a critical contribution to feminist efforts, largely by Third World women, to theorize the simultaneity of multiple oppressions. See Evelyn Torton Beck, ed., *Nice Jewish Girls: A Lesbian Anthology* (Watertown, MA: Persephone Press, 1982), xv. See also Beck's influential essay "The Politics of Invisibility," *NWSA Journal* 1 (1988): 93–102.

28   Although all the lesbian and lesbian-feminist anthologies and collections published throughout the 1980s and early 1990s are too numerous to cite here, a sampling of some of the influential texts includes Paula Gunn Allen, ed., *Spider Woman's Granddaughters: Traditional Tales and Contemporary Writing by Native American Women* (Boston: Beacon Press, 1989); Anzaldúa, *Making Face, Making Soul*; Beck, *Nice Jewish Girls*; Evelyn Torton Beck, Minnie Bruce Pratt, and Barbara Smith, ed., *Yours In Struggle: Three Feminist Perspectives on Anti-Semitism and Racism* (New York: Firebrand Books, 1984); Elly Bulkin, ed., *Lesbian Fiction: An Anthology* (Watertown, MA: Persephone Press, 1981); Hull, Scott, and Smith, *All the Women Are White, All the Blacks Are Men*; Kaye/Kantrowitz and Klepfisz, *The Tribe of Dina*; Sharon Lim-Hing, ed., *The Very Inside: An Anthology of Writing by Asian and Pacific Islander Lesbian and Bisexual Women* (Toronto: Sister Vision Press, 1994); Cherríe Moraga and Gloria Anzaldúa, eds., *This Bridge Called My Back: Writings By Radical Women of Color* (Persephone Press, 1981; New York: Kitchen Table: Women of Color Press, 1983); Juanita Ramos, ed., *Compañeras: Latina Lesbians* (Latina Lesbian History Project, 1987; New York: Routledge, 1994);

Makeda Silvera, ed., *Piece of My Heart: A Lesbian of Colour Anthology* (Toronto: Sister Vision Press, 1991); Smith, *Home Girls: A Black Feminist Anthology*; and Carla Trujillo, ed., *Chicana Lesbians: The Girls Our Mothers Warned Us About* (Berkeley: Third Woman Press, 1991). For recent writing by Asian-Canadian lesbians, see Sharon Fernandez, et al., eds., "Awakening Thunder: Asian Canadian Women," special issue of *Fireweed: A Feminist Quarterly* 30 (1990). For cogender collections, see Rakesh Ratti, ed., *A Lotus of Another Color: An Unfolding of the South Asian Gay and Lesbian Experience* (Boston: Alyson Publications, 1993); and Will Roscoe, ed., *Living the Spirit: A Gay American Indian Anthology* (New York: St. Martin's Press, 1988).

29   Focusing less on sexuality than on gender, Chandra Talpade Mohanty provides one of the most compelling discussions to date about the "interconnections of consciousness, identity, and writing" and the role of writing in Third World women's oppositional politics and engagements with feminism ("Introduction: Cartographies of Struggle," 33). For analyses of the political dimensions of Latina autobiographies, see Lourdes Torres, "The Construction of Self in U.S. Latina Autobiographies," *Third World Women*, 271–287; Norma Alarcón, "The Theoretical Subject(s) of *This Bridge Called My Back* and Anglo-American Feminism." For a cogent treatment of bilingualism as a form of linguistic/literary alienation, exile or "deterritorialization"—"the displacement of identities, persons, and meanings that is endemic to the postmodern world system" (188)—see Caren Kaplan, "Deterritorializations: The Rewriting of Home and Exile in Western Feminist Discourse," *Cultural Critique* 6 (1987): 187–198; and Anzaldúa, *Making Face, Making Soul*, xxii–xxiv.

30   In "Bridge, Drawbridge, Sandbar or Island," Gloria Anzaldúa registers the potential danger of collectivist appeals for people of color when they are imposed upon rather than asserted by them:

> Because people-of-color are treated generically by the dominant culture—their seeing and treating us as parts of a whole, rather than just as individuals—this forces us to experience ourselves collectively. I have been held accountable by some white people for Richard Rodriguez's views and have been asked to justify Cesar Chavez's political strategies. . . . Yet, were I to hold a white woman responsible for Ronald Reagan's acts, she would be shocked because to herself she is an individual (nor is her being white named because it is taken for granted as a norm).
>
> I think we people-of-color can turn this fusion or confusion of individual/collectivity around and use it as a tool for collective strength and not as an oppressive representation. We can subvert it and use it. It could serve as one base for intimate connection between personal and collective in solidarity work and in alliances across differences (220).

31   While the influential Third World feminist anthologies edited and published by lesbians of color, including *Home Girls*, *This Bridge Called My Back*, and *Making Face, Making Soul/Haciendo Caras*, have been central to the development of North American lesbians' political consciousness, the more pressing political desire of their editors, according to Cherríe Moraga, was to create a greatly needed "broad-based U.S. women-of-color movement capable of spanning borders of nation and ethnicity." See Moraga, "Refugees of a World on Fire: Foreword to the

Second Edition," *This Bridge Called My Back*. It is the recognition of their lesbian subjectivity that has nonetheless crucially informed some Third World writers' understanding of the interconnections between multiple interlocking axes of identity. As Moraga explains in the "La Güera" section of *Loving in the War Years: lo que nunca pasó sus labios*, "[M]y lesbianism is the avenue through which I have learned the most about silence and oppression, and it continues to be the most tactile reminder to me that we are not free human beings" (52).

32   Given the great many collaborative writing productions that both fostered a remarkable level of mutual understanding between lesbians from diverse backgrounds and informed the widespread theoretical interest in identity politics, it is ironic that critics have accorded Minnie Bruce Pratt's "Identity: Skin Blood Heart"—a moving account of a Southern white lesbian's effort to unlearn racism and anti-Semitism—precisely the level of cultural/critical dominance that Pratt herself tries to dismantle with her contribution to the jointly anchored text, *Yours In Struggle*. The frequency with which scholars invoke Pratt's essay as the model for understanding internalized dominance more than a decade since its publication indicates the critical need for a more thorough investigation of the vital connections between identity, experience, and politics that carried so many disparate lesbians to press during the 1970s and 1980s. For critical treatments of Pratt's essay, see Biddy Martin and Chandra Talpade Mohanty, "Feminist Politics: What's Home Got to Do with It?" in *Feminist Studies/Critical Studies*, ed. Teresa de Lauretis (Bloomington: University of Indiana Press, 1986), 191–212; Kaplan, "Deterritorializations: The Rewriting of Home and Exile," 187–198; Biddy Martin, "Lesbian Identity and Autobiographical Differences," *Life/Lines: Theorizing Women's Autobiography*, ed. Bella Brodzki and Celeste Schenck (Ithaca: Cornell University Press, 1988), 77–103; Ed Cohen, "Who Are 'We'? Gay 'Identity' as Political (E)motion: (A Theoretical Rumination)," in *Inside/Out: Lesbian Theories, Gay Theories*, ed. Diana Fuss (London: Routledge, 1991), 71–92; Teresa de Lauretis, "Queer Theory: Lesbian and Gay Sexualities—An Introduction," *Differences: A Journal of Feminist Cultural Studies* 3 (1991): iii–xviii; and Kathleen Martindale and Martha Saunders, "Realizing Love and Justice: Lesbian Ethics in the Upper and Lower Case," *Hypatia* 7 (4) (Fall 1992): 148–171.

33   Joseph Beam, "Introduction: Leaving the Shadows Behind," in *In the Life: A Black Gay Anthology*, ed. Joseph Beam (Boston: Alyson Publications, 1986) 13.

34   Barbara Smith, quoted in Tricia Lootens, "Third National Women In Print Conference," *Off Our Backs: A Women's News Journal* 15 (8) (1985): 23.

CHAPTER 4:

HERMAN, ALL IN THE FAMILY

1   I use the term "motherhood" to refer both to the biological status of some lesbian mothers and to the co-parenting, adoptive, or foster care status of others.

2   For more general reading in these areas, see Rita Arditti, Renate Duelli Klein, and Shelley Minden, eds., *Test-Tube Women: What Future for Motherhood?*

(Boston: Pandora Press, 1984); Susan Faludi, *Backlash: The Undeclared War Against American Women* (New York: Anchor Books, 1991); and Marlene Gerber Fried, *From Abortion to Reproductive Freedom: Transforming a Movement* (Boston: South End Press, 1990).

3   Stephanie Coontz, *The Way We Never Were: American Families and the Nostalgia Trap* (New York: Basic Books, 1992).

4   Brian McGrory, "Gays see growing backlash: Face potential defeats on rights across US," *Boston Globe*, 28 November 1993, sec. 1, p. 20.

5   For updates on legal developments, contact The Lambda Legal Defense and Education Fund, Inc., 666 Broadway, New York, NY 10012; the Lesbian Mothers' National Defense Fund, P.O. Box 21567, Seattle, WA 98111; or the National Center for Lesbian Rights, 1363 Mission St., San Francisco, CA 94103.

6   Quoted in Sasha Gregory Lewis, *Sunday's Women: A Report on Lesbian Life Today* (Boston: Beacon Press, 1975), 116. For more on lesbian custody cases, see Ellen Lewin, "Lesbianism and Motherhood: Implications for Child Custody," *Human Organization* 40 (1) (1981): 6–14.

7   M–6219, Mass. Sup. Jud. Ct., September 10, 1993.

8   For an analysis of these contrasting cases, see Nancy D. Polikoff, "Lesbian and Gay Parenting: What's at Stake," *Gay Community News*, special fall 1993 issue, 3, 14.

9   Phyllis Burke, *Family Values: Two Moms and Their Son* (New York: Random House, 1993).

10   Ellen Herman, *Psychiatry, Psychology, and Homosexuality* (New York: Chelsea House Publishers, 1995).

11   Caitlin Ryan and Judith Bradford, "The National Lesbian Health Care Survey: An Overview," in *Psychological Perspectives on Lesbian & Gay Male Experiences*, eds. Linda D. Garnets & Douglas C. Kimmel (New York: Columbia University Press, 1993), 550, 552–54.

12   For those not already familiar with this jargon, an addiction is generally defined as any substance or process over which a person is powerless, while codependence refers to any intimate relationship—past or present—with an addict, or to the consequences of growing up in a dysfunctional family.

13   Susan Forward, *Toxic Parents: Overcoming Their Hurtful Legacy and Reclaiming Your Life* (New York: Bantam Books, 1989), 166.

14   John Bradshaw, *Bradshaw on: The Family: A Revolutionary Way of Self-Discovery* (Deerfield Beach, FL: Health Communications, Inc., 1988), 31, emphasis in original.

15   Observers sometimes note the similarities between "adult childhood" and posttraumatic stress disorder, an array of symptoms first identified in Vietnam War veterans and now associated with a wide range of traumatic experiences, including a number that often take place within the familial context, such as child sexual abuse.

16   Anne Wilson Schaef, *When Society Becomes an Addict* (New York: Harper & Row, 1987), 15.

17   Dennis Wholey, *Becoming Your Own Parent: The Solution for Adult Children of Alcoholic and Other Dysfunctional Families* (New York: Doubleday, 1988), 22–23.

18   Bradshaw, *Bradshaw on: The Family*, 154.

19   Wholey, *Becoming Your Own Parent*, 162.

20   Forward, *Toxic Parents*, 317.

21   Nancy Chodorow, *The Reproduction of Mothering: Psychoanalysis and the Sociology of Gender* (Berkeley: University of California Press, 1978); Dorothy Dinnerstein, *The Mermaid and the Minotaur* (New York: Harper and Row, 1976).

22   Schaef, *When Society Becomes an Addict*, 37.

23   Schaef, *When Society Becomes an Addict*, 17.

24   Janet Mary Gottler, "Cultural Pioneers: The New Lesbian Families" (master's thesis, Smith School of Social Work, 1984), 54.

25   Quoted in Deborah Goleman Wolf, *The Lesbian Community* (Berkeley: University of California Press, 1979), 150–51, emphasis in original.

26   Ellen Lewin, *Lesbian Mothers: Accounts of Gender in American Culture* (Ithaca: Cornell University Press, 1993).

27   For a very thoughtful piece on these questions by a lesbian mother, see Nancy D. Polikoff, "Lesbians Choosing Children: The Personal Is Political Revisited," in *Politics of the Heart: A Lesbian Parenting Anthology*, eds. Sandra Pollack and Jeanne Vaughn (Ithaca: Firebrand Books, 1987), 48–54.

28   For an interesting story about coming out as a family, see Kt. Vermeulen, "A Family Comes Out," *Outlook* 3(3) (1991): 46–48.

CHAPTER 5:
LEWIN, "WHY IN THE WORLD WOULD YOU
WANT TO DO THAT?"

Earlier versions of this paper were presented at the University of California, Riverside; San Diego State University; the University of Chicago; Sonoma State University; the University of California, Santa Cruz; the Sixth North American Lesbian, Gay and Bisexual Studies Conference; the American Anthropological Association; the University of California, Los Angeles; and the Institute for Research on Women and Gender, Stanford University. I want particularly to thank Esther Newton, William Leap, and Liz Goodman for their comments and to acknowledge the support of the National Endowment for the Humanities and the Institute for Research on Women and Gender.

1   Paula L. Ettelbrick, "Since When Is Marriage a Path to Liberation?" and Thomas B. Stoddard, "Why Gay People Should Seek the Right to Marry," in Suzanne Sherman, ed., *Gay and Lesbian Marriage: Private Commitments, Public Ceremonies* (Philadelphia: Temple University Press, 1992), 20–26 and 13–19, respectively.

2   Suzanne Sherman, ed., *Gay and Lesbian Marriage: Private Commitments, Public Ceremonies* (Philadelphia: Temple University Press, 1992), 1–2.

3   Gilbert Herdt, "Introduction: Culture, History, and Life Course of Gay Men," in *Gay Culture in America* (Boston: Beacon Press, 1992), 1–28.

4   See, for example, George Chauncey, *Gay New York: Gender, Urban Cul-*

ture, and the Making of the Gay Male World, 1890–1940 (New York: Basic Books, 1994); John D'Emilio, *Sexual Politics, Sexual Communities: The Making of a Homosexual Minority in the United States, 1940–1970* (Chicago: University of Chicago Press, 1983); Martin Bauml Duberman, Martha Vicinus, and George C. Chauncey Jr., eds., *Hidden From History: Reclaiming the Gay and Lesbian Past* (New York: New American Library, 1989); Lillian Faderman, *Odd Girls and Twilight Lovers: A History of Lesbian Life in Twentieth-Century America* (New York: Columbia University Press, 1991); Gilbert Herdt and Andrew Boxer, *Children of Horizons* (Boston: Beacon Press, 1993); Elizabeth L. Kennedy and Madeline D. Davis, *Boots of Leather, Slippers of Gold: The History of a Lesbian Community* (New York: Routledge, 1993); Esther Newton, *Cherry Grove, Fire Island: Sixty Years in America's First Gay and Lesbian Town* (Boston: Beacon Press, 1993); Kath Weston, *Families We Choose: Lesbians, Gays, Kinship* (New York: Columbia University Press, 1991).

5   Lila Abu-Lughod, "The Romance of Resistance: Tracing Transformations of Power through Bedouin Women," *American Ethnologist*, 17(1)(1990): 41–55.

6   James Scott, *Weapons of the Weak: Everyday Forms of Peasant Resistance* (New Haven: Yale University Press, 1985).

7   Jean Comaroff, *Body of Power, Spirit of Resistance: The Culture and History of a South African People* (Chicago: University of Chicago Press, 1985); David I. Kertzer, *Ritual, Power, and Politics* (New Haven: Yale University Press, 1988).

8   Ellen Lewin, *Lesbian Mothers: Accounts of Gender in American Culture* (Ithaca, NY: Cornell University Press, 1993).

9   Anita Diamant, *The New Jewish Wedding* (New York: Summit Books, 1985).

10   All subjects quoted in this paper are identified by pseudonyms.

11   A later conversation with the rabbi confirmed my suspicion that Conservative Judaism does, in fact, oppose same-sex marriages as a matter of policy, though sanctions imposed on rabbis who perform such ceremonies are only informal. (In contrast, rabbis who perform or even attend interfaith weddings risk expulsion from the Conservative rabbinate.)

12   The Seven Blessings (with the "eighth blessing" inserted between the fourth and fifth) are as follows (emphasis mine):

1. Blessed is Ha Shem, Source of All Creation, creator of fruit of the vine.

2. Blessed is Ha Shem, Source of All Creation, creator of the universe.

3. Blessed is Ha Shem, Source of All Creation, creator of humanity.

4. Blessed is Ha Shem, Source of All Creation, creator of human beings in the divine image. Blessed are You, Adonai our God, You endow each of us with life, with the power of creation, with a bond to all humankind through Your Oneness.

4a. Blessed is Ha Shem, Source of All Creation, creator of love and passion between woman and woman, man and man, woman and man. Blessed are you, Adonai our God, you open our hearts to love, and strengthen us to walk with dignity among those who are different from us.

5. May the dream of Zion inspire us to create a life of goodness, wisdom and generosity, a world of compassion, justice and peace. Blessed are you, Adonai

our God, You rejoice, as a mother reunited with her children, when the promise of humanity is fulfilled.

6. May the perfect joy of the Garden of Eden envelop these two beloved companions. Blessed are you, Adonai our God, You sanctify the rejoicing of these unique souls united in love.

7. Blessed is the Mystery, Source of All Creation, creator of joy and gladness, lover and beloved, awe and exultation, pleasure and delight, love and harmony, peace and friendship. Soon may we hear from the streets of every city and the paths of every field the voice of joy and gladness, the voice of the lover and the voice of *her* beloved, the voices of *brides* rising from beneath the chuppah, the voices of celebrants lifted in song at their wedding feasts. You Abound in Blessings, Adonai our God, You rejoice with these lovers united in marriage.

13 A San Francisco ordinance in effect since February 14, 1991 allows gay and straight couples to register as domestic partners. Like similar provisions in many other localities, the measure provides a minimal level of official recognition though it extends virtually none of the legal benefits of marriage to the couples who register. In some cases, employers who provide benefits to employees' domestic partners may require the registration to verify their status.

14 The Sisters of Perpetual Indulgence are a group of gay men who have been performing a particularly outrageous form of political street theatre in San Francisco for many years. The Sisters dress as nuns, but in the exaggeratedly incongruous style of "gender fuck"; typically their "habits" are worn with such accessories as full beards, motorcycle boots, and chains. The Sisters adopt pseudonyms such as Sister Missionary Position and often focus their performances around political but sexually charged themes.

15 *Namaste* means "I salute you" in Hindi.

16 This is most likely a reference to John Boswell's well-known research on early Christianity, later published as *Same-Sex Unions in Premodern Europe* (New York: Villard, 1994), although this book had not yet appeared at the time of this ceremony.

17 Barbara Myerhoff, "We Don't Wrap Herring in a Printed Page: Fusion, Fictions and Continuity in a Secular Ritual," in Sally Falk Moore and Barbara G. Myerhoff, eds., *Secular Ritual* (Amsterdam: Van Gorcum, 1977), 199–224.

18 Barbara Myerhoff, "A Death in Due Time: Conviction, Order, and Continuity in Ritual Drama," in Marc Kaminsky, ed., *Remembered Lives: The Work of Ritual, Storytelling, and Growing Older* (Ann Arbor: University of Michigan Press, 1992), 159–190.

19 Bruce Bawer, *A Place at the Table* (New York: Poseidon Press, 1993).

CHAPTER 6:
WESTON, REQUIEM FOR A STREET FIGHTER

Many thanks to Esther Newton and Geeta Patel for their insightful comments on an earlier draft of this chapter. A draft of the essay was presented at the 1991 Out-

Write: National Gay and Lesbian Writers Conference, in San Francisco. An earlier version appeared in *Out in the Field: Reflections of Lesbian and Gay Anthropologists*, ed. Ellen Lewin and William Leap (Urbana: University of Illinois Press, 1996), pp. 274–285.

1   "As to my *Requiem*, perhaps I have also instinctively sought to escape from what is thought right and proper, after all the years of accompanying burial services on the organ! I know it all by heart. I wanted to write something different" (translated in Robert Orledge, *Gabriel Fauré* [London: Eulenburg Books, 1979], 113). On Fauré's attempt to develop to develop a composition that could meld classical structure with artistic innovations, see Jean-Michel Nectoux, *Gabriel Fauré: A Musical Life*, trans. Roger Nichols (New York: Cambridge University Press, 1991). Subheadings in this essay derive from the expanded orchestral version of Fauré's *Requiem*, Opus 48.

2   On the lack of any necessary correspondence between "insider" status and nearness to the people who end up at the focus of a research study, see José Limón, "Representation, Ethnicity, and the Precursory Ethnography: Notes of a Native Anthropologist," in *Recapturing Anthropology: Working in the Present*, ed. Richard G. Fox (Santa Fe: School of American Research Press, 1991), 115–135; and Greg Sarris, "What I'm Talking about When I'm Talking about My Baskets: Conversations with Mabel McKay," in *De/Colonizing the Subject: The Politics of Gender in Women's Autobiography*, ed. Sidonie Smith and Julia Watson (Minneapolis: University of Minnesota Press, 1991), 20–33. Dorinne Kondo, in *Crafting Selves: Power, Gender, and Discourses of Identity in a Japanese Workplace* (Chicago: University of Chicago Press, 1990), discusses her experience of a "collapse of identity" as a Japanese-American woman conducting research in Japan. For Ruth Behar, fieldwork precipitated a "personal crisis of representation" that entailed situating herself as (among other things) "another new mestiza who has infiltrated the academy" (*Translated Woman: Crossing the Border with Esperanza's Story* [Boston: Beacon Press, 1993], 339). On the ever-shifting category "self," see also Judith Butler, "Imitation and Gender Insubordination," in *Inside/Out: Lesbian Theories, Gay Theories*, ed. Diana Fuss, (New York: Routledge, 1991), 13–31.

3   Jill Johnston, *Lesbian Nation* (New York: Simon and Schuster, 1973); Lila Abu-Lughod, *Veiled Sentiments: Honor and Poetry in a Bedouin Society* (Berkeley: University of California Press, 1986), Richard Handler, *Nationalism and the Politics of Culture in Quebec* (Madison: University of Wisconsin Press, 1988), Audre Lorde, *The Black Unicorn* (New York: Norton, 1978).

4   Gloria Anzaldúa, *Borderlands/La Frontera* (San Francisco: Spinsters/Aunt Lute, 1987); David Bergman, ed., *Camp Grounds: Style and Homosexuality* (Amherst: University of Massachusetts Press, 1993); Gay American Indians and Will Roscoe, eds., *Living the Spirit: A Gay American Indian Anthology* (New York: St. Martin's Press, 1988).

5   Taken, respectively, from Judith Butler, *Gender Trouble: Feminism and the Subversion of Identity* (New York: Routledge, 1990); Catherine Lutz, *Unnatural Emotions: Everyday Sentiments on a Micronesian Atoll and Their Challenge to Western Theory* (Chicago: University of Chicago Press, 1988), James T. Sears, *Growing Up Gay in the South: Race, Gender, and Journeys of the Spirit* (New York: Haworth Press,

1991), and Elizabeth A. Povinelli, *Labor's Lot: The Power, History, and Culture of Aboriginal Action* (Chicago: University of Chicago Press, 1993).

6   Robert R. Alvarez, Jr., *Familia: Migration and Adaptation in Baja and Alta California 1800–1975* (Berkeley: University of California Press, 1987); Vincent Crapanzano, *Waiting: The Whites of South Africa* (New York: Random House, 1985); Jonathan Boyarin, *Storm from Paradise: The Politics of Jewish Memory* (Minneapolis: University of Minnesota Press, 1992).

7   Kath Weston, *Families We Choose: Lesbians, Gays, Kinship* (New York: Columbia University Press, 1991).

8   B. Jaye Miller, "From Silence to Suicide: Measuring a Mother's Loss," in *Homophobia: How We All Pay the Price*, ed. Warren J. Blumenfeld (Boston: Beacon Press, 1992), 79–94; Gary Remafedi, ed., *Death By Denial: Studies of Suicide in Gay and Lesbian Teenagers* (Boston: Alyson Publications, 1994); Eric E. Rofes, "*I Thought People Like That Killed Themselves*": *Lesbians, Gay Men, and Suicide* (San Francisco: Grey Fox Press, 1983).

CHAPTER 7:
AMORY, CLUB Q

1   The club reappeared again in 1994, but has never regained the phenomenal popularity it enjoyed in those early years.

2   Karen Everett, *Framing Lesbian Fashion* (1992). Distributed by Wolfe Video, P.O. Box 64, New Almaden, CA 95042; (408) 268-6782.

3   Many friends and colleagues have contributed to my thinking about the world in general and this article in particular. I would like to thank: Ellen Lewin, Jacqueline Nassy Brown, Karen Stroud, Asale Ajani, Jared Braiterman, Mrs. Gigi L'Amoure, William Maurer, Joel Streiker, and Donald Moore. Finally, I thank the smartest girl I know, Pattie Wall.

4   Public discussion of the term "lipstick lesbian" seems to date back to the famous *Wall Street Journal* article on lesbians at Yale that described tensions between "lipstick lesbians" and "crunchies" (granola-heads who followed more traditional lesbian-feminist codes of dress and politics). The term was certainly in common use by the late eighties, and is cited by Lisa Duggan, "The Anguished Cry of an Eighties Fem: 'I Want to be a Drag Queen,'" *Out/Look* 1(1) (1988):63–65, and Arlene Stein, "Style Wars and the New Lesbianism," *Out/Look* 1(4) (1989): 34–42.

5   For example, see Terralee Bensinger, "Lesbian Pornography: The Re/Making of (a) Community," *Discourse* 15(1) (1992): 69–93; Lisa Duggan, "Making it Perfectly Queer," *Socialist Review* 22 (1) (1992): 11–31; and various essays in Arlene Stein's edited volume, *Sisters, Sexperts, Queers* (New York: Plume, 1993), including Camille Roy, "Speaking in Tongues," 6–12; Arlene Stein, "The Year of the Lustful Lesbian," 13–34, and Vera Whisman, "Identity Crises: Who is a Lesbian, Anyway?" 47–60. Finally, Karen Everett's video, *Framing Lesbian Fashion*, visually documents this history.

6   Editors of several volumes of feminist theory raise the issues of race and class, including Sue Ellen Case's introduction to *Performing Feminisms: Feminist Critical Theory and Theater* (Baltimore: Johns Hopkins University Press, 1990), and Linda Nicholson's introduction to *Feminism/Postmodernism* (New York: Routledge, 1990). For important analyses that integrate race and class into discussions of sexuality, see Richard Fung, "Looking for My Penis: The Eroticized Asian in Gay Video Porn," in *How Do I Look?* ed. Bad Object Choices (Seattle: Bay Press, 1991), 145–168; Jackie Goldsby, "What it Means to be Colored Me," *Out/Look* 3(1): 8–17; and Biddy Martin's essays, including "Sexual Practice and Changing Lesbian Identities," in *Destabilizing Theory: Contemporary Feminist Debates*, ed. Michele Barrett and Anne Phillips (Stanford: Stanford University Press), 93–119; and "Lesbian Identity and Autobiographical Difference[s]," in *Life/Lines: Theorizing Women's Autobiography*, ed. Bella Brodzki and Celeste Schenck (Ithaca: Cornell University Press, 1988), 77–103.

7   Ruth Frankenburg has recently begun the important work of theorizing "whiteness" as a racial category in *White Women, Race Matters* (Minneapolis: University of Minnesota Press, 1993).

8   Norma Alarcón addresses issues of race (and racism) in feminist theory in her essay, "The Theoretical Subject(s) of *This Bridge Called My Back* and Anglo-American Feminism," *Making Face, Making Soul: Haciendo Caras*, ed. Gloria Anzaldúa (San Francisco: Aunt Lute, 1990), 356–369.

9   My emphasis on "sameness and difference" comes from my own idiosyncratic reading of Case's introduction to *Performing Feminisms*.

10   Although cruising is regarded as a time-honored gay male activity, the art seems to have been only recently introduced to more academic discussions of lesbian lives.

11   Elizabeth Kennedy and Madeline Davis's *Boots of Leather, Slippers of Gold* departs from this tradition by explicitly examining the history of Buffalo's lesbian communities in terms of both race and class.

12   The research for this article was conducted during 1989 and 1990, including numerous trips to Club Q, interviews with club-goers, and a survey conducted in August of 1990, six months after the club started to meet weekly. I would like to thank Donna Daniels for originally working with me on this project, Sami Sparks for invaluable assistance as my official research assistant, and Page Hodel for her gracious cooperation.

13   Gloria Anzaldúa, *Borderlands: La Frontera* (San Francisco: Spinsters/Aunt Lute, 1987).

14   In particular, these challenges have been located in debates about feminist epistemology. See, for example, Donna Haraway, "Situated Knowledges: The Science Question in Feminism and the Privilege of Partial Perspective," *Feminist Studies* 14(3) (1988): 575–599; Linda Nicholson's edited volume, *Feminism/Postmodernism*, including the articles by Jane Flax, "Postmodernism and Gender Relations in Feminist Theory," 39–62, and Sandra Harding, "Feminism, Science, and the Anti-Enlightenment Critiques," 83–106.

15   See, for example, Norma Alarcón's "The Theoretical Subjects of *This Bridge Called My Back*"; Teresa de Lauretis, "Eccentric Subjects: Feminist Theory

and Historical Consciousness," *Feminist Studies* 16 (1) (1990): 115–150; and Chandra Mohanty, "Feminist Encounters: Locating the Politics of Experience," in *Destabilizing Theory: Contemporary Feminist Debates*, ed. Michele Barrett and Anne Phillips (Stanford: Stanford University Press, 1990), 74–92.

16   In many ways this critique grew out of the publication of anthologies by women of color in the early eighties, including *This Bridge Called My Back: Writings by Radical Women of Color*, ed. Cherríe Moraga and Gloria Anzaldúa (Watertown: Persephone Press, 1981) and *All the Women are White, All the Blacks are Men, But Some of Us Are Brave: Black Women's Studies*, ed. Gloria T. Hull, et al. (Old Westbury, N.Y.: The Feminist Press, 1982). Gloria Anzaldúa's edited volume, *Making Face, Making Soul: Hacienda Caras* (San Francisco: Aunt Lute, 1990) continues in this same tradition. Writings concerning "postcoloniality" have further enriched the debate. See, for example, Trinh T. Minh-ha, *Woman, Native, Other: Writing Postcoloniality and Feminism* (Bloomington: Indiana University Press, 1989).

17   Judith Butler's theorization of gender as a performative act is most comprehensively described in her book *Gender Trouble* and further developed in *Bodies that Matter: On the Discursive Limits of 'Sex'* (New York: Routledge, 1993). In my account here I also draw on Teresa de Lauretis' *Technologies of Gender* (Bloomington and Indianapolis: Indiana University Press, 1987) and Monique Wittig, *The Straight Mind and Other Essays* (Boston, Beacon Press, 1992).

18   Local term for a DJ who mixes or plays records.

19   "Clean and sober" is a phrase from twelve-step programs (based on Alcoholics Anonymous) that refers to people who are no longer using alcohol or drugs. For a critical look at the addiction industry that indicates its importance to the lesbian and gay communities, see Ellen Herman, "Getting to Serenity: Do Addiction Programs Sap Our Political Vitality?" *Out/Look* 1(2) (1988): 10–21.

20   Funk has its roots in rhythm and blues. Developed by (most notably) James Brown in the late sixties, the style combines rudimentary melodies with complex rhythmic patterns created by bass and drums, as well as horns and keyboards. Sly and the Family Stone further popularized funk in the early seventies with hits like "I Want to Take You Higher," and "Thank You (Falettinme Be Mice Elf Agin)." Parliament/Funkadelic, headed by George Clinton, also redefined the notion of funk ("One Nation Under a Groove" is a good example), and Prince would be a contemporary artist working in the funk tradition. Thanks to Karen Stroud, local funk expert, for providing these details; see also Nelson George, *The Death of Rhythm and Blues* (New York: Penguin Books, 1988), especially 98–111, 153–159.

21   Thanks to Jacqueline Nassy Brown for our conversations about the links between music, music videos, dance, and border crossings at the Q.

22   Mrs. Gigi L'Amoure, personal communication with the author.

23   Renato Rosaldo, *Culture and Truth* (Boston: Beacon, 1989), 20.

24   House music came out of black gay clubs in Chicago in the early eighties; see Anthony Thomas, "The House the Kids Built: The Gay Black Imprint on American Dance Music," *Out/Look* 2(1): (1989): 24–33. House sounds something like disco but has a faster beat and fewer vocals. Thomas describes house as "pure

dance music" that highlights drums and percussion, with instrumental tracks added electronically. DJs pioneered this music as they spun records and sampled off of classic soul and disco hits. Also see Nelson George, *Buppies, B-Boys, Baps and Bohos* (New York: Harper, 1992) for essays on post-soul African-American music and identity.

25   Interestingly enough, gays and lesbians are often represented as having higher incomes than the "general" population. Clearly, the poor lesbian and gays aren't being counted. Danae Clark includes statistics on gay and lesbian income in her article, "Commodity Lesbianism," *Camera Obscura* 25 / 26 (1991): 180–201; reprinted in *The Lesbian and Gay Studies Reader*, ed. Abelove, Barale, and Halperin (New York: Routledge, 1992), 186–201. Clark argues that (middle-class) lesbian identity is constructed in response to marketing strategies of major corporations, among other things.

26   For an important discussion of fifties butch / femme style as a working class aesthetic and practice, see Kennedy and Davis, *Boots of Leather*. Joan Nestle's collection of essays, *A Restricted Country* (New York: Firebrand Books, 1987) is also a classic, and the more recent volume edited by Nestle, *The Persistent Desire: A Butch-Femme Reader* (Boston: Alyson Publications, 1992) includes a helpful survey of different writings. For a description of S / M style as the practice of a working class, urban gender terrorist, see anonymous, "S / M Aesthetic," *Out/Look* 1(4) (1989): 42–43.

27   Other people have discussed this issue, including Lisa Kahaleole Chang Hall, "Bitches in Solitude: Identity Politics and Lesbian Community," in Stein ed. *Sisters, Sexperts, Queers*, 218–229; and Ruthann Robson, "Lesbian Lesbian: A Text on Lesbian Identity with a Subtext on Essentialism / Constructionalism," *Out/Look* 3(2) (1990): 26–29.

28   "Butchbonding" refers to things two butches do together in the absence of femmes. Following the classic working-class butch / femme model, our butchbonding explicitly did not include having sex.

29   See also Teralee Bensinger, "Lesbian Pornography."

30   Stuart Hall, "What is this 'Black' in Black Popular Culture?" in *Black Popular Culture*, ed. Gina Dent (Seattle: Bay Press, 1992), 21–36, 32.

31   Ann Cvetkovich, "The Powers of Seeing and Being Seen: *Truth or Dare* and *Paris is Burning*," in *Film Theory Goes to the Movies*, ed. Collins, Radner and Collins (New York: Routledge, 1993), 155–169.

32   Ann Cvetkovich, "The Powers of Seeing and Being Seen," 158.

33   Stuart Hall reminds us: "Identities are the names we give to the different ways we are positioned by and position ourselves within the narrative of the past"; from "Cultural Identity and Diaspora," in *Identity: Community, Culture, Difference*, ed. Jonathan Rutherford (London: Lawrence & Wishart, 1990), 222–237, 225. Thanks to Jacqueline Nassy Brown for sharing her inspirational quotes with me.

34   Thanks to Bill Maurer for our conversations on this topic.

35   Here I am thinking of the work of *This Bridge* and *But Some of Us Are Brave*; other classic examples might include the essays by Elly Bulkin, Minnie Bruce Pratt, and Barbara Smith in *Yours in Struggle: Three Feminist Perspectives on Anti-Semitism and Racism* (Brooklyn: Long Haul Press, 1984); and Biddy Martin

and Chandra Talpade Mohanty, "What's Home Got to do with It?" in *Feminist Studies/Critical Studies*, ed. Teresa de Lauretis (Bloomington: Indiana University Press, 1986), 191–212.

36   Again, on butch/femme style and sexuality of the fifties, see Kennedy and Davis, *Boots of Leather*. Martha Vicinus also attempts to create more complex models for the historical roots of lesbian identity as part of her project of constructing and theorizing a history of diversity. See "'They Wonder to Which Sex I Belong': The Historical Roots of Modern Lesbian Identity," in *Homosexuality, Which Homosexuality?* ed. Dennis Altman, Carole Vance, Martha Vicinus, and Jeffrey Weeks (Amsterdam: An Dekker, 1989), reprinted in *The Lesbian and Gay Studies Reader*, ed. Abelove, Barale, and Halperin (New York: Routledge, 1992), 432–452.

37   Stuart Hall, "What is this 'Black' in Black Popular Culture?" 27.

38   Anthony Thomas, "The House the Kids Built: The Gay Black Imprint on American Dance Music."

39   Nelson George describes disco's "movers and shakers" as gay male DJs who ignored male performers and instead popularized female vocalists like Diana Ross and Donna Summer. Indeed, he seems a little crabby about the whole thing; see *The Death of Rhythm and Blues*, 154.

40   Tracy Morgan, "Butch-Femme and the Politics of Identity," in *Sisters, Sexperts, Queers*, ed. Arlene Stein (New York: Plume, 1993), 35–46.

41   In "Making it Perfectly Queer," Lisa Duggan mentions this possibility and how it reinforces binary notions of gender.

42   See, for example, Kobena Mercer, "'1968': Periodizing Postmodern Politics and Identity," in *Cultural Studies*, ed. Lawrence Grossberg, Cary Nelson, and Paula Treichler (New York: Routledge, 1992), 424–437.

CHAPTER 8:
NEWTON, "DICK(LESS) TRACY"

Holly Hughes, to whom this essay mysteriously led me, had an insider's knowledge of the performance scene and a clarity that deepened my understanding and gave me confidence in my interpretation.

A much shorter version of this essay was presented at the INQueery, INTheory, INDeed Conference at the University of Iowa in November 1994; at the Annual Meetings of the American Anthropological Association in Atlanta in December of the same year, and at the First Annual Performance Studies Conference: the Future of the Field, at NYU in March 1995. Audience response at those meetings helped me to refine my arguments.

I am very much indebted to Jill Falzoi, who whetted my preexisting appetite for lesbian performance and theater, deluged me with many books and articles by performance theorists I had not known about, and commented on a draft of this essay. Lisa Duggan's astute and friendly reading helped me sort out the issues and do the last difficult revisions.

Epigraph: Quoted in Dorothy Chansky, "WOW Cafe: A Stage of Their Own," in *Theatre Week* (Sept 1990): 39–41.

1   My work on female impersonators, who are known in the gay world as drag queens, was originally published in *Mother Camp: Female Impersonators in America* (Englewood Cliffs, N.J.: Prentice-Hall, 1972. Reissued by the University of Chicago Press in 1979; the page numbering is identical). In that book I defined "drag" as "the clothing of one sex when worn by the other sex (a suit and tie worn by a woman also constitute drag)" (3). Sarah Murray's definition is more developed: "a tradition of enacting the essential characteristics of the opposite gender through cross-dressing and use of other symbols and gestures strongly associated with that gender. I distinguish between cross-dressing as an individual practice, drag as a theatrical convention, and drag as a developed theatrical genre." (Sarah E. Murray, "Dragon Ladies, Draggin' Men: Some Reflections on Gender, Drag and Homosexual Communities," in *Public Culture* [1994] 6: 345).

2   See Elizabeth Drorbaugh, "Sliding Scales: Notes on Stormé DeLarverie and the Jewel Box Revue, the Cross-dressed Woman on the Contemporary Stage, and the Invert," Lesley Ferris, ed., *Crossing the Stage: Controversies on Cross-Dressing* (London and New York: Routledge, 1993), 120–143.

3   According to Drorbaugh (133), Stormé's performance was "seldom if ever" mentioned in newspaper reviews, even though she was the emcee and the only male impersonator.

4   Murray, 343–344. Murray emphasizes what she thinks are collective psychological differences between men and women that make drag more satisfying to men, and also the difficulties of sending up masculinity, lines of argument I do not engage here. What our approaches share is grounding in ethnography and a concern with how power shapes representation.

5   Sue-Ellen Case, "Toward a Butch / Femme Aesthetic," in *The Lesbian and Gay Studies Reader*, ed. Henry Abelove, Michèle Aina Barale, and David M. Halperin (New York and London: Routledge, 1993), 294–306.

6   I follow Gayle Rubin in defining butch as "a category of lesbian gender that is constituted through the deployment and manipulation of masculine gender codes and symbols." "Of Catamites and Kings: Reflections on Butch, Gender, and Boundaries," in *The Persistent Desire: A Femme Butch Reader*, Joan Nestle, ed. (Boston: Alyson Publications, 1992), 467.

7   Newton, 106–111.

8   Judith Butler, *Gender Trouble: Feminism and the Subversion of Identity* (New York and London: Routledge, 1990), 146, and "Imitation and Gender Insubordination," *The Lesbian and Gay Studies Reader*, 314.

9   This point has been made by performance theorist Kate Davy in "Fe/male Impersonation: The Discourse of Camp," in Janelle G. Reinelt and Joseph R. Roach, *Critical Theory and Performance* (Ann Arbor, University of Michigan Press, 1992), 231–247.

10   Kath Weston, "Do Clothes Make the Woman? Gender, Performance Theory, and Lesbian Eroticism," in *Genders* 17 (fall 1993): 6, cites an earlier example by Marilyn Frye in 1983 that conflates butch-femme with gay male drag in the term "queer role-playing," which she contrasts favorably to heterosexual gender

performance, as the latter lacks the former's humor and theatricality. However, it was Case's piece, along with Judith Butler's work, that seems to have stimulated the current flutter in performance studies over butch-femme.

Murray and I aren't the first anthropologists to engage with the performance theorists' ideas about butch-femme. Although they refer only briefly to Case's essay, Elizabeth Lapovsky Kennedy and her co-author Madeline Davis ("'They was no one to mess with': The construction of the butch role in the lesbian community of the 1940s and 1950s," in *The Persistent Desire*, ed. Joan Nestle [Boston: Alyson Publications, 1992], 62–79) specifically compare "the role of the butch with that of the queen" (63) in order to "illuminate this puzzling *lack* of camp" (62; emphasis added) in the butch-femme system of the 1940s and 1950s. I am in substantial agreement with their conclusions, including that "No cultural aesthetic seems to have developed around male impersonation" (75).

Kath Weston's essay is a more direct challenge to performance theory. Her formulation, with different data, was similar to mine: "How do recent attempts to retheorize gender in literary studies, theater/film criticism, and philosophy stack up against an ethnographic analysis that examines what lesbians of different backgrounds and political persuasions have been doing and saying while scholars debate gender's fate?"(1). Deb Amory also calls for ethnographic siting of gender "performance" ("Club Q: Dancing With (a) Difference" in chapter 7). For two attempts to take a broader view of the relationship between social theory and performance theory, see Lisa Duggan, "Making it Perfectly Queer," *Socialist Review*, 22 (1) (1992): 11–31, and Michael Warner's introduction to *Fear of a Queer Planet: Queer Politics and Social Theory* (Minneapolis: University of Minnesota Press, 1993), vii–xxxi.

In a 1995 e-mail response to this essay that I quote with her permission, Sue-Ellen Case herself agreed that "Toward . . ." should have been more embodied. "[T]here was a 'king' in San Francisco in North Beach from the early 1970s on. So 'history' is local. I don't think B[utch]-F[emme] [in San Francisco] is anything like what they describe in upstate New York, for example. So, I think S[an] F[rancisco] had a different sense of it, and you're right—I should have said at Maud's in the 1970s in S[an] F[rancisco] this is the way I saw it [but] I agree with much of what you said."

11   The logical opposition/attraction between (lesbian) butch and (gay male) queen has been enacted theatrically by Peggy Shaw and Bette Bourne, who played Stanley Kowalski and Blanche DuBois, respectively, in the 1991 Bloolips productions of *Belle Reprieve*; see Alisa Solomon, "It's Never Too Late to Switch: Crossing Toward Power," in *Crossing the Stage: Controversies on Cross-Dressing*, ed. Lesley Ferris (London and New York: Routledge, 1993), 153.

12   Even when the term "queer" is not used, I notice an increasing disinclination to distinguish gay male experience from lesbian experience. For instance, "Gay men and lesbians are the people of drama. . . . From the moment of that first entry into 'the community' or 'the life,' we're embedded in a legendary network of gossip, tale-telling, and multiple interpretations of the same events. . . . Identity becomes an art form at times, a pastiche of meanings, affiliations, and self-parody that can be baroque." (Lisa Kahaleole Chang Hall, "Bitches in Solitude: Identity

Politics and Lesbian Community," in *Sisters, Sexperts, Queers: Beyond the Lesbian Nation*, ed. Arlene Stein [New York: Plume, 1993], 229). For a critique of the tendency toward genderless queers, see Biddy Martin, "Sexuality Without Genders and Other Queer Utopias," in *diacritics* 24.2–3 (1994) 104–121. For essays that both exhibit and "interrogate" the lesbian attraction toward queer, see the Stein collection and two other essays: Cathy Griggers, "Lesbian Bodies in the Age of (Post)mechanical Reproduction," in *Fear of A Queer Planet*, 178–192, and in the same collection, Lauren Berlant and Elizabeth Freeman, "Queer Nationality," 193–229.

13   On this point Case and I agree. She specifically complains about "heterosexual feminist critics" who disappear historical butches and femmes into concepts of cross-dressing and "carnavalesque" (299). Eve Sedgwick, one of the foremost partisans of the "queer" concept, makes the same observation: "[O]ne of the most striking aspects of the current popular and academic mania for language about cross-dressing is its virtual erasure of the connection between transvestism and— dare I utter it—homosexuality." (Eve Sedgwick and Michael Moon, "Divinity," in *Tendencies* (Durham: Duke University Press, 1993), 220.

14   Of course, Susan Sontag first appropriated camp for modernism by "disappearing" gay men ("Notes on Camp," *Against Interpretation* (New York: Dell, 1969), 277–293, a move elaborated by Andrew Ross for postmodernism ("Uses of Camp," in *No Respect: Intellectuals and Popular Culture* (New York: Routledge, 1989), 135–170).

15   It seems to me that in gay bar life, in the 1950s and 1960s, "drag butch" was a term occasionally used for a masculine lesbian who was passing as a boy or man on the street (not necessarily the same as a "stone butch," who would not have her genitals touched by her partner), whereas a "drag queen" was a gay man who was either hustling on the street in female clothing or performing for an audience, wearing any permutation of feminine clothing. In Elizabeth Lapovsky Kennedy and Madeline D. Davis' history of the Buffalo lesbian community, there is no index heading for "butch drag" or "drag butch," despite detailed descriptions of butches' masculine dress (*Boots of Leather, Slippers of Gold* [New York: Routledge, 1993], 154–167).

PART 2
Epigraph: Irene Elizabeth Stroud in "The Best of Times, the Worse of Times," in *The Women's Review of Books* 7(2) (November 1994): 5.

16   These points are developed with particular clarity in Kath Weston's essay.

17   This dissatisfaction was not limited to the younger generation (or even to lesbians) as is often asserted. Indeed the majority of the planners of and participants in (I was both) the 1982 Barnard Conference on Sexuality, which made opposition to anti-pornography feminism so visible, were heterosexual and verging on middle age. I well remember Ann Snitow coming to one of the Barnard planning meetings waving a manuscript copy of Gayle Rubin's essay "Thinking Sex" (in *Pleasure and Danger*, ed. Carole Vance [New York: Routledge, 1984]), and exclaiming, 'I'm holding revolutionary work in my hand; after this essay we'll never think about sex the same way!'"

18   Case, 297.

19   "Wandering Through Herland," in Stein, *Sisters, Sexperts, Queers*, 249.

20   Very preliminary income data *not* based on advertising hype indicate the average lesbian makes $22,397 per year, compared to the average gay man's $28,432—a difference that intuitively seems understated ("Beyond Biased Samples: Challenging the Myths on the Economic Status of Lesbians and Gay Men," March 1994, pamphlet published by the National Organization of Gay and Lesbian Scientists and Technical Professionals and the Institute for Gay & Lesbian Strategic Studies).

21   *The Advocate*, 26 July 1994, p. 19.

22   "Lesbofile," in *Deneuve* (August 1994) 4(4): 48. Lisa Duggan believes that "Any gay politics based on the primacy of sexual identity defined as unitary and 'essential,' residing clearly, intelligibly and unalterably in the body or psyche, and fixing desire in a gendered direction, ultimately represents the view from the subject position '20th-century Western white gay male.'" "Making it Perfectly Queer," 18.

PART 3

Epigraph: Needless to say, the "she" to whom Skip Arnold alludes is a gay man. Newton, *Mother Camp*, 110.

23   For more on this community, see my ethnohistory, *Cherry Grove, Fire Island: Sixty Years in America's First Gay and Lesbian Town* (Boston: Beacon Press, 1993). For the origins of the queen role, see Randolph Trumbach, "The Birth of the Queen," in *Hidden From History: Reclaiming the Gay and Lesbian Past*, ed. Martin Bauml Duberman, Martha Vicinus, and George Chauncey, Jr. (New York: New American Library, 1989), 129–140. Gay men in the Grove, like gay men in general before Stonewall, called each other "she," and many had effeminate names.

Carole-Anne Tyler expresses amazement that people like Vito Russo and Jack Babuscio would actually appeal to the notion of gay sensibility to contextualize drag in camp ("Boys Will Be Girls: The Politics of Gay Drag," in Diana Fuss, ed., *Inside/Out: Lesbian Theories, Gay Theories* (New York and London: Routledge, 1991), 32–70. But if there is any such thing as a sensibility, a gay male one exists. Jill Falzoi, a graduate student in performance studies at New York University, also advised me, in some alarm, to drop this passé term "sensibility," but if so, how to describe coherent aesthetic perspectives associated with social groups? Why would some other word be better? To those who doubt the existence of a critter such as camp humor, I say get out from behind your e-mail and go meet some gay men, or at least go to the movies, to see, for example, the new documentary film about gay fashion designer Izaac Mizrahi, *Unzipped*.

24   Newton, *Cherry Grove*, 81. For more detail about prominent Grove fag hags, see 24, 81–82.

25   To avoid confusion, Grove names and pronouns that refer to gay or cross-gender identities are italicized the first time they occur.

26   From the beginning of this episode Joan's narrative has been consistent in newspaper interviews and in informal Grove conversations. These quotes are

from Jeanne Sidebottom, "Homecoming Queen Overcomes Furor in the Grove," *Sappho's Isle* (August 1994): 19.

27   In lighter moments Joan was willing to play with some subthemes about the meaning of her performance in ways that might please performance theorists. Once, when Joan was dressed as Queen Scarlet Ooh, I remarked that she had every qualification for the position except one, and I pointed to her crotch. "You never know," she cautioned, laughing, "you never know."

28   "Without further specification of why butch / femme should represent a subversive activity for its practitioners and its 'audiences,' *as opposed to its theorists*, its political implications remain indeterminate and subject to romanticization" (Weston, 12, emphasis mine). In a paper that I saw in published form too late to integrate into this essay, Case criticizes "[poststructuralists who] operate in the refined atmosphere of 'pure' theory and writing, abandoning earlier materialist discourses that signalled to activist, grass-roots coalitions, while claiming a less essentialist base" ("Performing Lesbian in the Space of Technology: Part 1," in *Theatre Journal* 47 [1] [March 1995]: 1–18).

PART 4

29   For example, in the fifties Natalia Murray had attended a theme party as "Europa," in a female body suit, riding a male "bull." Though this is a variant on the Grove trope of the drag queen being carried by bearers, no one referred to Natalia as a "drag queen" or "drag king."

30   The possibility that lesbian femmes might want to be, or perhaps *were*, some kind of drag queens was first suggested in print by Lisa Duggan ("The Anguished Cry of an 80s Fem: 'I Want to be a Drag Queen'," *Out/Look* 1[1] [Spring 1988]: 63–65. In a spirited defense of feminism and femmeness, Biddy Martin (112) seconds Duggan.

31   This perfectly illustrates the importance of ethnography. Kate Davy asks, "Can women, as embodied on the stage, engender parody, or, as a function of gender, are they always already constituted as the material, or fodder, of parody? Many camp aficionados claim that there is no such thing as 'lesbian camp'—this may be why." ("From Lady Dick to Ladylike: The Work of Holly Hughes," *Acting Out: Feminist Performances*, ed. Lynda Hart and Peggy Phelan [Ann Arbor: University of Michigan Press, 1993], 84). Well, can lesbians be campy or not? This issue cannot be settled by appeals to Freud or Lacan, but only by observing lesbian performance and behavior in relation to what Jill Dolan usefully calls "spectatorial communities." See "Desire Cloaked in a Trenchcoat," in *Acting Out: Feminist Performances*, 105–118. Men and women in the Grove, a prime audience for camp performance, considered Lynne and some other lesbians to be camps; indeed in the summer of 1995 Lynne became the second lesbian to write a Grove revue.

32   The only reference to lesbian sexuality I recall was late in the eighties, made by a drag queen named *High Camp*, who played a lesbian lip-synching a song by lesbian comic Lynn Lavner.

33   During the years that *Candy* Stevens was the Ice Palace Disco emcee, she brought in any number of black drag queens, some pathetic and some amazingly talented. One of the latter was Paris Dupree, the namesake of Jenny Livingston's

acclaimed documentary film, *Paris Is Burning*. Paris ultimately declined to appear in Livingston's film and is seen only in silhouette in the breathtaking opening moments. See Phillip Brian Harper, " 'The Subversive Edge': *Paris Is Burning*, Social Critique, and the Limits of Subjective Agency," in *diacritics*, 24 (2–3): 90–103. Harper's essay is a devastating critique, based on objections similar to mine, of the voluntarist approach to gender found in so much performance theory.

34   Performance artist Holly Hughes, encased in a giant lobster costume, had lip synched "It's Not the Meat, It's the Motion" to a Maria Muldaur cover of the original Andrews Sisters song (perhaps the same recording used by the Jersey Girls) back in 1982 or 1983, proving once again that artists are ahead of the curve. This was part of Hughes' first production, titled *Shrimp in a Basket*, at the WOW cafe in New York City (personal communication with the author). As to the crowd's spontaneous enthusiasm for the butchest Jersey Girl, Amber Hollibaugh has long maintained in conversations that, culturally speaking, the butch is the central object of lesbian eroticism. This interesting subject is beyond the scope of my essay, but see Alisa Solomon's excellent essay on butchness, especially her description of butches Leslie Feinberg and Peggy Shaw dancing together in an off-Broadway performance ("Not Just a Passing Fancy: Notes on Butch," *Theatre* [November 1993] 42).

35   Whether this is cause and effect, as some suspected, is open to question. More likely there were many factors involved in the shift.

36   See Newton, *Cherry Grove, Fire Island*, chapter 6, for a fuller discussion of ethnic, racial, and class discrimination among Grovers. In the late eighties and early nineties many white male Grovers were upset, primarily about lesbians coming to the Grove to buy, rent, and day-trip, but also about groups of African-American day-trippers. Prior to this time, African-Americans had mostly come as individual workers or partners of whites.

PART 5

Epigraph: Sarah Murray, 344.

37   Weston, in an all-lesbian context, also raised this question: "What about the power relations embedded in my own presence as a lesbian ethnographer who found herself simultaneously 'natived' and 'othered,' desiring and desired, observing and observed? How to depict my participation?" (16). Also see my discussion of the problems of being a lesbian field-worker in the Grove in "My Best Informant's Dress: The Erotic Equation in Fieldwork," in *Out in the Field: Reflections of Lesbian and Gay Anthropologists*, ed. Ellen Lewin and William Leap (Urbana, IL: University of Illinois Press, 1996), 212–235.

38   Lorraine's butch appearance raised what I considered to be interesting questions about Joan's willingness to portray a drag queen, but Grovers did not comment on it in my hearing. There was, however, gossip about the fact that Joan and Lorraine formed the second apparently butch-butch relationship among prominent Grove lesbians in recent years.

39   Peter Worth, nearing eighty, was approached by one of Joan's lesbian supporters to bless Joan as Homecoming Queen at the tea, presumably to symbolize continuity between the lesbian generations. Peter declined, explaining it was too

drafty at Cherry's and that she's not a "public person." I reminded her that Kay, the grandest of all Grove "lady" lesbians, "would have loved to do it!" Peter agreed. "Kay was the one person who *could* have done it, but she's no longer with us."

40   "A First for Cherry Grove," in *The New York Times*, Long Island Section, 19 June 1994, p. 3, and Elizabeth Wasserman, "This Queen Crosses Some on Fire Island," *Newsday*, 16 June 1994. Wasserman did a follow-up article after the Invasion: "Cherry Grove Queen Proves She's No Drag," *Newsday*, 5 July 1994.

41   "Talk of the Grove," P. A., *Fire Island Tide*, 17 June 1994, p. 34.

42   "Homecoming Queen is a Woman," letter to the editor by Barbara Bozzone, *Fire Island Tide*, 1 July 1994, p. 12.

43   "Homecoming Queen is a Woman," letter to the editor by Helen Schwartz, *Fire Island Tide* 1 July 1994, p. 12.

44   Panzi said the number of cross-dressers going over on the ferry had peaked at about 170 eight or nine years previously, then decreased for several years, and increased to about 175 in 1994.

PART 6

Epigraph: Kate Davy, "From Lady Dick to Ladylike," 56–57. Davy goes on to write that lesbians, like women in general, are still defined by what they are not, i.e., they cannot be "phallic signifiers." It is just this construction that Holly Hughes, and the Jersey Girls, were contesting by performing, as lesbians, "It's Not the Meat It's the Motion" (lyrics that were perhaps originally intended as sex advice for men). Despite Davy's attacks on the work of the Five Lesbian Brothers (especially their play *Voyage to Lesbos*) and of Hughes, as essentially too male-identified, in my view their work does just what Davy advocates: "The challenge for lesbian and feminist theater, it seems to me, is to devise strategies for not only foregrounding the ways in which female sexuality is denied access to the phallus, as signifier of desire, but for seizing the phallus, as it were, and forcing it to function representationally in the service of an autonomous female sexuality" ("Visibility Troubles and Literate Perverts, *Women and Performance*, 7 [1] [1994]: 153). See C. Carr, "The Lady Is a Dick: The Dyke Noir Theater of Holly Hughes," in *On Edge: Performance at the End of the Twentieth Century* (Hanover and London: Wesleyan University Press, 1993), 132–137. In any case it seems to me that Davy, the performance artists, and I are all contesting Audre Lorde's famous dictum, "The master's tools will never dismantle the master's house."

As I wrote this section I was watching the televised celebration for Martina Navratilova's retirement at the Virginia Slims Tournament (November 15, 1994). Martina, more than any other public lesbian, attained the status of mainstream phallic signifier when she became the first woman in history to have her banner raised to the roof of Madison Square Garden. On this occasion, she was also given a black silver-studded motorcycle while the song "Born to be Wild" blasted over the p.a. system.

45   Besides works already cited, see Lynda Hart, "Identity and Seduction: Lesbians in the Mainstream," and Hilary Harris, "Toward a Lesbian Theory of Performance: Refunctioning Gender," in *Acting Out: Feminist Performances*, ed.

Lynda Hart and Peggy Phelan (Ann Arbor: University of Michigan Press, 1993) 119–137, and 257–276, respectively.

For an article by a self-declared femme that critiques the "emphasis on the visible" in lesbian culture, see Lisa M. Walker, "How to Recognize a Lesbian: The Cultural Politics of Looking Like What You Are," *Signs*, 18 (4) (1993): 866–890.

46   Some lesbians were so acutely aware of male fears of exclusion that one woman suggested that Joan should have been escorted to the tea at Cherry's by a gay male escort dressed as a man, rather than by her partner dressed in a tux.

47   Kate Davy thinks male impersonation can never serve lesbians the way female impersonation has served gay men, for Lacanian and also historical reasons. But she still thinks that "the tools that camp provides—artifice, wit, irony, exaggeration—are available to butch-femme gender play separate from the ways in which they are inscribed by camp as a historically marked phenomenon" ("Fe/male Impersonation," 243). While I agree that lesbians can (and do) use camp, I disagree on the three fundamental points: first, that lesbians cannot use drag; second, that camp or drag as practiced by gay men is *intrinsically* either mysogynist or some kind of sellout; and third, that lesbians could use drag or camp in a separatist historical vacuum. These points have been addressed with a different emphasis and in a somewhat different context by José Estéban Muñoz in an appreciation of the Cuban-American lesbian performer Carmelita Tropicana, whom he sees as successfully practicing both drag and camp to create a persona who is a queer "hybrid diasporic subject" ("Choteo/Camp Style Politics: Carmelita Tropicana's Performance of Self-Enactment," *Women & Performance: A Journal of Feminist Theory*, 7 [2–8] [1], issue 14, 15, 38–51 [forthcoming]).

48   The concept of "gay gender" in regard to butch-femme was first suggested to me by Amber Hollibaugh in the early eighties.

49   "Nellie"—an adjective, not a noun—is the gay male concept that corresponds to lesbian femme. It has become somewhat disused.

It is ironic, as Kath Weston has pointed out, that "femme- and butch-*identified* lesbians" have been marginalized just as performance theory has reclaimed butch-femme *performances* as subversive (Weston, 8). Alisa Solomon makes a related point: "Because it subverts male privilege, butchness can be the most dangerous queer image—and that's exactly why it is increasingly invisible even as gays and lesbians find ourselves in the news for good or ill. And that's why when it does appear, it's tamed, even commodified" ("Not Just a Passing Fancy," 45).

50   Judith Butler has more recently tried to counter the postmodern tendency to think of gender as a something like a clothing style: "Gender performativity is not a matter of choosing which gender one will be today. Performativity is a matter of reiterating or repeating the norms by which one is constituted: it is not a radical fabrication of a gendered self" ("Critically Queer," in *GLQ*, 1 [1993]: 22). Although I believe genders *are* psychosocially created, that does not mean they are fluid or easily changeable, on either the macro (social) or micro (subjective) levels.

51   Quoted in Michiko Kakutani, "The Rise of a Self-Proclaimed Phenomenon," *New York Times*, 15 November 1994, sec. C, p. 19.

52   Davy, "From Lady Dick to Ladylike," 84; for Carmelita Tropicana, see

Muñoz, and Jill Dolan, "Carmelita Tropicana Chats at the Club Chandelier," in *TDR: The Drama Review*, 29 (1) (1985): 26–32.

53   Hart, "Identity and Seduction," 129.

54   Davy, "Fe/male Impersonation," 234. In her 1994 piece, "Visibility Troubles and Literate Perverts," Davy softens her repudiation of gay male camp, but still worries about "the shift away from gender and feminism, [and] the simultaneous move toward the sensibilities of gay male sexuality. In the same breath that feminism was disavowed [at the 1991 Rutgers Queer Studies Conference], gay male practices, aesthetics, and representational strategies were hailed as sites not only of new alliances, but of new ways of imagining and imaging lesbian sexuality," 143.

55   Davy quotes Peggy Shaw as saying, "When lesbians make it to Off Broadway, it's the boys who are doing it," referring to Charles Busch's long-running show *Lesbian Vampires of Sodom* ("Fe/male Impersonation," 234). For an overview of the development of lesbian and feminist theater, see Emily L. Sisley, "Notes on Lesbian Theatre," *TDR* (*The Drama Review*), 25 (1) (T89) (March 1981): 47–56. For descriptions of the WOW cafe, besides Davy's other articles see "Heart of the Scorpion at the WOW Cafe," *TDR*, 29 (1) (Spring 1985) (T105): 52–56; Chansky (fn 1); Solomon, "Never Too Late," in *Crossing Toward Power*, 151–153, and "The WOW Cafe," *TDR*, 92–101, and C. Carr, "The Queer Frontier," in *On Edge: Performance at the End of the Twentieth Century* (Hanover and London: Wesleyan University Press, 1993), 84–87.

According to Holly Hughes (personal communication), several WOW performers have now received Obies and respectful reviews in *The New York Times*, and have performed in off-Broadway venues. However, only Lisa Kron's 1994 solo monologue, *101 Humiliating Stories*, has broken through to receive a Drama Desk nomination and three reviews in the *Times*. None of the lesbian work, Hughes told me, has "anywhere near" the recognition that gay male theater work now routinely gets.

56   Murray, 344 (emphasis in original). In a later phone conversation, Murray and I agreed that the recent flourishing of lesbian drag and camp is based more than anything on increasing confidence and power. Shane Phelan makes a very similar point: "Lesbians have been denied the right to be heard not just by forced silence but also by having "lesbian" voices and words deprived of authority. So the first need for our politics is the guarantee that these will be heard" ("[Be] Coming Out: Lesbian Identity and Politics," in *Signs*, 18 [4] [Summer 1993]: 779).

CONTRIBUTORS

Deborah P. Amory is assistant professor of anthropology at the State University of New York College at Purchase. She has conducted research in East Africa and San Francisco on issues of identity, race, and sexuality.

Ellen Herman is a historian who teaches in the social studies program at Harvard University. She is the author of *The Romance of American Psychology: Political Culture in the Age of Experts* (University of California, 1995) and *Psychiatry, Psychology, and Homosexuality* (Chelsea House, 1995). She lives with her family in Jamaica Plain, Massachusetts.

Elizabeth Lapovsky Kennedy is a founder of women's studies at the State University of New York, Buffalo, where she is a professor in the department of American studies. She is a coauthor of *Feminist Scholarship: Kindling in the Groves of Academe* and (with Madeline Davis) of *Boots of Leather, Slippers of Gold: The History of a Lesbian Community*.

Alisa Klinger is an assistant professor of English at York University, where she teaches contemporary/postmodern literature and film; lesbian, gay, and bisexual studies; and cultural studies. She is working on a cultural history of lesbian-feminist publishers and the apparatus of lesbian literary production.

Ellen Lewin is an affiliated scholar at the Institute for Research on Women and Gender at Stanford University. She is the author of *Lesbian Mothers: Accounts of Gender in American Culture*, and coeditor (with William Leap) of *Out in the Field: Reflections of Lesbian and Gay Anthropologists*. She is at work on an ethnographic study of lesbian and gay commitment ceremonies, tentatively titled *Recognizing Ourselves*.

Esther Newton is professor of anthropology at the State University of New York College at Purchase. Her major interest is in American culture, especially in lesbian and gay ethnohistory and representational practices, and she is a founder of the lesbian and gay studies program at the college. She is the author of *Mother Camp: Female Impersonators in America* and *Cherry Grove, Fire Island: Sixty Years in America's First Lesbian and Gay Town*.

Rochella Thorpe is finishing her doctoral dissertation at Binghamton University. She is also serving her first term as a councilwoman in Ithaca, New York.

Kath Weston is a member of the National Writers Union and an associate professor of anthropology at Arizona State University West in Phoenix. Before that, she flirted with the prospect of becoming a mechanic. With the money from a day job (mechanics), or a night-and-day job (academics), she wanted to write about the ways that sexuality is intertwined with race and class. She is the author of *Families We Choose: Lesbians, Gays, Kinship* and a coeditor of *The Lesbian Issue: Essays from SIGNS*. Her latest book is *Render Me, Gender Me: Lesbians Talk Sex, Class, Color, Nation, Studmuffins & Such*.